Suicide

SOCIAL ISSUES AND SOCIAL PROBLEMS INFORMATION GUIDE SERIES

Series Editors: Kenneth D. Sell, Chairman, Department of Sociology, Catawba College, Salisbury, North Carolina and Betty H. Sell, Director, Catawba College Library, Salisbury, North Carolina

Also in this series:

CHILD CARE ISSUES FOR PARENTS AND SOCIETY—*Edited by Andrew Garoogian and Rhoda Garoogian*

DIVORCE IN THE UNITED STATES, CANADA, AND GREAT BRITAIN—*Edited by Kenneth D. Sell and Betty H. Sell*

The above series is part of the
GALE INFORMATION GUIDE LIBRARY

The Library consists of a number of separate series of guides covering major areas in the social sciences, humanities, and current affairs.

General Editor: Paul Wasserman, Professor and former Dean, School of Library and Information Services, University of Maryland

Managing Editor: Denise Allard Adzigian, Gale Research Company

Suicide

A GUIDE TO INFORMATION SOURCES

Volume 3 in the Social Issues and Social Problems Information Guide Series

David Lester

*Professor of Psychology
and
Criminal Justice
Richard Stockton State College
Pomona, New Jersey*

Betty H. Sell

*Director of the Library
Catawba College
Salisbury, North Carolina*

Kenneth D. Sell

*Professor of Sociology
and
Chairman of the Department
Catawba College
Salisbury, North Carolina*

Gale Research Company
Book Tower, Detroit, Michigan 48226

Library of Congress Cataloging in Publication Data

Lester, David, 1942—
    Suicide : a guide to information sources.

    (Social issues and social problems information
guide series ; v. 3) (Gale information guide library)
    Includes indexes.
    1. Suicide—Information services. 2. Suicide
—Bibliography. 3. Suicide—Indexes. I. Sell,
Betty H., joint author. II. Sell, Kenneth D.,
joint author. III. Title. IV. Series.
RC569.L47   616.85'8445'007   80-71
ISBN 0-8103-1415-0

VITAE

David Lester is professor of psychology and criminal justice at Richard Stockton State College at Pomona, New Jersey. He received his Ph.D. from Brandeis University and his B.A. from Cambridge University. He has written two books on suicide and over one hundred scholarly articles on the subject since beginning his studies on suicidal behavior in 1965. For two years he was director of research and evaluation at the Suicide Prevention and Crisis Service in Buffalo, New York, where he founded a journal, CRISIS INTERVENTION, which dealt with the problems faced by suicide prevention centers.

Betty Haas Sell is director of the library at Catawba College, Salisbury, North Carolina, since 1970, and previously served as a librarian at The Florida State University Library and at Livingstone College in North Carolina. She is a doctoral candidate in the School of Library Science at The Florida State University, where she received her M.S. and Advanced Masters degrees in library science. Mrs. Sell also earned an M.R.E. from the Lancaster Theological Seminary, Lancaster, Pennsylvania. She is a member of Beta Phi Mu International Library Science Honor Society. She has held offices in professional library organizations in North Carolina.

Kenneth Daniel Sell is professor of sociology and chairman of the department at Catawba College, Salisbury, North Carolina. He received his Ph.D. from The Florida State University through its interdivisional program in marriage and the family, in 1968. He has published articles in the FAMILY LAW QUARTERLY, the FAMILY COORDINATOR, RQ, and NEW DIRECTIONS IN LEGAL SERVICES, and a bibliography on DIVORCE IN THE 1970S.

Dr. and Mrs. Sell are the authors of DIVORCE IN THE UNITED STATES, CANADA, AND GREAT BRITAIN (Gale Research Co., 1978) which was selected by the American Library Association's Outstanding Reference Book Committee as one of the outstanding reference books of 1978.

CONTENTS

Contents

Contents

Contents

Contents

INTRODUCTION

Suicide is a subject of great personal meaning for most people. As Camus has said, suicide and the question of whether or not one should kill oneself is a major question about our existence. Scholars in many disciplines, including the social sciences, various branches of the medical sciences, law, philosophy, religion, and literature, have long been fascinated by the topic and study of suicide and suicidal behavior.

Despite this continuing fascination with suicide and suicidal behavior, it remains a very difficult behavior to study. For almost all other behaviors which are studied and analyzed, the persons performing the behaviors are living, and thus can communicate and interact with other persons. However, for the person completing suicide, we must rely on the memories of relatives and on any residual documents left behind after the person's death.

This combination of continuing high interest and difficulty of study leads to the appearance each year of many hundreds of articles, and other publications, on suicide, most of which add very little information to our knowledge of this topic. Articles and books, of all kinds, however, continue to be published on suicide, as the editors often tend to apply less stringent criteria in recognition of the public interest and the research difficulties in this area.

The problem of identifying substantive and nonredundant publications on suicide is also compounded by the interdisciplinary nature of this subject. Information on suicide is scattered throughout the literature of many disciplines, in a variety of formats. Without a systematic approach, searching this literature can be a difficult and discouraging effort.

In this information guide, therefore, two major approaches have been provided to help the student, scholar, educator, clinician, researcher, or otherwise interested person, find the kind of information he or she needs. In Part I, the user who wishes to identify for himself general or specific information on suicide, both retrospective and current, is provided with sources for doing so. A systematic methodology is also provided throughout whereby the user, by means of periodically checking suggested ongoing sources or by being able to find new sources as they appear, may in the future keep up with suicide publications and information in his special area of interest. If comprehensiveness is required, by using all of Part I this can be accomplished to a very high degree. The user thus becomes skilled in independently searching the literature, in all of its variety of format and type, thereby selecting items deemed significant for his own purposes.

In the remaining parts of this information guide, Parts II through V, the various aspects of suicide most commonly studied by scholars are treated in separate sections. Each section provides selected references to the major seminal articles and books pertinent to that aspect. The articles and books cited, with brief annotations, are essentially those most cited in current writing about suicidal behavior.

Several special features are provided by this information guide. In Part I, the relevant subject headings in current usage in the on-going information sources described are indicated in order to facilitate searching by the user. Also, for types of materials that are particularly difficult for the user to locate, special preliminary checklists have been prepared. These include a checklist of doctoral dissertations on suicide, a checklist of authors who have completed suicide, a checklist of suicides in literature, and a listing of references to suicide in mythology. For effective use of this information guide, the user should be aware that by examining the table of contents carefully, and by making extensive use of the three indexes at the back of the guide, particularly the subject index, the user can efficiently and effectively find information on a specific aspect, often in whatever type of material or format desired.

Part I

SOURCES FOR LOCATING INFORMATION
AND MATERIALS ON SUICIDE

Chapter 1
INTRODUCTIONS TO THE STUDY OF SUICIDE

A large number of books have appeared on the topic of suicide. These are written from a variety of points of view and with different aims in mind. This chapter presents a selection of outstanding books which discuss general issues in suicidal behavior and which can serve as introductions to the subject of suicide. Selected specialized books on specific aspects are presented in later chapters of this information guide. Chapters 2 and 3 present strategies and sources for identifying more books on suicide in general, or on the various related aspects and issues, according to the needs of the individual user of this guide.

1.1 GENERAL INTRODUCTORY BOOKS: SELECTED REFERENCES

The following are a number of selected books on suicide that have been written for the student or educated layperson. Unless otherwise noted, these are very general and balanced introductions.

1.101   Alvarez, Alfred. THE SAVAGE GOD: A STUDY OF SUICIDE. New York: Random House, 1971. 229 p.

> This work is chiefly concerned with suicide in literature.

1.102   Brooke, Eileen M. SUICIDE AND ATTEMPTED SUICIDE. Geneva: World Health Organization, 1974. 127 p.

> This book contains articles on the incidence of suicide in different countries, especially among the young, and on the practices of medical examiners and coroners in different countries.

1.103   Choron, Jacques. SUICIDE. New York: Scribner, 1972. 182 p.

1.104   Dublin, Louis I. SUICIDE: A SOCIOLOGICAL AND STATISTICAL STUDY. New York: Ronald Press, 1963. 240 p.

1.105   Farberow, Norman L., and Shneidman, Edwin S., eds. THE CRY FOR HELP. New York: McGraw-Hill, 1961. 398 p.

Essentially a collection of articles on attempted suicide, part 1 of this book presents ten original articles. Part 2 presents a case study of a man who attempted suicide, with a discussion of the case by eight leading personality theorists. Part 3 is a bibliography on suicide for 1897-1957.

1.106   Gibbs, Jack, ed. SUICIDE. New York: Harper & Row, 1968. 338 p.

This is a collection of articles intended to introduce the subject of suicide. Somewhat narrow in scope, most of these articles have been reprinted from other sources.

1.107   Grollman, Earl A. SUICIDE: PREVENTION, INTERVENTION, POSTVENTION. Boston: Beacon Press, 1971. 145 p.

1.108   Hafen, Brent Q., and Faux, Eugene J., eds. SELF DESTRUCTIVE BEHAVIOR. Minneapolis: Burgess, 1972. 330 p.

A collection of articles reprinted from popular rather than scholarly sources, the emphasis of this work is on suicidal behavior in adolescents and on prevention.

1.109   Lester, Gene, and Lester, David. SUICIDE: THE GAMBLE WITH DEATH. Englewood Cliffs, N.J.: Prentice-Hall, 1971. 176 p.

1.110   Perlin, Seymour, ed. A HANDBOOK FOR THE STUDY OF SUICIDE. New York: Oxford University Press, 1975. 236 p.

As a collection of articles on suicide by a historian, a literature expert, a philosopher, an anthropologist, a sociologist, a biologist, a psychiatrist, an epidemiologist, a medical sociologist, and a community psychiatrist, this handbook is very broad in scope. It is unique in its interdisciplinary aspect.

1.111   Pretzel, Paul W. UNDERSTANDING AND COUNSELING THE SUICIDAL PERSON. Nashville: Abingdon, 1972. 251 p.

1.112   Resnik, H.L.P., ed. SUICIDAL BEHAVIORS: DIAGNOSIS AND MANAGEMENT. Boston: Little, Brown, 1968. 536 p.

Including a large selection of articles on all aspects of suicidal behavior, written by experts in the field, this book is an excellent and broad-based selection which covers most of the perspectives of suicidal behavior.

Introductions to the Study of Suicide

1.113 Resnik, H.L.P., and Hathorne, Berkley C., eds. SUICIDE PREVEN-
TION IN THE 70S. DHEW Publication No. (HSM) 72-9054. Rockville, Md.: National Institute of Mental Health, Center for Studies
of Suicide Prevention, 1973. 109 p. HE 20.2402:Su3.

Committee reports from a meeting convened to decide upon
trends in suicide research for the 1970s are collected into
this book. Sections cover nomenclature, education and
training, research, delivery of services for preventing suicide, and new treatment approaches.

1.114 Shneidman, Edwin S., ed. ESSAYS IN SELF-DESTRUCTION. New
York: Science House, 1967. 554 p.

This book consists of a collection of original essays covering
literary, philosophical, sociological, ethnographic, psychological, psychiatric, taxonomic, and forensic topics.

1.115 _____. ON THE NATURE OF SUICIDE. San Francisco: Jossey-Bass,
1969. 146 p.

1.116 _____. SUICIDOLOGY: CONTEMPORARY DEVELOPMENTS. New
York: Grune & Stratton, 1976. 571 p.

This work consists of a collection of articles by various authors on the demography of suicide, methodological developments in suicide research, the thinking of the suicidal person, philosophical and legal aspects of suicide, and suicide
prevention.

1.117 Shneidman, Edwin S., and Farberow, Norman L., eds. CLUES TO
SUICIDE. New York: McGraw-Hill, 1957. 227 p.

A collection of original articles, this work treats aspects
of the topic of completed suicide.

1.118 Stengel, Erwin. SUICIDE AND ATTEMPTED SUICIDE. Baltimore:
Penguin Books, 1964. 135 p.

1.119 Waldenstom, Jan; Larsson, Tage; and Ljungstedt, Nils, eds. SUICIDE
AND ATTEMPTED SUICIDE. Stockholm: Nordiska Bokhandelns-Forlag,
1972. 320 p.

This collection of articles on suicide is written by European
scholars.

1.120 Wolman, Benjamin B., ed. BETWEEN SURVIVAL AND SUICIDE. New
York: Gardner Press, 1976. 195 p.

This collection of general essays on the topic of suicide is

5

Introductions to the Study of Suicide

varied in content and represents the idiosyncratic views on the phenomenon of suicide held by the eight authors. The collection does not attempt to survey the field of suicidology, but rather to present original views on relevant issues in the motivation of suicide.

1.2 PROFESSIONAL SURVEYS: SELECTED REFERENCES

A number of books have appeared that are written for professionals, and which attempt to discuss limited aspects of suicidal behavior. Typically, they do not attempt a comprehensive or balanced view of the field. These are, however, good introductions to the aspects treated.

1.201 Bosselman, Beulah C. SELF-DESTRUCTION: A STUDY OF THE SUICIDAL IMPULSE. Springfield, Ill.: Charles Thomas, 1958. 94 p.

Containing psychiatric information about suicidal behavior, this book also includes case studies for illustrative purposes.

1.202 Fedden, Henry R. SUICIDE: A SOCIAL AND HISTORICAL STUDY. 1938. Reprint. New York: Benjamin Blom, 1972. 351 p.

An excellent review of the thoughts of philosophers through the ages on suicidal behavior, this book also reviews the ideas of early suicidologists from the nineteenth and twentieth centuries.

1.203 Leonard, Calista V. UNDERSTANDING AND PREVENTING SUICIDE. Springfield, Ill.: Charles Thomas, 1967. 351 p.

This book is a professional review of some aspects of suicidal behavior.

1.204 Lester, David. WHY PEOPLE KILL THEMSELVES. Springfield, Ill.: Charles Thomas, 1972. 353 p.

This book is the only extensive general review of research on suicide to date. Refer to item 2.303.

1.205 McCulloch, James W., and Philip, Alistair E. SUICIDAL BEHAVIOR. Elmsford, N.Y.: Pergamon, 1972. 123 p.

A general professional introduction to suicide, based primarily on the authors' research, this work includes a general survey of relevant issues.

1.206 Resnik, H.L.P., and Hathorne, Berkley C. TEACHING OUTLINES IN SUICIDE STUDIES AND CRISIS INTERVENTION. Bowie, Md.: Charles Press, 1974. 169 p.

This book covers the field of suicidology in outline form, with bibliographies and reading references for each section. It presents the reader with an overview of key elements concerning suicide, and indicates where specific information about each element can be found. It is not a textbook, but rather a sourcebook for instructors who are planning courses in suicidology, and for students in the helping professions.

1.207   Sprott, Samuel E. THE ENGLISH DEBATE ON SUICIDE. LaSalle, Ill.: Open Court Publishing Co., 1961. 168 p.

This work presents a discussion of philosophical views on suicide in England from the time of Donne to the time of Hume.

Chapter 2
BIBLIOGRAPHIES ON SUICIDE

When a person looks for information on a subject such as suicide, very often only a small amount of information on a particular aspect of suicide is all that is required. Sources of information of this type will be treated in later chapters of this information guide. Other times, however, especially when a research project or an in-depth study is being started, much more information is needed. In this latter case, the researcher must aim for comprehensiveness in searching the literature on suicide, in all possible formats, by using more comprehensive sources prepared for this purpose.

In either case the researcher or investigator is advised not to waste time and needless effort by using a haphazard or serendipitous approach to his search for information. A main purpose of this book is to lead the user through a systematic search strategy when the aim is for comprehensiveness, and, in later chapters of the book, to lead the user quickly to specific sources for brief factual, statistical, or specialized information if the need is not as extensive or general.

In the beginning of a comprehensive search of the literature on suicide, an effective way is to make use of the efforts of other persons who have amassed pertinent citations or references to books, periodical articles, newspaper articles, reports, documents, pamphlets, and similar materials on the subject. These lists of references are usually published as bibliographies on suicide or relating to suicide. Bibliographies with annotated listings are particularly helpful.

When using an already prepared bibliography on suicide, one should determine what parameters or limitations the compilers admittedly or inadvertently followed in compiling the bibliographies. Also it is well to determine, if possible, the sources and the subject headings that the compilers searched or consulted in compiling the bibliographies. In this way the user can identify what areas, types of materials, and time periods are not included in the bibliographies being consulted. Often, for example, published bibliographies, although very helpful, may not be as up-to-date as the user requires. Keeping any limitations in mind, one can then determine exactly what additional specific sources of information should be searched to meet the requirements of the study or research being undertaken. The remaining chapters of this information guide may be consulted to locate additional sources of information.

Bibliographies on Suicide

Section 2.1 of this chapter describes well-known ongoing sources for locating subject bibliographies as described above. Sections 2.2 and 2.3 of this chapter describe significant current and retrospective bibliographies to date which are useful for suicide information, as well as significant scholarly reviews of the research literature.

2.1 LOCATING SUBJECT BIBLIOGRAPHIES ON SUICIDE

An important source for locating bibliographies on suicide is the library card catalog. Library holdings of bibliographies on suicide, in the form of entire books, can be found under subject headings such as the following:

Suicide--Bibliography
Suicide--U.S.--Bibliography
Suicide--Canada--Bibliography
Suicide--Prevention--Bibliography
Suicide in literature--Bibliography

Also, since most college, university, and research libraries in the United States use subject headings adopted by the Library of Congress, most of the subject headings listed in item 3.104 can be searched in these libraries, when they are followed by the word "bibliography"; for example, Children--Suicidal behavior--Bibliography. Of course, these headings are subject to change and new headings may be added from time to time.

For research purposes, especially, it should also be remembered that the bibliographies which are included in doctoral dissertations and masters' theses on suicide may be extremely valuable in locating books, as well as other published and unpublished materials, on suicide. Dissertations on suicide are discussed in chapter 6 of this information guide. Other sources of bibliographies are cited below.

2.101   Besterman, Theodore. A WORLD BIBLIOGRAPHY OF BIBLIOGRAPHIES AND BIBLIOGRAPHICAL CATALOGUES, CALENDARS, ABSTRACTS, DIGESTS, INDEXES, AND THE LIKE. 4th ed., rev. 5 vols. Lausanne, Switzerland: Societas Bibliographica, 1965.

   Although this work is broad in scope and attempts universal coverage, it has somewhat limited usefulness for the subject of suicide. The bibliographies are arranged by subject in the first four volumes. Volume 5 is an author-title index. A two-volume decennial supplement to this work was prepared by Alice F. Toomey, entitled A WORLD BIBLIOG-RAPHY OF BIBLIOGRAPHIES, 1964-1974 (Roman & Little-field, 1977). Further supplements should certainly be consulted as they appear.

   Consult: Suicide

2.102   BIBLIOGRAPHIC INDEX: A CUMULATIVE BIBLIOGRAPHY OF BIB-
          LIOGRAPHIES, 1937-- . New York: H.W. Wilson Co., 1938-- .
          Three issues per year cumulated annually, with triennial cumulative
          volumes.

          The best source of information on new bibliographies each
          year, this work is a subject listing of books, periodical ar-
          ticles, and pamphlets that include bibliographies of fifty or
          more items, as well as a subject listing of separately pub-
          lished bibliographies. Over twenty-two hundred American
          and European periodical titles are examined regularly for
          such bibliographies.

          Consult: Children--Suicidal behavior
                     Suicide
                     Right to die
                     Suicide prevention
                     Youth--Suicidal behavior

2.2 SIGNIFICANT BIBLIOGRAPHIES ON SUICIDE

2.201   Brooke, Eileen M., ed. SUICIDE AND ATTEMPTED SUICIDE. Public
          Health Paper, no. 58. Geneva: World Health Organization, 1977.
          127 p.

2.202   Farberow, Norman L. BIBLIOGRAPHY ON SUICIDE AND SUICIDE
          PREVENTION; 1897-1957, 1958-1970. Chevy Chase, Md.: National
          Institute of Mental Health, 1972. Pt 1, 126 p.; pt. 2, 143 p. HE
          20.2417:Su3.

          Part 1 of the bibliography is a reprint of the bibliography
          from Farberow's previous work, in collaboration with E.S.
          Shneidman, THE CRY FOR HELP (see item 1.105), covering
          the years 1897-1957. In part 2, Farberow has added a bib-
          liography for the years 1958-70. Neither bibliography is
          annotated. There is, however, a subject index for this ex-
          panded work.

2.203   Motta, Emilio. BIBLIOGRAFIA DEL SUICIDIO. Bellizona: Tip. di
          C. Salvioni, 1890. viii, 102 p.

          Arranged by time periods, this work contains 647 references
          to various-language publications on suicide from 1551 to
          1889. There is an author and subject index.

2.204   Nick, William V. INDEX TO LEGAL MEDICINE, 1940-1970. Columbus,
          Ohio: Legal Medicine Press, 1970. iv, 694 p.

          This annotated bibliography has an extensive section on sui-
          cide, including such aspects as suicide attempts, etiology,

diagnosis, legal questions, methods, prevention and control, and occurrence.

2.205   Prentice, Anne E. SUICIDE: A SELECTIVE BIBLIOGRAPHY. Metuchen, N.J.: Scarecrow Press, 1974. 227 p.

Primarily for the period 1960-73, this work lists 2,218 items, including articles, literary works, scholarly works, works in popular magazines, and films and tape recordings. An author and a subject index are provided. Although not an exhaustive listing, the scope and extent of this work make it useful.

2.206   Rost, Hans. BIBLIOGRAPHIE DES SELBSTMORDS MIT TEXTLICHEN EINFUHRUNGEN ZU JEDEM KAPITEL. Augsburg, Germany: Haas & Grabherr, 1927. xv, 391 p.

Over 3,775 items on suicide are listed in this extensive retrospective bibliography.

Although not a bibliographic source specifically on suicide, the following massive bibliographic work provides extensive and detailed references to suicide in numerous cultures and nations.

2.207   Human Relations Area Files, Inc. HRAF Master Index. New Haven, Conn.: 1979-- .

Multidisciplinary in nature, covering anthropology, sociology, psychology, political science, and, to some extent, the life sciences and the humanities, this system is a page-by-page subject index to over forty-five hundred carefully selected books, periodical articles, and manuscripts processed by the Human Relations Area Files, Inc., and covering more than twenty-three hundred cultures, nations, and areas. It consists of the original INDEX TO THE HUMAN RELATIONS AREA FILES, by Raoul Naroll and Donald Morisson, 1972, and its SUPPLEMENT I (through 1977), a total of sixteen volumes. To use the above HRAF volumes, the following HRAF publications must be consulted: George P. Murdock's OUTLINE OF WORLD CULTURES (5th ed., 1975); OUTLINE OF CULTURAL MATERIALS, by George P. Murdock et al., (4th ed., 1971, c1961), which classified cultural materials into over seven hundred categories, one of which is suicide; and HRAF SOURCE BIBLIOGRAPHY, CUMULATIVE HUMAN RELATIONS AREA FILES, one looseleaf volume. This system is a rich continuing bibliographic source for suicide information, providing, as of May 1979, references to at least 425 items.

Consult: Suicide (762)
Offenses against life (regarding punishment for
attempted suicide) (682)

2.3 CRITICAL REVIEWS OF THE RESEARCH AND SCHOLARLY LITERATURE ON SUICIDE

2.301   Adam, Kenneth S. "Suicide: A Critical Review of the Literature."
CANADIAN PSYCHIATRIC ASSOCIATION JOURNAL 12 (1967): 413-20.

2.302   Beall, Lynnette. "The Dynamics of Suicide: A Review of the Literature, 1897-1965." BULLETIN OF SUICIDOLOGY (March 1969): 2-16.

2.303   Lester, David. WHY PEOPLE KILL THEMSELVES. Springfield, Ill.:
Charles Thomas, 1972. 353 p.

This book is the only extensive general review of research
on suicide published in English to date. It aims to cover
all research up to 1969 and presents a critical evaluation
of the findings. Written for the professional, it is a well-
rounded scholarly review of what we know about suicide.

2.304   Seiden, Richard H. SUICIDE AMONG YOUTH: A REVIEW OF THE
LITERATURE, 1900-1967. Chevy Chase, Md.: National Institute of
Mental Health, 1969. iv, 62 p. HE 20.2413/2:Y8.

Sixty-five references reviewed in this work include such areas
as suicide rates among American youth by age, race, and
sex, for the period 1900-1964.

A related source, which is not entirely on suicide, but is useful for surveying
research, is described below.

2.305   Documentation Associates. DRUGS AND DEATH: THE NON-MEDICAL
USE OF DRUGS RELATED TO ALL MODELS OF DEATH. Rockville,
Md.: National Institute on Drug Abuse, 1975. vii, 151 p. HE 20.814:6.

This work is a summary of research, 1958-74, which includes
suicide by use of drugs.

Chapter 3
LOCATING BOOKS ON SUICIDE
FROM GENERAL BIBLIOGRAPHIC SOURCES

Many books are recommended both in chapter 1 of this information guide, in regard to general introductions to suicide, and also in later chapters of this guide, in regard to specific aspects and areas of suicide. For persons who have a need for more books, especially new books as they come out, or older books for historical purposes, this chapter provides both strategies and sources.

As noted in chapter 2, one effective way to identify books on the subject of suicide is to make use of specially prepared bibliographies on the subject. When these special subject bibliographies are not sufficient or adequate, or are not sufficiently up to date for the purposes of the research or investigation at hand, books on suicide may have to be identified through more general bibliographic sources. These general bibliographic sources, described in this chapter, are usually arranged by subject, have subject indexes, or are subject indexes or listings. Following the descriptions of each general source, subject headings used to locate books on suicide in that source are listed, where possible.

Books on suicide which can be located through these general bibliographic sources may be on all aspects of suicide, including historical, legal, medical, psychological, religious, and sociological. They may range from research studies to personal reports or suggestions for prevention.

The card catalogs of local libraries as well as the printed catalogs of large libraries such as the Library of Congress and the British Library, now including the library of the British Museum, are good general bibliographic sources for locating books on suicide. These are described in section 3.1 of this chapter. Some of these printed library catalogs are considered national bibliographies in that they contain complete bibliographic information for most of the books copyrighted and cataloged in that country. They are accurate and authoritative.

Trade bibliographies, described in section 3.2 of this chapter, are lists of books in print which have been compiled from publishers' listings and brochures. For this reason, these works are often not as accurate as the national bibliographies. These trade bibliographies are mainly concerned with "trade" books, that is, books that are of general interest to the reading public. Some smaller publishers in more specialized fields, as well as some university presses and association publishers, may not be included in these works. However, trade bibliographies are very useful for quick information on current publications.

The retrospective book sources, described in section 3.3 of this chapter, are listings of earlier works and vary in accuracy. Since these sources often lack any kind of subject approach, much patience is required to scan the items listed in them in order to find a limited amount of material on suicide. For historical research on suicide, however, this material may be very important.

Sources for finding reviews of books on suicide are described in section 3.4. Some of these sources, those with subject indexes, can also be used to locate additional books on suicide.

The problem of finding the relevant chapters on suicide in various types of composite books is treated in section 3.5.

3.1 SUBJECT INDEXES TO LIBRARY CATALOGS AND NATIONAL BIBLIOGRAPHIES

An important source for locating books on suicide are library card catalogs, especially those of the larger university and research libraries. By using the card catalogs, the researcher or other interested person has the advantage of examining the books on location. Since most college, university, and large public libraries in the United States use subject headings adopted by the Library of Congress, the subject headings listed in item 3.104 are appropriate to use when searching for books on suicide in these library catalogs, keeping in mind that these headings may change over time and new ones may be added. Librarians can provide assistance with these changes and additions. Printed library catalogs in book form and national bibliographies are also good sources. The most significant of these for books on suicide are described below. These works are ongoing sets which began publication at the time of the imprint date noted in the citation and are continuing to date. This currency is indicated by the dash following the imprint dates.

3.101   British Museum. Department of Printed Books. SUBJECT INDEX OF MODERN BOOKS ACQUIRED. London: Trustees of the British Museum, 1902-- .

An excellent source for identifying books on suicide in English and other languages, this index is an alphabetical listing of the books added since 1881 to the collection of the British Museum, now part of the British Library. The collection is worldwide in scope and spans centuries of publication. The first cumulation of the index covers the period of acquisition from 1881 to 1900. Subsequent cumulations have been issued every five years. Although the subject

index was not initially highly developed, it has the longest
run of any existing subject index. At present, there is a
fifteen-year time lag. The earlier title of this work was
SUBJECT INDEX OF THE MODERN WORKS ADDED TO
THE LIBRARY OF THE BRITISH MUSEUM, FROM 1881 TO
1900. For a subject approach to works on suicide, with a
British emphasis, before 1881, the selective indexes by R.A.
Peddie (item 3.309) are somewhat helpful.

Consult: Suicide

3.102   THE BRITISH NATIONAL BIBLIOGRAPHY. London: British Library
        Bibliographic Services Division, 1950-- . Weekly, with quarterly,
        annual, and quinquennial cumulations.

        A basic reference source for British copyrighted materials,
        this work essentially lists and describes bibliographically
        every new book published in Great Britain. It provides an
        author index, a title index, and, at the end of each month,
        a subject index.

        Consult: Suicide

3.103   CANADIANA: PUBLICATIONS OF INTEREST RECEIVED BY THE NA-
        TIONAL LIBRARY, 1950-- . Ottawa: National Library, 1951-- .
        Monthly, with annual cumulations.

        A basic source for Canadian materials on suicide, this bib-
        liography lists all of the materials cataloged at the National
        Library of Canada, which serves as a depository for Canadian
        books and other materials. The work is divided into eight
        sections: (1) monographs and microfilms, (2) theses in mi-
        croform, (3) serials, (4) pamphlets, (5) sound recordings,
        (6) films and filmstrips, (7) publications of the government
        of Canada, and (8) publications of the provincial govern-
        ments. There is a subject index in English, a subject index
        in French, and a general index in English only. Because
        this set is difficult to use, CANADIAN REFERENCE SOURCES:
        A SELECTIVE GUIDE (item 4.302) and its SUPPLEMENT
        should be consulted. CANADIANA was preceded by the
        CANADIAN CATALOGUE OF BOOKS PUBLISHED IN CAN-
        ADA, ABOUT CANADA, AS WELL AS THOSE WRITTEN
        ABOUT CANADIANS, 1921-1949, published by Toronto
        Public Libraries, 1959. There were two decennial cumula-
        tion of this earlier work.

        Consult: Suicide

3.104   U.S. Library of Congress. LIBRARY OF CONGRESS CATALOGS--
        SUBJECT CATALOG. Washington, D.C.: 1950-- . Quarterly, with
        annual and quinquennial cumulations.

Locating Books on Suicide

A subject guide to all of the books cataloged by the Library of Congress since 1950, with imprints since 1945, this basic index is worldwide in scope. It lists government documents and serials, in addition to books. Each citation is bibliographically complete, accurate, and authoritative. The subject headings are quite detailed and follow the Library of Congress's SUBJECT HEADINGS USED IN THE DICTIONARY CATALOGS OF THE LIBRARY OF CONGRESS. There is a time lag of several months to more than a year before a new book appears in this listing. Prior to 1975, this work was entitled LIBRARY OF CONGRESS CATALOG. BOOKS: SUBJECTS. A CUMULATIVE LIST OF WORKS REPRESENTED BY LIBRARY OF CONGRESS PRINTED CARDS. The following subject headings are used in this subject listing. Any book may appear under more than one heading. It should be noted that these headings are subject to change and that new headings may be added from time to time. Librarians can provide assistance with these changes and additions.

Consult: Afro-Americans--Suicidal behavior
Children--Suicidal behavior
College students--Suicidal behavior
Indians of North America--Suicidal behavior
Kamikaze aeroplanes
Prisoners--Suicidal behavior
Right to die
Sallekhana
Self poisoning
Seppuku
Suicide
Suicide--Addresses, essays, lectures
Suicide--Bibliographies
Suicide--Case studies
Suicide--Congresses
Suicide--Indexes
Suicide--(local subdivisions)
Suicide--Periodicals
Suicide--Prevention
Suicide (Jewish law)
Suicide in literature
Widow suicide
Young adults--Suicidal behavior
Youth--Suicidal behavior

Other national bibliographies, as well as printed catalogs to other major national libraries, may be referred to if one is interested in publications on suicide in other languages and cultures. Consult librarians in large research libraries for guidance in this area.

Bibliographies of government publications, published by the governments themselves, may be considered special types of national bibliographies. These are
often very useful for identifying current, accurate, and very authoritative publications. National governments often publish extensively. For example, the
U.S. Government Printing Office is considered the largest publisher in the world.
Several of the ongoing national bibliographies of government publications, in
English, are listed below. For information on similar works from other countries,
consult librarians.

3.105   Canada. Information Canada. CANADIAN GOVERNMENT PUBLICA-
        TIONS. Ottawa, 1954-- . Annual. Published in two series. MONTHLY
        CATALOGUE, 1953-- . Subject indexes.

        An English-French listing of all government documents, both
        parliamentary and departmental, this work includes legal
        publications as well as other official publications, such as
        census and vital statistics reports. In addition to a general
        subject index, a subject index to government periodicals is
        included. This latter has a two-year time lag from the time
        the articles appear until they are cited. This work suc-
        ceeded the CATALOGUE OF OFFICIAL PUBLICATIONS OF
        THE PARLIAMENT AND GOVERNMENT OF CANADA, 1928-
        1954, which is similarly arranged.

        Consult: Suicide

3.106   Great Britain. Stationery Office. GOVERNMENT PUBLICATIONS.
        London: 1936-- . Monthly, with annual cumulations.

        This index to the official documents published by the British
        government has a subject index and a quinquennial cumula-
        tion of the index. Former titles were GOVERNMENT PUB-
        LICATIONS: CONSOLIDATED LIST 1922-53; GOVERN-
        MENT PUBLICATIONS CATALOG 1954-55; and CATALOGUE
        OF GOVERNMENT PUBLICATIONS 1956-57. For documents
        published from 1922 to 1972, a two-volume cumulative index
        is available.

        Consult: Suicide

3.107   U.S. Superintendent of Documents. MONTHLY CATALOG OF UNITED
        STATES GOVERNMENT PUBLICATIONS. Washington, D.C.: Govern-
        ment Printing Office, 1895-- . Monthly, with annual cumulative index.
        GP3.8:yr./no.

        This current bibliography includes publications by all branches
        of the government in a variety of formats, including books.
        For documents issued between 1900 and 1970, refer to item
        8.302.

        Consult: Suicide
                From July 1976 to date, consult also the headings
                listed in item 3.104.

3.2 GENERAL TRADE BIBLIOGRAPHIES

3.201 AMERICAN BOOK PUBLISHING RECORD. New York: R.R. Bowker Co., 1960-- . Monthly, with annual and quinquennial cumulations.

Often referred to as the BPR, this publication is a record of the books published each month in the United States. Generally excluded are government publications, serial publications including periodicals, and dissertations. This monthly record is compiled from the WEEKLY RECORD, an author listing published by the R.R. Bowker Company. The BPR ANNUAL CUMULATIVE started in 1965. Several quinquennial cumulations have appeared. The BPR entries are arranged by Dewey decimal classification numbers, as cataloged by the Library of Congress, with author and title indexes. Since 1976 a subject index was added, which refers the user to one or more Dewey decimal classification numbers for each subject consulted. Before 1976, when no subject index was included, use of the BPR in searching on a subject was very difficult. One had to know the Dewey number to find books in a subject area, and as a result valuable items may have been missed. The user is advised, when using pre-1976 volumes, to consult the latest subject indexes to ascertain all possible Dewey numbers applicable to suicide as a subject. The following subject headings are suggested at present, although many additional headings may be used in future volumes.

Consult: Suicide
Suicide--United States
Suicide--Early works to 1800
Suicide in literature

3.202 BRITISH BOOKS IN PRINT: THE REFERENCE CATALOGUE OF CURRENT LITERATURE. London: J. Whitaker and Sons, 1874-- . Annual.

Information on over 260,000 books marketed in any given year in England is included in this listing of books. The books are arranged by subject, author, and title. Publication data included are the price, place, and date of publication. This trade publication has a long history, dating back to the REFERENCE CATALOGUE OF CURRENT LITERATURE, founded by Joseph Whitaker in 1874.

Consult: Attempted suicide
Suicide

3.203 CUMULATIVE BOOK INDEX: A WORLD LIST OF BOOKS IN THE ENGLISH LANGUAGE. New York: H.W. Wilson Co., 1898-- . Monthly (except August), cumulated quarterly, annually since 1969, and at least biennially since 1957.

As the title indicates, this very useful publication attempts to list all of the U.S., British, Canadian, and other English-language books published throughout the world. Before 1928 it was mainly a list of books published in the United States. The contents are alphabetized by subject, author, and title in one list. Government documents, most pamphlets, and inexpensive paperbound books are generally not included. Since this is a monthly index, it gives rapid access to new books in many fields and it is easy to use. Although the bibliographic information provided may not be as complete as, or concur with, that of the library of Congress catalogs, inaccuracies are very few. The CBI was issued for 1899-1928 under the title UNITED STATES CATALOG: BOOKS IN PRINT.

Consult: Suicide
Suicide--Addresses, essays, lectures
Suicide--Bibliographies
Suicide--Congresses
Suicide--Outlines, syllabi
Suicide--Prevention
Suicide--Statistics

3.204   PAPERBACKS IN PRINT. London: J. Whitaker and Sons, 1960-- . Annual.

Over forty-three thousand paperbacks for sale in Great Britain are listed by author, title, and by some fifty-two subject headings in this guide. The subject index is a keyword-in-title index. Care must be taken in using this type of index because, unless the user can anticipate all of the possible words referring to suicide that authors may use in the titles, some significant books may be missed.

Consult: Suicide; or subject headings such as those suggested in item 5.133.

3.205   PAPERBOUND BOOKS IN PRINT. New York: R.R. Bowker Co., 1955-- . Annual, with supplements in May and September.

Over 130,000 titles of paperbound books sold each year by American publishers are listed by subject, title, and author. The subject listing is difficult to use because the headings are very broad and general. The main use for this work appears to be for personal purchase of inexpensive books.

Consult: Psychology--General
Sociology--General

3.206   PUBLISHERS' TRADE LIST ANNUAL. SUBJECT GUIDE TO BOOKS IN PRINT; AN INDEX TO THE PUBLISHERS' TRADE LIST ANNUAL. 2 vols. New York: R.R. Bowker Co., 1957-- . Annual, with a mid-year supplement.

Over 367,000 book titles from U.S. publishers are listed
under 62,000 subject headings, including subdivided headings, that generally conform to the Library of Congress subject headings. Legal books, fiction, drama, juvenile fiction, and government documents are usually not included.
This is a good source of information for new U.S. books on
suicide, and is easy to use. The price, date of publication,
and the publisher are given for most titles. Since this guide
at times contains inaccurate bibliographic information, the
CUMULATIVE BOOK INDEX (item 3.203) and preferably
the NATIONAL UNION CATALOG compiled by the Library of Congress should be consulted for accuracy.

Consult: Kamikaze airplanes
Suicide

3.207 SUBJECT GUIDE TO FORTHCOMING BOOKS; A BIMONTHLY SUBJECT
FORECAST OF BOOKS TO COME. New York: R.R. Bowker Co.,
1967-- . Bimonthly, each issue revising and updating the previous
issue.

A companion to FORTHCOMING BOOKS by the same publisher, this work announces books that are scheduled to be
published in the United States within the next five months.
The expected title, author, month of publication (if set),
the price, and the publisher are given for each book. Entries are arranged by title under subject headings, which
were revised in 1976. A title may appear under several
headings. Care should be exercised in using this work because listed titles may be changed upon publication and
some books may never be published. It is a useful work,
however, in that it alerts the reader to books forthcoming
in his area of interest.

Consult: Suicide

3.3 RETROSPECTIVE GENERAL BIBLIOGRAPHIES AND CHECKLISTS OF EARLY WORKS

Except for the early bibliographies on suicide by Motta (item 2.203) and Rost
(2.206), and the early volumes of several of the ongoing works cited in sections
3.1 and 3.2, books on suicide written prior to 1890 are difficult to identify.
The general retrospective bibliographies and checklists of early works listed
below are those that can be considered most useful to the researcher in locating
any further references to early books on suicide. Fortunately many of these
early books cited in the general bibliographies and checklists described below
are available in microform. However, these works are not easy to search because most of them lack subject indexes.

3.301 THE AMERICAN CATALOGUE, 1876-1910. 1880-1911. Reprint. 8
vols. New York: Peter Smith, 1941.

> This valuable work attempts to list all of the books that
> were printed in the United States from July 1, 1876 to
> December 31, 1910. The listings are by author and title;
> the subject index was published as a separate work (item
> 3.302).
>
> Consult: Suicide

3.302 THE AMERICAN CATALOGUE: SUBJECTS. 1880-1900. Reprint. 5
vols. New York: Peter Smith, 1941.

> This work represents the only adequate subject index to
> American books in the nineteenth century. By the turn of
> the century the CUMULATIVE BOOK INDEX (item 3.203)
> took over this task and is much superior.
>
> Consult: Suicide

3.303 Bristol, Roger P., comp. SUPPLEMENT TO CHARLES EVANS' AMERICAN
BIBLIOGRAPHY. Charlottesville: University of Virginia Press, 1970.
xix, 636 p.

> This supplement to Evans's bibliography (item 3.306) contains
> an additional eleven thousand imprints for the years 1646-
> 1800. The author attempted to locate all of the works
> missed by Evans. The books are arranged in chronological
> order. There is a separate author and title index, but no
> subject index, thereby requiring much perseverance in search-
> ing for books on suicide. Over ten thousand of these ad-
> ditional works are also available in many large university
> libraries on microcards, grouped under the heading "Early
> American Imprints 1639-1800. First Series (Evans)."

3.304 Bruntjen, Scott, and Bruntjen, Carol. A CHECKLIST OF AMERICAN
IMPRINTS, 1831-- . Metuchen, N.J.: Scarecrow Press, 1975-- .

> About ten thousand books are listed in the first two volumes
> of this set, covering books published in 1831 and 1832.
> They are listed by author and title, using secondary sources.
> No indexes are included.

3.305 Cooper, Gayle. A CHECKLIST OF AMERICAN IMPRINTS FOR 1830.
Metuchen, N.J.: Scarecrow Press, 1972. 493 p.

> This volume completed Shoemaker's project (item 3.313)
> which was incomplete at the time of Shoemaker's death.

3.306 Evans, Charles, comp. AMERICAN BIBLIOGRAPHY. 1903-34. Reprint. 12 vols. New York: Peter Smith, 1941-42.

Over thirty-nine thousand early American imprints from 1639 to 1800, including books, pamphlets, and periodicals, are arranged in chronological order in this basic work. Each volume contains an author list and a very general, as well as inadequate, subject list. This bibliography of Americana is incomplete (refer to item 3.303). It also contains some books never published. About thirty thousand of the works included in this bibliography are available on microcards in the collections of many large university libraries, grouped under the title "Early American Imprints 1639-1800. First Series (Evans)." The inadequate subject index in this work makes it difficult to estimate the number of works published on suicide in the United States during this period.

Consult: Suicide

3.307   Haight, Willet R. CANADIAN CATALOGUE OF BOOKS: 1791-1897. 1896-1904. Reprint. 3 vols. Vancouver: Devlin; London: H. Pordes, 1958.

As an incomplete listing of Canadian books from the nineteenth century, arranged alphabetically by author with no subject index, this work may be of very little value for locating books on suicide.'

3.308   Kelly, James, comp. THE AMERICAN CATALOGUE OF BOOKS PUBLISHED IN THE UNITED STATES FROM JAN. 1861 TO JAN. 1871. 1866-77. Reprint. 2 quinquennial vols. New York: Peter Smith, 1938.

Kelly's work, like its predecessor by Roorbach (item 3.311), is also incomplete. Especially lacking are books published in the South during the Civil War. Books are listed by author only, which makes searches for books on suicide in this source very tedious.

3.309   Peddie, Robert Alexander. SUBJECT INDEX OF BOOKS PUBLISHED BEFORE 1880. 4 vols. London: Grafton, 1933-48.

A valuable reference that provides a subject approach to nearly 200,000 books in the British Museum and elsewhere, this work is an important source for locating, by subject, books published prior to the publication of the British Museum's SUBJECT INDEX OF MODERN BOOKS ACQUIRED (item 3.101). Under each subject heading, the titles are listed chronologically from the late 1400s to 1880.

Consult: Suicide

3.310   Pollard, Alfred W., and Redgrave, G.R., comps. A SHORT-TITLE CATALOGUE OF BOOKS PRINTED IN ENGLAND, SCOTLAND AND

IRELAND AND OF ENGLISH BOOKS PRINTED ABROAD, 1475-1640.
London: Bibliographical Society, 1926. xvi, 609 p.

Approximately 26,500 titles are arranged in this work by
author with no subject index. This listing represents most
of the known books for the period. Locations in 133 British
libraries and 15 American libraries are noted. Many of
these titles, however, are available in microform in many
large university libraries, grouped into a series entitled
"Early English Books, 1475-1640."

3.311   Roorbach, Orville A., comp. BIBLIOTHECA AMERICANA: CATALOGUE
OF AMERICAN PUBLICATIONS, INCLUDING REPRINTS AND ORIGI-
NAL WORKS, FROM 1820 TO JANUARY 1861. 1849-61. Reprint.
4 vols. New York: Peter Smith, 1939.

Although Roorbach's record of American book production
from 1820 to 1861 is very incomplete, it is the only work
covering most of the period. Books are listed by author.
The lack of a subject index makes searching for books on
suicide very difficult.

3.312   Shaw, Ralph R., and Shoemaker, Richard H., comps. AMERICAN BIB-
LIOGRAPHY: A PRELIMINARY CHECKLIST. 19 vols. New York:
Scarecrow Press, 1958-63.

This checklist, which lists books from American presses for
the first two decades of the nineteenth century, contains
over fifty thousand titles. Each volume lists the books produced for a single year. The works are listed by author,
with separate cumulated author and title indexes, but no
subject index. This makes searching for books on suicide
very difficult. The accuracy of the work may be somewhat
questionable in that only secondary sources were used in
compiling this checklist. The majority of these titles are
now available on microcards in many large university libraries under the heading "Early American Imprints 1801-
1819. Second Series (Shaw-Shoemaker)."

3.313   Shoemaker, Richard H., comp. A CHECKLIST OF AMERICAN IM-
PRINTS, FOR 1820-1829. 11 vols. New York: Scarecrow Press,
1964-73.

Over forty-seven thousand titles are contained in this con-
tinuation of the AMERICAN BIBLIOGRAPHY (item 3.306)
for the years 1820-30. The titles are listed chronologically
by author. As with the preceding volumes, this set does
not contain a subject index, which makes it very difficult
to use. There are separate cumulative author and title indexes. Locations for the works cited are indicated. This
checklist was also compiled from secondary sources; that is,

the original works were not examined, which may result in
occasional inaccuracies. Refer to item 3.305.

3.314   Tod, Dorothea, and Cordingley, Audrey. A CHECKLIST OF CANADIAN
IMPRINTS, 1900-25. Ottawa: Canadian Bibliographic Center, Public
Archives of Canada, 1950. 370 p.

This work lists books and pamphlets of more than fifty pages.
No government documents are included. Entries are by author, with no title or subject indexes.

3.315   Tremaine, Marie. A BIBLIOGRAPHY OF CANADIAN IMPRINTS, 1751-
1800. Toronto: University of Toronto Press, 1952. xxvii, 705 p.

This list of 1,204 early imprints is arranged in chronological
order with good bibliographic descriptions of each work.
It appears to contain very few items on suicide. Entries
are made by author, title, and subject.

3.4 RELATED BIBLIOGRAPHIC SOURCES

3.401   INTERNATIONAL BIBLIOGRAPHY OF SOCIAL AND CULTURAL AN-
THROPOLOGY, 1955-- . Paris: UNESCO, 1955-59; Chicago: Aldine; London: Tavistock Publications, 1960-- . Annual.

This extensive work lists books, periodical articles, and
duplicated materials in many languages. Access is through
an author index and subject index.

Consult: Suicide

3.402   INTERNATIONAL BIBLIOGRAPHY OF SOCIOLOGY. Vol. 1, 1951-- .
Paris: UNESCO, 1951-60; Chicago: Aldine, 1961-- .; London:
Tavistock Publications, 1962-- . Annual.

This extensive bibliography lists books, periodical articles,
pamphlets, and government publications in many languages.
It has author and subject indexes. There is about a two-
year time lag until a published work appears in the annual
volumes.

Consult: Suicide

3.403   MEDICAL BOOKS AND SERIALS IN PRINT: AN INDEX TO LITERA-
TURE IN THE HEALTH SCIENCES. New York: R.R. Bowker Co.,
1978-- . Annual.

This work continues and expands the former MEDICAL BOOKS
IN PRINT, which started in 1972. There are separate subject indexes for books and for serials. This is a good and

easy-to-use source of books in print each year on suicide,
with approximately seventy-five items listed, some of which
are also listed in the SUBJECT GUIDE TO BOOKS IN
PRINT (3.206).

Consult: Suicide

3.404   Walters, LeRoy. BIBLIOGRAPHY OF BIOETHICS. Detroit: Gale
Research Co., 1975-- . Annual.

Refer to item 5.103.

In addition, selected books on suicide may also be identified by using the following works: ABSTRACTS ON CRIMINOLOGY AND PENOLOGY (5.202);
INDEX MEDICUS (5.115); PAIS BULLETIN (5.131); PSYCHOLOGICAL ABSTRACTS
(5.219); and SOCIOLOGICAL ABSTRACTS (5.225).

3.5 LOCATING REVIEWS OF BOOKS ON SUICIDE

Book reviews are useful sources of critical opinion on books, usually appearing
within a year or two of a book's publication. In addition to providing favorable
or unfavorable contemporary impressions about a book, reviews often summarize
the contents of the book. The main reference sources for finding reviews of
books in English on suicide are described below. These review sources, when
subject indexes are included, may also serve as aids for finding books on suicide.

3.501   BOOK REVIEW DIGEST. New York: H.W. Wilson Co., 1905-- .
Monthly (except February and July) with annual cumulations, and five-
year cumulative indexes.

Selected reviews from approximately seventy-five American
and British general periodicals are indexed by this ongoing
work. In addition to citing reviews of a book in the various
periodicals, excerpts from several of the reviews are provided. The reviews are selected for inclusion according to
the publisher's stated criteria, noted in the preface: "To
qualify for inclusion a book must have been published or
distributed in the United States. A work of non-fiction
must have received two or more reviews and one of fiction
four or more reviews in the journals selected." Generally,
this statement on number of reviews applies to a time period
of within eighteen months of publication of the book. This
may eliminate some scholarly books because of the time lag
in reviewing in the major professional journals. The book
reviews are arranged by author, with title and subject indexes. This latter is very important when using this work
to identify books on suicide. The citations of the reviews
in the BOOK REVIEW DIGEST are cumulated in the NA-
TIONAL LIBRARY SERVICE CUMULATED BOOK REVIEW

INDEX (item 3.504), the use of which results in a great reduction in searching time.

Consult, when using the subject index:
Fiction--Suicide
Suicide

3.502 BOOK REVIEW INDEX. Detroit: Gale Research Co., 1965-- . Bi-monthly, with annual cumulations.

About 35,000 reviews from over 225 popular and scholarly American periodicals are cited annually by this work, making it a more comprehensive source for locating reviews than the BOOK REVIEW DIGEST (item 3.501). The citations are arranged by the authors of the books. This index is particularly useful for the researcher who is looking for reviews of a specific book on suicide. Since reviews for any particular book may appear over a period of several years, several volumes of this work may have to be consulted to locate all of the reviews indexed by this work. Excerpts from the reviews are not included in this work, only the abbreviated citations to the reviews printed in the various periodicals. There is a time lag of generally less than six months from the time that the review is published until it is indexed.

3.503 CURRENT BOOK REVIEW CITATIONS. New York: H.W. Wilson Co., 1976-- . Monthly, except August.

This excellent book review index has broad coverage, indexing reviews from over twelve hundred American periodicals for fiction, nonfiction, and children's books. The reviews are simply cited, with no excerpts, and are indexed by author and title.

3.504 National Library Service Corporation. NATIONAL LIBRARY SERVICE CUMULATED BOOK REVIEW INDEX, 1905-1974. 6 vols. Princeton, N.J.: 1975.

This work is a cumulative index to all of the reviews cited in the BOOK REVIEW DIGEST (item 3.501) for the seventy-year period. There is one listing for authors and one for titles, with no subject listing.

In addition to the above sources for locating reviews of books on suicide, various periodical indexes and abstract journals noted in sections 1 and 2 of chapter 5 may be consulted, as well as the newspapers cited in items 10.106, 10.108, and 10.109. For a review of a book on suicide which has been published too recently for any review of it to be indexed and cited in the above sources, the reader is advised to consult recent issues of the periodicals listed in section 5.5.

3.6 LOCATING CHAPTERS ON SUICIDE IN COMPOSITE BOOKS

The previous sections of this chapter deal with the identification of whole books on suicide. As can be seen, there is little difficulty in identifying these if one systematically searches for them as described in this chapter. However, when it comes to identifying significant chapters in books, particularly in composite books, there is very little aid available. As a result, much relevant information is often lost.

Composite books are of several types. There are those in which the author deals in each chapter with a fairly distinctive topic, one of which may be some aspect of suicide. Such a chapter on suicide may have information and insight not found elsewhere. But since it is only one chapter in a book covering a fairly broad range of topics, the subject of suicide will not normally be noted for that book in library catalogs, or in the other general bibliographic indexes previously listed. In the catalogs and indexes mentioned, a subject heading must be ascribed which is broad enough to cover the entire composite book, for example, "Social Problems," with no mention of suicide as a subject. In this way the information on suicide may be essentially lost.

There is another type of composite book, often on a broad general theme, in which each chapter is written by a different individual on some distinctive aspect of the general theme, some chapters perhaps being only loosely related to the theme. This may be the case with conference proceedings. Again, in the general bibliographic system, only a broad subject heading is assigned to the book, and thus a chapter specifically on suicide may be lost bibliographically.

The researcher has limited recourse in his efforts to identify significant chapters in these types of books. Various periodical indexes and abstract journals cite selected chapters in composite books. These include the ARTS AND HUMANI-TIES CITATION INDEX (5.102), BIBLIOGRAPHY OF BIOETHICS (5.103), BIO-RESEARCH INDEX (5.104), SCIENCE CITATION INDEX (5.133), SOCIAL SCI-ENCES CITATION INDEX (5.134), PSYCHOLOGICAL ABSTRACTS (5.219), and the several CURRENT CONTENTS indexes (5.401-5.403).

Since conference proceedings volumes may be considered composite books, section 12.4 of this information guide describes indexing sources useful for identifying conference papers and reports.

The only other aids available are the works described in section 9.7 of this information guide. Of particular importance for current studies is item 9.703, ESSAY AND GENERAL LITERATURE INDEX. Although to date this latter has very little on suicide, it does provide information often not otherwise available.

Chapter 4
SUICIDE INFORMATION IN BASIC REFERENCE WORKS

Several types of basic reference works are especially convenient sources of suicide information. Among these are encyclopedias, almanacs, yearbooks, and handbooks. Fortunately many of these basic reference works are readily available to the public in libraries and bookstores. These are useful because they provide suicide information in succinct form for a wide cross-section of the general public, from the relatively uninformed person wanting a short general overview of the subject to the specialist wanting a quick update on recent data or research on some aspect of suicide.

This chapter will describe the most useful basic reference works for suicide and the type of suicide information provided by each. Sources for more detailed and extensive information on suicide are described in later chapters of this information guide, and are best found by using the subject index. Following the description of each work cited in this chapter is a listing of subject headings under which information on suicide may be found in that work. This can potentially save the user considerable time. However, one should be aware that subject headings for later editions of the works may change or new relevant headings may be added.

The last section, 4.3, of this chapter describes means by which the person particularly interested in being able to identify new reference works specifically on the subject of suicide, as they are published can do so.

4.1 ENCYCLOPEDIAS AND HANDBOOKS

For persons relatively uninformed in the area of suicide, articles from some of the general encyclopedias listed below can provide very good points of entry into the subject. Some encyclopedias and handbooks listed are more specialized and contain very useful summaries for the student or the researcher in this area.

4.101 AMERICAN HANDBOOK OF PSYCHIATRY. Silvano Arieti, editor-in-chief. 2d rev. and expanded ed. 6 vols. New York: Basic Books, 1974-75.

Volume 2 of this work contains an article entitled "Community Programs in Suicidology," and volume 3 contains a major article entitled "Suicide." In addition, throughout the set, there are many references to suicide. There is a separate subject index for each volume.

Consult: Suicidal behaviors
Suicide
Suicide attempts
Suicide prevention programs

4.102   CHAMBER'S ENCYCLOPAEDIA. New rev. ed. 15 vols. Oxford and New York: Pergamon Press, 1967.

There is no general article on suicide in this well-known British encyclopedia but there are eight short references which include suicide and folklore, suicide and vampires, psychology of suicide, and burial customs for suicide victims.

Consult: Suicide (in the general index)

4.103   COLLIER'S ENCYCLOPEDIA. 24 vols. New York: Crowell-Collier Educational Corp., 1949-- .

The 1979 edition contains a number of short references to suicide and psychology, poisons, legal aspects, and life insurance, with particular regard to the present day United States.

Consult: Suicide (in the general index)

4.104   ENCYCLOPEDIA AMERICANA. 30 vols. New York: Grolier Educational Corp., Americana Division, 1829-- . New editions issued annually under a policy of continuous revision. Annual supplements.

A good article in the 1978 edition treats comparative and modern concepts of suicide. Comparative suicide rates and other statistics according to age groups are also provided in this article. A number of short additional references in the set include suicide and crime, insurance, mental illness, and legal aspects.

Consult: Suicide (in the general index)

4.105   ENCYCLOPAEDIA BRITANNICA. ca. 30 vols. Chicago: Encyclopaedia Britannica, 1929-- . New editions issued annually under a policy of continuous revision. The 1974 edition started a radically different format and content. Annual supplements.

An extensive article in the 1979 edition treats definitions of suicide in modern and premodern societies, theories, and treatment and prevention. It also provides statistics through 1965. A number of short additional references in the set relate suicide to drug abuse, life insurance, and medical aspects.

Consult: Suicide (in the general index)

4.106 ENCYCLOPAEDIA JUDAICA. Jerusalem and New York: Macmillan, 1971-72. Supplements.

This specialized Jewish encyclopedia contains a short article on suicide in Judaism. Several short references to suicide are made throughout the work. A short bibliography on Jewish suicide is included.

Consult: Suicide (in the general index)

4.107 ENCYCLOPEDIA OF PHILOSOPHY. Paul Edwards, editor-in-chief. 8 vols. New York: Macmillan, 1967.

Largely concerned with philosophical aspects of suicide only, this work has a very good general article under "Suicide," with excellent footnotes and bibliography. Treatment of euthanasia is also included in the article. A number of short references throughout the set lead one to the views on suicide of various philosophers.

Consult: Suicide (in the general index)

4.108 ENCYCLOPEDIA OF RELIGION AND ETHICS. James Hastings et al., eds. 12 vols. plus index vol. New York: Charles Scribner's Sons, 1908-27.

This very scholarly work provides a twenty-page article on suicide which is excellent for historical purposes and for comparative studies of suicide in ancient cultures and primitive societies, as well as of suicide in various other areas and countries of the world through the nineteenth century. The notes and bibliography are excellent as well. Numerous other references may be found throughout the set relating suicide to aspects such as alcoholism, burial practices, and crime. See also item 9.905.

Consult: Suicide (in the general index)

4.109 ENCYCLOPAEDIA OF THE SOCIAL SCIENCES. 15 vols. New York: Macmillan, 1930-35.

This classic work contains a three-page scholarly article on suicide. Comparative suicide statistics for North America and Europe for the period 1912-30 are presented. Also included is a bibliography of older scholarly works on suicide.

This work is particularly useful for the historical aspects of social science study on suicide.

Consult: Suicide

4.110 INTERNATIONAL ENCYCLOPEDIA OF PSYCHIATRY, PSYCHOLOGY, PSYCHOANALYSIS, AND NEUROLOGY. Benjamin B. Wolman, ed. 12 vols. New York: Produced for Aesculapuis Publishers by Van Nostrand Reinhold Co., 1977.

Suicide, hospital treatment of suicidal patients, and suicide prevention are each discussed in three one-page articles in this work. A brief bibliography follows each article. The general index leads to other references to suicide in the set.

Consult: Suicide (in the general index)

4.111 INTERNATIONAL ENCYCLOPEDIA OF THE SOCIAL SCIENCES. 17 vols. New York: Macmillan, 1968.

A twenty-page article on the social and psychological aspects of suicide and its theoretical perspectives is provided in this scholarly encyclopedia. The general index also contains short references to suicide and aging, suicide and mental disorders, and suicide and social class. Some bibliography is also included.

Consult: Suicide (in the general index)

4.112 NEW CATHOLIC ENCYCLOPEDIA. Prepared by an editorial staff at the Catholic University of America. 15 vols. New York: McGraw-Hill, 1967. Supplements.

A short article in this encyclopedia deals with the kinds of suicide, the morality of suicide, and ecclesiastical penalties for suicide. There are other short references in the set in regard to adolescent suicide, burial laws relating to suicide, and medical experimentation related to suicide.

Consult: Suicide (in the general index)

4.113 Perlin, Seymour, ed. A HANDBOOK FOR THE STUDY OF SUICIDE. New York: Oxford University Press, 1975. 236 p.

Refer to item 1.110.

4.2 ALMANACS AND YEARBOOKS

Almanacs and yearbooks provide quick, fairly recent factual information on specific subjects but with little interpretation of the facts. There are a number of these general reference works available, and each contains some distinctive information on suicide. In addition to the works which are described below, basic suicidal statistical information is provided in the following annuals: CANADA YEAR BOOK (item 7.101); DEMOGRAPHIC YEARBOOK (item 7.303); ANNUAL ABSTRACT OF STATISTICS (item 7.103); STATISTICAL ABSTRACT OF THE UNITED STATES (item 7.107); STATISTICS CANADA CATALOGUE (item 7.302); VITAL STATISTICS OF THE UNITED STATES (item 7.212). Yearbooks to the encyclopedias described in section 4.1 often are good sources for current information.

4.201 INFORMATION PLEASE ALMANAC. New York: Simon & Schuster, 1947-- . Annual.

> Suicide rates for selected countries around the world are provided by this source. There is generally a three-year time lag on the information at the time of its publication.
>
> Consult: Suicide

4.202 READER'S DIGEST ALMANAC AND YEARBOOK. Pleasantville, N.Y.: Reader's Digest Association, 1966-- . Annual.

> This source provides very brief information on suicide. It reports the number of suicides and the suicide rates in the United States for the previous year and for several selected prior years.
>
> Consult: Suicides

4.203 WORLD ALMANAC AND BOOK OF FACTS. New York: Newspaper Enterprise Associates, 1868-- . Annual.

> Information is provided on the number of suicides and the suicide rate for the United States, by race, age, and sex. There is a two-year time lag in reporting the annual information.
>
> Consult: Suicide

4.204 WORLD HEALTH STATISTICS ANNUAL. Geneva: World Health Organization, 1962-- . Annual.

> This is a basic source for suicide statistics. Refer to item 7.308.

4.3 IDENTIFYING NEW REFERENCE WORKS

Completely new reference books are being published each year, some of which may become important for suicide information. One way to find out about them, as they are added to library collections, is to periodically search in library card catalogs under subject headings such as:

> Suicide--Handbooks, manuals, etc.

Suicide--Dictionaries
Suicide--Yearbooks

or many of the subject headings listed in item 3.104, followed by the above
subdivisions.

Reference books on suicide may be identified also by keeping up with the following general guides to reference books as they are supplemented or as new
editions are published.

4.301   AMERICAN REFERENCE BOOKS ANNUAL. Edited by Bohdan S. Wynar.
        Littleton, Colo.: Libraries Unlimited, 1970-- . Annual, with quin-
        quennial cumulative index.

        Each annual volume describes and evaluates reference books
        which have been published the previous year. Citations to
        other reviews of the reference books are included. This
        carefully prepared work is arranged by subject areas with
        subdivisions. An author, specific subject, and title index
        is very helpful.

4.302   Ryder, Dorothy E., ed. CANADIAN REFERENCE SOURCES: A SE-
        LECTIVE GUIDE. Ottawa: Canadian Library Association, 1973. x,
        185 p. Supplement.

        This well-annotated guide to specifically Canadian reference
        works is arranged in five general areas with subdivisions and
        with full indexing.

4.303   Sheehy, Eugene Paul; Keckeissen, Rita G.; McIlvaine, Eileen. GUIDE
        TO REFERENCE BOOKS. 9th ed. Chicago: American Library Asso-
        ciation, 1976. xviii, 1,015 p.

        This is a revised, expanded, and updated version of the
        eighth edition by Constance M. Winchell. This annotated
        worldwide basic listing of selected reference works is an
        essential source for locating new reference works which may
        contain information on suicide. Supplements and forthcoming
        editions of this work should be watched for.

4.304   Walford, Albert John, ed. GUIDE TO REFERENCE MATERIAL. 3d ed.
        3 vols. London: Library Association, 1973-75.

        A worldwide, carefully annotated listing of important ref-
        erence books, this work emphasizes materials published in
        Great Britain. The annotations often include citations to
        reviews of the works.

New works such as those described above may be watched for in the future under subject headings in library card catalogs such as:

Reference books--Bibliography

An additional source for identifying new reference books which may contain suicide information is the index cited below.

4.305 LIBRARY LITERATURE: INDEX TO LIBRARY AND INFORMATION SCI-
ENCE, 1921/32-- . New York: H.W. Wilson Co., 1934-- . Bimonthly, with annual cumulative volumes. Subtitle varies.

In addition to indexing library and information science materials, this work also selectively indexes nonlibrary science
materials of reference and research value. In this manner
basic reference books of all types and periodical articles on
the literature of special subjects, as well as book lists, are
included.

Consult: Book lists--Special subjects--Suicide
Reference books--Bibliography
Reference books--Reviews
Research materials--Special subjects--Suicide

Chapter 5

LOCATING PERIODICAL ARTICLES ON SUICIDE

A large number of periodical articles on suicide appear each year, written on a variety of different aspects and for a variety of purposes. In later chapters of this information guide, which treat specific areas of suicide, selected articles are cited as being most informative among those published to date. The purpose of this chapter is to present strategies and sources for identifying other periodical or journal articles according to the specific needs of the individual user of this guide, especially new articles as they are published.

For study and research on suicide, periodical articles have certain characteristics that may make them more useful than books. First, if timeliness is of utmost importance, the periodical article is usually more current, since the time between writing and publication is usually shorter for periodical articles. Second, the article may contain succinct information on a specific aspect, a current trend, or a recent finding in suicidology not easily found elsewhere. Third, the length of a periodical article may be adequate and sufficient to describe the methodology and findings of a research project or other investigation without need for the more lengthy format of a book. One of the main disadvantages in using periodical articles, however, is the difficulty that the uninformed person may have in identifying pertinent articles on suicide from the thousands of periodicals published each year.

It is not possible to locate pertinent articles efficiently in periodicals without the aid of standard periodical indexes and abstract journals, which index a large number of different periodicals at one time. In sections 5.1 and 5.2 of this chapter, the most important of these standard indexes and abstract journals are described and evaluated according to their usefulness in locating articles on suicide. Current subject headings useful for locating the articles in each source are listed after the description. It should be remembered, however, that these headings may change with time and new headings may be used in the future.

Most of the periodical indexes and abstract journals must be searched manually for relevant articles. Some of the more important ones, however, may also be computer searched. This option is noted in the description of each source where applicable.

Locating Periodical Articles

For the researcher, educator, clinician, or other specialist in suicidology and suicidal behavior, a discussion of current awareness services is provided in section 5.4. For those who wish to keep an even closer watch on the current output of information on suicide in the periodical literature, a listing of periodicals which most frequently publish articles on suicide is provided in section 5.5.

5.1 INDEXES TO PERIODICALS

Periodical indexes, unlike abstract journals, in general provide only citations to periodical articles. They do not provide abstracts of the contents of the articles in addition to the citations, as do the abstracting journals. Indexes are thereby usually more current than abstract journals because of the increased time consumed in the abstracting process of the latter. A citation of a periodical article usually includes the author of the article, the title of the article, the title, volume number, and issue number of the periodical in which the article is found, as well as the page numbers.

Two of the most important indexes for research articles on suicide are the IN-DEX MEDICUS (item 5.115) and the SOCIAL SCIENCES CITATION INDEX (5.134). On the other hand, one of the most important indexes for locating periodical articles of more general interest on suicide is the READERS' GUIDE TO PERIODICAL LITERATURE (item 5.132). Other indexes described in this section, which cite articles on or related to suicide, are from such areas as ethics, medical services, biology, arts and humanities, business, religion, education, psychology, sociology, and law. After the description of each index, in order to save the user considerable time, the subject headings used in each index to locate articles on suicide are indicated. A real attempt has been made to provide all of the pertinent subject headings currently used in each index. However, the user should be aware that subject headings may change over time and relevant new headings may be added at any time. The average number of suicide citations per year appearing in each source for the past two or three years is also indicated.

5.101   ACCESS: THE SUPPLEMENTARY INDEX TO PERIODICALS. Syracuse, N.Y.: J.G. Burke, distributed by Gaylord Bros., 1975-- .

> Access to the contents of about 125 popular periodicals, not previously indexed but widely held by public libraries, is supplied by this index. An author and a subject index are provided. Reviews of books and films are included. Average usefulness for this topic.
>
> Consult: Negro youth--Suicide
> Suicide
> Suicide--Geographical places
> Suicide prevention centers
> Women--Suicide
> Youth--Suicidal Behavior

5.102   ARTS AND HUMANITIES CITATION INDEX. Philadelphia: Institute for Scientific Information, 1978-- . Three issues per year, including annual cumulations.

This work indexes over eight hundred periodicals in art, architecture, the classics, film, folklore, history, linguistics, literature, music, poetry, theatre, theology and religious studies, and philosophy from twenty-eight countries. About half of the journals indexed are from the United States. Book reviews are also provided. This multidisciplinary index to the humanities periodical literature is in the same format as the SOCIAL SCIENCES CITATION INDEX (item 5.134) and the SCIENCE CITATION INDEX (item 5.133). See item 5.133 on how to use this index. One of the chief deficiencies of a keyword-in-title approach such as is used in this index is that, unless the user can anticipate all of the possible words referring to suicide that the authors may use in the titles, some significant articles may be missed.

Consult: The list of words suggested in item 5.133, remembering that these keywords may change with time and new ones may be used in the future.

5.103   BIBLIOGRAPHY OF BIOETHICS. Detroit: Gale Research Co., 1975-- . Annual.

This index cites journal articles, books, chapters in books, newspaper articles, court decisions, and audiovisuals that deal with ethical implications of biological research and medicine. On-line computer searching is available from the National Library of Medicine's MEDLINE network (5.115). About five citations to periodical articles on suicide appear each year.

Consult: Suicide

5.104   BIORESEARCH INDEX, 1965-- . Philadelphia: BioSciences Information Service, 1965-- . Monthly.

This source indexes research articles and reports that are published in volumes resulting from regular international congresses and symposia on biological research, as well as in annual reports from foundations promoting biological research. These are not covered by BIOLOGICAL ABSTRACTS. A keyword-in-title approach, with supplementary keywords, requires sophistication in using the index if comprehensiveness is required. Approximately fifty citations a year on suicide are provided. The title will be changed to BIOLOGICAL ABSTRACTS/RRM beginning January 1980, vol. 18.

Consult: Suicide

5.105   BRITISH HUMANITIES INDEX. London: Library Association, 1915-- .
        Quarterly, with annual cumulations.

        Nearly four hundred periodicals in the social sciences and
        humanities published principally in England, Australia, and
        New Zealand are indexed by means of separate subject and
        author indexes. The time lag for current listings is from
        three to six months. This work was formerly entitled the
        SUBJECT INDEX TO PERIODICALS, 1915-1961. This source
        provides about one to three citations on suicide per year.

        Consult: Suicide

5.106   BUSINESS PERIODICALS INDEX. New York: H.W. Wilson Co.,
        1958-- . Monthly (except August), with annual cumulations.

        Dealing with the topic of suicide in its business aspects,
        such as suicide and insurance, and pharmacist liability in
        suicide, this index cites articles and book reviews from over
        170 English-language periodicals in accounting, advertising
        and public relations, automation, banking, communications,
        economics, finance and investments, labor, management,
        and taxation. This index is one of the successors to the
        INDUSTRIAL ARTS INDEX, 1913-57. Approximately one
        or two articles per year on suicide are cited by this index.

        Consult: Suicide

5.107   CANADIAN PERIODICAL INDEX. Ottawa: Canadian Library Asso-
        ciation, 1948-- . Monthly, with annual cumulations.

        Articles and book reviews from English and French-Canadian
        periodicals in the social sciences and humanities are indexed
        by this work.   Coverage was expanded to nearly one hun-
        dred periodical titles in 1976.   Indexing is essentially by
        author and subject. For current listings there is a six-month
        time lag. This work was formerly entitled CANADIAN IN-
        DEX TO PERIODICALS AND DOCUMENTARY FILMS, 1948-
        1963. Approximately one to three articles on suicide are
        cited each year.

        Consult: Suicide

5.108   CATHOLIC PERIODICAL AND LITERATURE INDEX. Vol. 14-- , 1967/
        68-- . Haverford, Pa.: Catholic Library Association, 1968-- . Bi-
        monthly, with biennial cumulations.

        Articles and book reviews from approximately 135 Catholic
        periodicals, about 2,500 selected adult books each year by
        and about Catholics, as well as papal, diocesan, conciliar,
        and other official church documents are indexed by this
        work. Most of the above indexed materials originate in

the United States, with some, however, from Europe and Latin America. Access is provided by means of author, title (books only), and subject indexes. The time lag for current listings is approximately six months. This index was formed from two previous works: the CATHOLIC PERIODICAL INDEX, 1930-67, vols. 1-13, and the GUIDE TO CATHOLIC LITERATURE, 1888-1967. Approximately three articles on suicide are cited per year.

Consult: Suicide

5.109 CHRISTIAN PERIODICAL INDEX. West Seneca, N.Y.: Christian Librarians' Fellowship, distributed by Houghton College, 1958-- . Quarterly, with annual and quinquennial cumulations.

Approximately thirty-five conservative evangelical Protestant periodicals, from the United States, Canada, and England, not usually indexed elsewhere, are indexed by author and subject in this work. The time lag for current listing is approximately one year. One or two articles on suicide are cited per year.

Consult: Suicide

5.110 CUMULATIVE INDEX TO NURSING LITERATURE. Vol. 1, 1956-- . Glendale, Calif.: Seventh-Day Adventist Hospital Association, 1961-- . Bimonthly, with annual cumulations.

About three hundred English-language nursing journals are wholly or partially indexed in this work, including some journals not indexed in INDEX MEDICUS. In addition to journal articles, references to pamphlets, book reviews, and audiovisuals are included. Access is through separate author and subject indexes. The time lag for current listings is from six to nine months. Approximately twenty to thirty articles on suicide are cited per year.

Consult: Suicide

5.111 EDUCATION INDEX. New York: H.W. Wilson Co., 1929-- . Monthly (except July and August), with annual cumulations.

Articles about suicide among children and students are indexed in this work. By means of a subject-author index, articles from approximately 250 education periodicals, proceedings of conferences and other meetings, yearbooks, and U.S. government documents are cited. This index has a broader coverage of nonjournal materials than the CURRENT INDEX TO JOURNALS IN EDUCATION (5.207). For current listings there is a time lag of less than six months. Approximately five to ten references to suicide are provided each year.

Consult: Suicide
         Suicide in literature

5.112   GUIDE TO SOCIAL SCIENCE AND RELIGION IN PERIODICAL LITERA-
        TURE. Flint, Mich.: National Periodical Library, 1964/65-- . Quar-
        terly, with annual and triennial cumulations.

        General information on the psychological and religious as-
        pects of suicide can be located by this work, which indexes
        more than eighty denominational and interdenominational
        Protestant, Roman Catholic, and Jewish periodicals of a
        general rather than a more scholarly nature. The work is
        essentially a subject index. Most of the periodicals in-
        dexed are not covered by the RELIGION INDEX/ONE:
        PERIODICALS (5.221). The GUIDE TO SOCIAL SCIENCE
        AND RELIGION IN PERIODICAL LITERATURE was formerly
        entitled the GUIDE TO RELIGIOUS AND SEMI-RELIGIOUS
        PERIODICALS. There is a time lag of about one year for
        current listings. Approximately three articles are cited per
        year.

        Consult: Mental health--Suicide

5.113   HOSPITAL LITERATURE INDEX. Chicago: American Hospital Associa-
        tion, 1945-- . Quarterly, with annual and quinquennial cumulations.
        Title varies.

        Approximately 550 periodicals related to hospitals, health
        centers of all types, and to the administrative aspects of
        delivery of health and medical care, are indexed in this
        work. From twenty to thirty articles related to suicide are
        cited each year. Computer searching is available through
        MEDLINE services (5.115).

        Consult: Suicide
                 Suicide, attempted.

5.114   HUMANITIES INDEX. New York: H.W. Wilson Co., 1974-- . Quar-
        terly, with annual cumulations.

        A recently expanded index covering at least 260 English-
        language periodicals in archaeology, classical studies, folk-
        lore, history, language and literature, performing arts,
        philosophy, religion, and theology, this work can be anti-
        cipated to provide information on suicide from some of the
        disciplines represented. The HUMANITIES INDEX is not
        as extensive in its coverage of humanities journals as is the
        ARTS AND HUMANITIES CITATION INDEX, but it is easier
        to use with its subject approach. About twelve articles per
        year on suicide are cited.

        Consult: Suicide
                 Suicide in literature

5.115   INDEX MEDICUS. Bethesda, Md.: National Library of Medicine,
         National Institutes of Health, 1960-- . Monthly, cumulates annually
         into the CUMULATED INDEX MEDICUS.

         References to the medical and psychiatric aspects of suicide
         are provided by this massive index, which cites nearly a
         quarter of a million research articles and books annually
         from the general medical and psychiatric literature. This
         includes approximately thirty-four hundred journals. Access
         is by separate subject and author indexes. There is a time
         lag of three to nine months for current listings. A com-
         puterized search service is available through the library's
         MEDLINE network. The time lag is greatly shortened by
         using the on-line MEDLINE service or its continuing SDI-
         LINE service for current listings. The CUMULATED INDEX
         MEDICUS supersedes the CURRENT LIST OF MEDICAL LIT-
         ERATURE, 1941-59. Antecedents to the INDEX MEDICUS
         date back to 1879. Refer to Sheehy (4.303), page 805,
         for information on these. The INDEX MEDICUS is a major
         source for citations on suicide, providing from two hundred
         to three hundred references each year.

         Consult: Suicide
                  Suicide--History
                  Suicide--Occurrence
                  Suicide--Prevention and control
                  Suicide, attempted
                  Suicide, attempted--Occurrence
                  Suicide, attempted--Prevention and control
                  Suicide, attempted--Therapy

5.116   INDEX TO CANADIAN LEGAL PERIODICAL LITERATURE. Montreal:
         Canadian Association of Law Libraries, 1961-- . Bimonthly, with
         annual cumulations.

         Refer to item 8.501.

5.117   INDEX TO DENTAL LITERATURE. Vol. I, 1939-- . Chicago: American
         Dental Association, 1943-- . Quarterly, with annual cumulations.

         Dealing mostly with suicide among dentists, this is only a
         marginal source, in that approximately one or two articles
         are cited per year. A subject and a name index are pro-
         vided.

         Consult: Suicide

5.118   INDEX TO JEWISH PERIODICALS. Cleveland Heights, Ohio: College
         of Jewish Studies Press, 1963-- . Semiannual.

         Approximately forty scholarly and general Jewish periodicals
         in the English language are indexed by author and subject

in this work. Book reviews are also included. There is a time lag of more than one year for current listings. Only about one or two articles on suicide are cited each year.

Consult: Suicide

5.119   INDEX TO LEGAL PERIODICAL LITERATURE, 1888-1937. Edited by Leonard A. Jones (vols. 1-2) and Frank E. Chipman (vols. 3-6). 6 vols. Boston: Boston Book Co., 1888-1937.

Refer to item 8.502.

5.120   INDEX TO LEGAL PERIODICALS, 1908-- . New York: H.W. Wilson Co., in cooperation with the American Association of Law Libraries, 1908-- . Monthly (except September), with annual cumulations.

Refer to item 8.503.

5.121   INDEX TO PERIODICALS OF THE CHURCH OF JESUS CHRIST OF LATTER-DAY SAINTS. Provo, Utah: Brigham Young University, Library, 1966-- . Annual, with quinquennial cumulations.

Information on suicide from five official church periodicals is indexed by subject and author in this work. The time lag for annual listings is at least five months. Marginal usefulness.

Consult: Suicide

5.122   INDEX TO U.S. GOVERNMENT PERIODICALS, 1970-- . Chicago: Infordata International, 1975-- . Quarterly, with annual cumulations.

This index to over 140 U.S. government periodicals, many of which are not indexed elsewhere, is easy to use. There are currently about one or two articles per year on suicide cited in the index. For further information refer to item 8.504.

Consult: Suicide

5.123   INTERNATIONAL BIBLIOGRAPHY, INFORMATION, DOCUMENTATION. New York: Bowker and Unipub, 1973-- . Quarterly, with annual cumulative subject index.

This work provides worldwide bibliographic information on publications of the United Nations organizational system, which are often difficult to locate through other sources. It is particularly useful for locating articles on suicide in publications such as the WORLD HEALTH STATISTICS RE-PORTS (18.107). Several references on suicide are cited each year.

Consult: Suicide

5.124 INTERNATIONAL BIBLIOGRAPHY OF SOCIAL AND CULTURAL AN-
THROPOLOGY, 1955-- . Paris: UNESCO, 1955-59; Chicago: Aldine; London: Tavistock Publications, 1960-- . Annual.

> This worldwide index provides author and subject indexing
> to over eight hundred anthropological journals. There is a
> two- to three-year time lag for current publications. From
> two to five articles on suicide are cited in this source per
> year.

> Consult: Suicide

5.125 INTERNATIONAL BIBLIOGRAPHY OF SOCIOLOGY, 1951-- . Paris:
UNESCO, 1951-60; Chicago: Aldine, 1961-- ; London: Tavistock
Publications, 1962-- . Annual.

> Many of the one thousand periodicals indexed in this basic
> index of the sociological literature are indexed elsewhere.
> Books, pamphlets, and government publications are also in-
> dexed. Items are arranged within eleven subject areas,
> with a time lag of two to three years for current publica-
> tions. About ten to twenty articles on suicide are cited
> each year.

> Consult: Suicide

5.126 INTERNATIONAL NURSING INDEX. New York: American Journal
of Nursing, 1966-- . Quarterly, with annual cumulations.

> Over two hundred nursing journals are completely indexed,
> and more than twenty-two hundred nonnursing journals are
> scanned for articles to be indexed in this work. Selected
> books and doctoral dissertations by nurses are also cited.
> The indexing is included in the National Library of Medi-
> cine's computerized indexing system, and computerized
> searching is available through their MEDLINE SERVICE
> (5.115). From twenty to twenty-five articles on suicide
> are cited each year.

> Suicide: Suicide
> Suicide--Occurrence
> Suicide--Prevention and control
> Suicide, attempted

5.127 MAGAZINE INDEX, 1976-- . Los Altos, Calif.: 1978-- . Monthly,
with total cumulations on microform.

> The MAGAZINE INDEX indexes more than 370 journals of
> a popular nature. Sixty-nine of these titles are not in-
> dexed in other popular periodical indexes. However, some
> of these titles are included in the more scholarly indexes.
> A few of the popular periodicals that are unique to this

index are not likely to have much information on suicide,
for example, AMERICAN GIRL, COED, MS., and MODERN
BRIDE. Many of the other unique titles are of a very specialized recreational nature, such as BIKE WORLD, GUITAR
PLAYER, SAIL, SURFER, and WATER SKIER, and are not
likely to contain much material on suicide. Subject headings used in the index are those used by the Library of
Congress, as well as keywords from titles. This material
is available for searching on computer output microform and
also on-line at libraries and information centers that provide
facilities for computerized searching through Lockheed's
DIALOG services (5.301). The main advantage of this index is that of a rapid search of a large number of general
interest periodicals with a time lag of only a few weeks.
All of the magazines indexed in the READER'S GUIDE TO
PERIODICAL LITERATURE (5.132) are included in this index.

Consult: The list of subject headings used by the
Library of Congress (3.104)

5.128   NINETEENTH CENTURY READERS' GUIDE TO PERIODICAL LITERATURE,
1890-1899, WITH SUPPLEMENTARY INDEXING, 1900-1922. 2 vols.
Edited by Helen Grant Cushing and Adah V. Morris. New York:
H.W. Wilson Co., 1944.

This easy-to-use author-subject index to fifty-one scholarly
and general periodicals of the 1890s, including seven periodicals not indexed by POOLE'S INDEX TO PERIODICAL
LITERATURE (5.129), also includes book reviews. The main
emphases of the materials included in the index are history,
religion, education, geography, economics, and thereby
suicide information as related to these emphases.

Consult: Suicide
Suicide in literature

5.129   POOLE'S INDEX TO PERIODICAL LITERATURE. By William Frederic
Poole . . . with the assistance as associate editor of William I. Fletcher,
and the cooperation of the American Library Association and the Library Association of the United Kingdom. Rev. vol., 1802-81. Supplements. Reprint. New York: Peter Smith, 1938.

This basic subject index indexes nearly five hundred general,
rather than essentially scholarly, British and American periodicals, with book reviews, from the nineteenth and early
twentieth centuries. Novels, poems, and plays are indexed
by title as well. This work is somewhat difficult to use
because of the lack of dates in the citations to the periodical articles. A special table must be referred to in order
to find the year of publication of each article cited.

Consult: Suicide

5.130   POPULAR PERIODICAL INDEX. Camden, N.J.: Camden Library,
Rutgers University, 1973-- . Semiannual, noncumulative issues.

Approximately twenty popular periodicals such as MONEY,
TV GUIDE, and PLAYBOY are indexed in this work by
title and subject. The time lag for current listings is about
four months. Five to ten articles on suicide are cited each
year.

Consult: Suicide

5.131   Public Affairs Information Service (PAIS). BULLETIN. New York:
1915-- . Weekly, with quarterly and annual cumulations. CUMU-
LATIVE SUBJECT INDEX, 1915-1974. 15 vols. Arlington, Va.:
Carrollton Press, 1977-78.

Over one thousand periodicals published in English throughout the world are selectively indexed by this work, which
emphasizes public issues of high current interest. The PAIS
BULLETIN, as it is popularly called, also includes selected
current books, pamphlets, government publications, and reports of private agencies. The prices and sources of materials cited are given when applicable. Photocopies of
out-of-print pamphlets and reports are available from the
New York Public Library. Computer searching is available
since 1976 (refer to item 5.301). There is a time lag of
three to nine months for current listings. Two or three citations on suicide are provided per year.

Consult: Suicide
           Suicide--bibliography
           Suicide--statistics
           Suicide prevention

5.132   READERS' GUIDE TO PERIODICAL LITERATURE, 1900-- . New York:
H.W. Wilson Co., 1905-- . Semimonthly (except monthly in July and
August), with quarterly and annual cumulations.

This basic author-subject index to articles from approximately
180 periodicals of general interest also indexes reviews of
books, theatrical productions, and motion pictures. There
is a time lag of only one to two months for current listings.
About a dozen articles on suicide are cited annually in this
work, which is a basic index for nonresearch articles on
suicide. Computerized searching of this work may be done
by using the data base of the MAGAZINE INDEX. Refer
to item 5.127.

Consult: Self-mutilation
           Suicide
           Suicide--Prevention
           Suicide in literature

5.133   SCIENCE CITATION INDEX: AN INTERNATIONAL INTERDISCI-
        PLINARY INDEX TO THE LITERATURE OF SCIENCE, MEDICINE,
        AGRICULTURE, TECHNOLOGY, AND THE BEHAVIORAL SCIENCES.
        Philadelphia: Institute for Scientific Information, 1961-- . Three
        issues per year, including annual cumulations.

        This basic reference work indexes about twenty-seven hun-
        dred journals in the chemical, biological, life, and phy-
        sical sciences; clinical practice and engineering; plus pro-
        ceedings volumes, selected monographs, and composite books.
        Perhaps one-half of the journals are in the life sciences.
        U.S. journals make up about one-third of the total journals.
        There is considerable overlapping in the psychological and
        psychiatric journals indexed in this source and with those in-
        dexed in the SOCIAL SCIENCES CITATION INDEX (5.134).
        Some 115 psychological and psychiatric journals are indexed
        in both works. The SCIENCE CITATION INDEX indexes
        about fifty journals in psychology and psychiatry that are
        not indexed in the SOCIAL SCIENCE CITATION INDEX,
        while the SOCIAL SCIENCES CITATION INDEX indexes
        about 145 journals not indexed in the SCIENCE CITATION
        INDEX. Therefore both of these sources should be searched
        if comprehensiveness is desired. The SCIENCE CITATION
        INDEX is organized very much like the SOCIAL SCIENCES
        CITATION INDEX and the reader is referred to item 5.134
        for a description of these indexes. Below is a list of sug-
        gested keywords which may be searched for finding articles
        on suicide. Care should be exercised in regard to pairs
        of words which may be hyphenated; for example, "attempted-
        suicide" will be indexed in a location different from "at-
        tempted suicide," the former being indexed as one word.
        The user should really check both possible locations. This
        index is a very good source for articles on suicide. For
        computer searching, consult section 5.3.

        Consult: Attempted-suicide   Self-administered
                   Crisis intervention   Self destruction
                   Drowning   Self destructive
                   Hanging   Self harm
                   Hara-kiri   Self inflicted
                   Kamikaze   Self mutilation
                   Kill(ing) oneself   Self poisoning
                   Life threatening behavior Suicidal
                   Overdose   Suicide(s)
                   Poisoning   Suicidology
                   Psychiatric emergencies

5.134   SOCIAL SCIENCES CITATION INDEX: AN INTERNATIONAL MULTI-
        DISCIPLINARY INDEX TO LITERATURE OF THE SOCIAL, BEHAVIORAL,
        AND RELATED SCIENCES, 1969-- . Philadelphia: Institute for Sci-
        entific Information, 1973-- . Three issues per year, including annual
        cumulations.

About fifteen hundred social science journals are completely indexed by this work, and an additional twenty-six hundred journals are selectively indexed for social science information. This work is essentially a citation index, although it can be very effectively used as a standard retrieval source for information on suicide. As a citation index, the index is used as follows. For the person who has found a periodical article on suicide that is very pertinent to his research needs, this source, in its citation index, provides citations to related articles and reviews that may also be pertinent. These articles and reviews have cited the same article that the user found to be so valuable. The user can then read these additional articles and often may find that the new articles have expanded upon the original research or concept. Thus the user is able to follow the development of research in a very specific area. This particular function is performed by the first and second main parts of this work: (1) the Citation Index, and (2) the Source Index, which is arranged by author cited, providing full bibliographic information and even the current address of the author, when possible, for consultation if desired. Corporate authors, such as agencies, universities, and research centers are handled in the same way. The third main part of this work is the Permuterm Subject Index. This uses a technique of subject indexing which pairs every keyword in the title of an article with every other keyword, and then connects the name of the author with each pair of keywords. To find an article on suicide the user must anticipate all of the possible words referring to suicide that the authors may use in the titles. If this is not done, some significant articles may be missed. Care must be exercised in regard to pairs of words which may be hyphenated; for example, "attempted-suicide" will be indexed in a location different from "attempted suicide," the former being indexed as one word. The user should really check both possible locations in every case. This index is a very good source for articles on suicide. For computer searching refer to section 5.3.

Consult: The list of words suggested in item 5.133, remembering that these keywords may change with time and new ones may be used in the future.

5.135   SOCIAL SCIENCES INDEX. New York: H.W. Wilson Co., 1974-- . Quarterly, with annual cumulations.

Indexing over 265 scholarly English-language social science journals in the areas of anthropology, economics, geography, law, criminology, medical science, political science, psychology, public administration, and sociology, this author-title index provides articles on suicide from these disciplines. Book reviews are also indexed at the end of each volume.

There is a time lag of nine months to one year for current listings. Many journals not indexed in SOCIOLOGICAL ABSTRACTS (5.225) are covered by this work. This index was formerly part of the SOCIAL SCIENCES AND HUMANITIES INDEX, April 1965-March 1974, when the social science coverage was not as extensive. From 1907 to 1965 this latter index was entitled the INTERNATIONAL INDEX, with added coverage of many foreign language journals. Approximately thirty articles on suicide may be located each year through this easily used index.

Consult: Suicide

5.136   SOUTHERN BAPTIST PERIODICAL INDEX. Nashville, Tenn.: Historical Commission of the Southern Baptist Convention, 1965-- . Annual.

Approximately forty-five periodicals published by the Southern Baptist Convention are comprehensively indexed by author and subject in this work, which is the only index for many of these periodicals. A computer search is available on a limited basis. This index cites about two articles on suicide annually.

Consult: Suicide

5.137   TOXICITY BIBLIOGRAPHY: A BIBLIOGRAPHY COVERING REPORTS ON TOXICITY STUDIES, ADVERSE DRUG REACTIONS, AND POISONING IN MAN AND ANIMALS. Bethesda, Md.: National Library of Medicine, 1968-- . Quarterly.

This index cites about 150 articles per year on suicide by poisoning from a variety of chemicals and drugs. It has an author index and a good subject index. The references are selected from monthly issues of INDEX MEDICUS (5.115), but with more specific subject indexing. Computer searching is available through MEDLINE (see 5.115).

Consult: Suicide
          Suicide, attempted

5.138   UNITED METHODIST PERIODICAL INDEX: AN INDEX TO SELECTED UNITED METHODIST PERIODICALS. Nashville, Tenn.: Methodist Publishing House, 1961-- . Quarterly, with quinquennial cumulations.

Approximately sixty Methodist periodicals are indexed for general use of this denomination by this author-subject index, which includes book reviews. From 1961 to 1968 this work was entitled the METHODIST PERIODICAL INDEX. About two articles on suicide are cited annually.

Consult: Suicide
          Suicide prevention

5.139   U.S. Air University. Library. AIR UNIVERSITY LIBRARY INDEX TO
         MILITARY PERIODICALS. Maxwell Air Force Base, Ala.: 1949-- .
         Quarterly, with annual cumulations. Title varies.

> Nearly seventy English-language military and aeronautical
> periodicals, not generally indexed elsewhere, are included
> in this subject index. Significant news articles, news items,
> and editorials are also indexed. This index is preceded by
> the AIR UNIVERSITY PERIODICAL INDEX, 1949-1962. Ar-
> ticles cited on suicide often deal with suicide by aircraft.
> Generally about one article per year on suicide is cited.
>
> Consult: Suicide

5.140   VERTICAL FILE INDEX: A SUBJECT AND TITLE INDEX TO SELECTED
         PAMPHLET MATERIALS, 1932/34-- . New York: H.W. Wilson Co.,
         1935-- . Monthly (except August), with quarterly cumulations since
         1973.

> Although not a periodical index, this index is mentioned
> here as a source devoted exclusively to indexing pamphlet
> materials. Its former title was VERTICAL FILE SERVICE
> CATALOG, 1932-54. About two pamphlets on suicide are
> cited per year.
>
> Consult: Suicide
>   Young adults--Suicidal behavior

Pamphlets are also cited in the PAIS BULLETIN (5.131), the INTERNATIONAL
BIBLIOGRAPHY OF SOCIOLOGY (5.125), and the CUMULATIVE INDEX TO
NURSING LITERATURE (5.110).

Alternative and underground periodicals are indexed in the ALTERNATIVE PRESS
INDEX (10.201).

5.2 ABSTRACTS OF PERIODICAL ARTICLES

Abstracts are very useful because, in addition to citing periodical articles and
reports, they also summarize in a succinct manner the contents of the articles,
often describing the methodology and the major findings of research. They are
therefore great time savers in helping to select articles or reports which are most
pertinent to one's information needs. However, the extra time required in the
preparation of the abstracts generally increases the time lag from the time that
the article or report was published to the time it is cited and abstracted in the
abstract journal. This may be important if currency is an issue. On-line computer search services are often available for persons who require maximum currency.

The main sources for locating abstracts of published articles and reports on suicide are described in this section. The approximate number of abstracts per year on suicide which each abstract journal below provides is noted so that the researcher or investigator can more easily decide whether to search for suicide information in that abstract source or not, according to his specific information needs. It should be noted here that the most prolific and general scholarly sources for abstracts on suicide are PSYCHOLOGICAL ABSTRACTS (5.219), ABSTRACTS ON CRIMINOLOGY AND PENOLOGY (5.202), and EXCERPTA MEDICA (5.209). Others are very helpful within their specific emphases and should certainly be consulted if comprehensiveness is desired.

After the description of each abstract source, in order to save the user considerable time, the subject headings used in each source to locate the abstracts on suicide are indicated. A real attempt has been made to provide all of the pertinent usbject headings that are useful for suicide information. However, the user should be aware that subject headings may change over time and new relevant headings may be added at any time.

5.201   ABSTRACTS OF POPULAR CULTURE. Bowling Green Ohio: Bowling Green University Popular Press, 1976-- . Quarterly.

This source selectively abstracts over six hundred city, state, and regional periodicals in the fields of popular literature, folklore, television, films, theater, and the counter-culture. A few foreign magazines, including British and Canadian ones, are also abstracted. Copies of articles are available from the publisher. About three articles on suicide are cited per year.

Consult: Suicide

5.202   ABSTRACTS ON CRIMINOLOGY AND PENOLOGY. Amsterdam: Excerpta Criminologica Foundation, 1961-- . Bimonthly.

International in scope, this source abstracts periodical articles and books related to criminology. This work was entitles EXCERPTA CRIMINOLOGICA from 1961 to 1969. Approximately two hundred citations to suicide are provided by this source per year.

Consult: In section 6.14, Automutilation
Euthanasia
Suicide
Suicide, Attempted

5.203   ABSTRACTS ON POLICE SCIENCES: AN INTERNATIONAL ABSTRACTING SERVICE COVERING POLICE SCIENCE, THE FORENSIC SCIENCES AND FORENSIC MEDICINE. Deventer, Netherlands: Criminologica Foundation, 1971-- . Bimonthly with subject index, with annual cumulated subject and author indexes.

Of the approximately fifteen hundred abstracts per year in
this source, about twenty to twenty-five are on suicide.

Consult: Suicide

5.204 ALCOHOLISM DIGEST ANNUAL. Rockville, Md.: Information Planning Associates, 1972/73-- . Annual, with monthly supplements.

This work annually provides over twelve hundred brief abstracts of periodical articles, books, and reports on the
social, legal, family, and psychological problems resulting
from chronic and excessive abuse of alcohol. Access is
by an author and a subject index. Approximately five to
fifteen items are cited annually on alcohol abuse as it relates to suicide.

Consult: Suicide

5.205 BIOLOGICAL ABSTRACTS. Philadelphia: BioScience Information Service, 1926-- . Semimonthly, with semiannual cumulative indexes.

Over five thousand periodicals published in nearly one hundred countries are abstracted in this source. Subject areas
include bacteriology, behavioral sciences, biochemistry,
bioinstrumentation, biophysics, cell biology, environmental
biology, experimental medicine, genetics, immunology, mi-
crobiology, nutrition, parasitology, pathology and physiology
of animals and plants, public health, radiation biology,
systematic biology, toxicology, and virology. A keyword
indexing service, BASIC (Biological Abstracts Subjects in
Context) uses computer methods. Computer searches are
available at libraries or other information centers which
provide facilities for this type of data base searching (see
5.301 and 5.302), or directly by mail from the publisher.
This abstracting service is useful for articles on suicide.

Consult: Suicide

5.206 COLLEGE STUDENT PERSONNEL ABSTRACTS. Claremont, Calif.:
College Student Personnel Institute, 1965-- . Quarterly.

For easy access to information on suicide and suicidal behavior among college students, this is a useful source. However, nearly all of the references provided are found in the
more standard psychological and educational indexing and
abstracting services described in this chapter. From five to
ten articles are cited per year by this work.

Consult: Suicide

5.207 CURRENT INDEX TO JOURNALS IN EDUCATION. New York: Macmillan Information, 1969-- . Monthly, with annual cumulations.

This source, prepared by the U.S. Educational Resources Information Center (ERIC), although privately printed, indexes and abstracts research articles appearing in over seven hundred English-language journals on education and related areas. Contents are arranged in four parts: main entries, subject index, author index, and journal contents. The main entry, arranged by accession number, cites the article from the journal issue in which it appeared, and provides an abstract of the article, along with assigned subject descriptors and identifiers. The descriptors are those used by ERIC for its RESOURCES IN EDUCATION (6.302) as listed in its regularly updated THESAURUS OF ERIC DESCRIPTORS. Refer to item 6.302 for more information on the thesaurus. The time lag for current listings is from six to twelve months. Reprints of the articles are not available from the publisher or the center. Computer searches are available at libraries or other information centers which provide facilities for this type of data base searching (see section 5.3), or directly by mail from the center itself. This source annually cites about twenty to thirty articles generally relating suicide to children and students.

Consult: Suicide

5.208   EXCEPTIONAL CHILD EDUCATION RESOURCES. Reston, Va.: Council for Exceptional Children, 1969-- . Quarterly.

This source was previously entitled EXCEPTIONAL CHILD EDUCATION ABSTRACTS. About five citations related to suicide are provided per year.

Consult: Suicide

5.209   EXCERPTA MEDICA: THE INTERNATIONAL MEDICAL ABSTRACTING SERVICE. Amsterdam, Netherlands: 1947-- . Monthly.

Approximately three-hundred thousand articles are abstracted each year from about thirty-five hundred worldwide medical journals by this important service. The service is divided into a number of separate sections, corresponding to various medical specializations. Abstracts from journal articles corresponding to these specializations are published for each section, with a small amount of overlap among the sections. There are separate author and subject indexes for each volume published during the year by each of the sections. It is important when using the abstract service for any section to consult the index for each of the two or three volumes published per year for each section, not just the index for the final annual volume. There is a time lag of about one year for current listings. A computerized search service is available for materials published since 1968. The following sections (items 5.210 - 5.216) provide abstracts of articles on suicide.

5.210   _____. Section 40, DRUG DEPENDENCE, 1972/73-- .

Approximately ten to fifteen abstracts on suicide and drugs appear in this section annually.

Consult: Suicide

5.211   _____. Section 49, FORENSIC SCIENCE, 1975-- .

Each year about seventy-five medico-legal articles in regard to aspects of suicide are published.

Consult: Suicide
          Suicide attempts

5.212   _____. Section 5, GENERAL PATHOLOGY AND PATHOLOGICAL ANATOMY, 1948-- .

About ten articles on the anatomical and pathological aspects of suicide are abstracted in this section annually.

Consult: Suicide

5.213   _____. Section 20, GERONTOLOGY AND GERIATRICS, 1958-- .

Approximately five to ten articles on suicide and aging are abstracted annually in this section.

Consult: Suicide
          Suicide attempts

5.214   _____. Section 7, PEDIATRICS AND PEDIATRIC SURGERY, 1947-- .

A total of about five articles on adolescent suicide are abstracted in this section per year.

Consult: Suicide
          Suicide attempts

5.215   _____. Section 32, PSYCHIATRY, 1948-- .

One of the most important sections for suicidology, this section abstracts about 175 articles a year concerning the psychiatric aspects of suicide.

Consult: Suicide
          Suicide attempts

5.216   _____. Section 17, PUBLIC HEALTH, SOCIAL MEDICINE, AND HYGIENE, 1955-- .

Each year between seventy five to one hundred articles on social aspects of suicide are abstracted in this section. There is some degree of overlap with articles appearing in Section 32, PSYCHIATRY.

Consult: Suicide
Suicide attempts

5.217 INTERNATIONAL PHARMACEUTICAL ABSTRACTS. Washington, D.C.: American Society of Hospital Pharmacists, 1964-- . Semimonthly, with semiannual and annual author and subject index.

This abstract service provides information on suicides by drugs and combination of drugs. About ten abstracts appear each year on drug-related suicide. For computer searching of this source refer to item 5.301.

Consult: Suicide

5.218 PHILOSOPHER'S INDEX: AN INTERNATIONAL INDEX TO PHILO-SOPHICAL PERIODICALS. Bowling Green, Ohio: Bowling Green University, 1967-- . Quarterly, with annual cumulations.

Abstracts from about 275 American and western European periodicals in philosophy and closely related disciplines are provided in this work. A subject and author index is included. About three or four articles on suicide are abstracted annually.

Consult: Suicide

5.219 PSYCHOLOGICAL ABSTRACTS. Washington, D.C.: American Psychological Association, 1927-- . Monthly, with semiannual and triennial cumulated indexes. Imprint varies.

Research articles from nearly one thousand American and foreign journals in psychology and related areas are abstracted, along with at least fifteen hundred books, annually. Chapters in selected books, as well as dissertations and technical reports, are also abstracted by this basic source for research information on the psychological aspects of suicide. The abstracts and citations are arranged in each issue under sixteen topics, and then alphabetically by author under each topic. Brief author and subject indexes are included in each issue. These are expanded and cumulated semiannually. A two-volume CUMULATED SUBJECT INDEX TO PSYCHO-LOGICAL ABSTRACTS, 1927-1960 (Boston: G.K. Hall, 1966), has been followed by triennial supplements, all of which are very helpful. Care should be taken in the use of the subject indexing, because the subject headings are not consistent over time. A THESAURUS OF PSYCHOLOGI-CAL TERMS used in the subject indexing system is provided

as an aid for the user. Computerized literature searches
are available for the literature from 1967 to date at libraries
or other information and research centers that provide facilities for this type of data base searching (refer to section
5.3). The user can also arrange searches directly by mail
with the publisher. The final pages of each monthly issue
provide information on this latter service. The time lag
for current listings in the monthly issues varies, perhaps
averaging one year, but this can be shortened by use of
the computerized search service. This is a basic source for
suicide information, providing about three hundred citations
a year.

Consult: Attempted suicide
           Suicide
           Suicide prevention
           Suicide prevention centers

5.220   PSYCHOPHARMACOLOGY ABSTRACTS. Chevy Chase, Md.: National
        Clearinghouse for Mental Health Information, 1961-- . Quarterly, with
        annual cumulated index.

        This work abstracts articles on the treatment, causes, and
        prevention of mental disorders as related to pharmaceuticals.
        An author index and a subject index are provided. The
        subject index is a keyword-in-title index, and is cumulated
        annually. About five to seven abstracts on suicide in rela-
        tion to mental disorders involving pharmaceuticals are pro-
        vided each year.

        Consult: Suicide

5.221   RELIGION INDEX / ONE: PERIODICALS, 1949/52-- . Chicago: Ameri-
        can Theological Library Association, 1953-- . Semiannual, with bi-
        ennial cumulations. Title varies.

        Approximately two hundred scholarly Protestant, Roman
        Catholic, and Jewish periodicals mainly in the English
        language are indexed by author and subject. About eighty
        of these are abstracted in the RELIGIOUS AND THEOLOGI-
        CAL ABSTRACTS (5.222). The RELIGION INDEX was for-
        merly entitled INDEX TO RELIGIOUS PERIODICAL LITERA-
        TURE. About three abstracts on suicide appear each year.

        Consult: Suicide

5.222   RELIGIOUS AND THEOLOGICAL ABSTRACTS. Youngstown, Ohio:
        Theological Publications, 1958-- . Quarterly, with annual cumulative
        author and subject indexes.

        Abstracts of articles from approximately eighty U.S. and
        fifty European scholarly religious journals from the Protestant,

Catholic, Orthodox, and Jewish traditions are provided by
this source. Suicide information found here is mostly from
the biblical, theological, and historical perspectives. The
time lag for current listings is over one year. Although
this abstract journal has only about one article per year on
suicide, the scholarly nature of the journals abstracted
should make the search for the occasional article worthwhile.

Consult: Suicide

5.223   SOCIAL SCIENCE ABSTRACTS. 5 vols. New York: Social Science
Abstracts, Columbia University, 1929-33.

About five to ten abstracts of articles on suicide appeared
annually in this work, which includes over fifty thousand
abstracts from worldwide periodicals in the social sciences
for the period 1928-32. A cumulative author and subject
index is provided.

Consult: Suicide

5.224   SOCIAL WORK RESEARCH AND ABSTRACTS. New York: National
Association of Social Workers, 1965-- . Quarterly, with annual cumulated author and subject indexes.

This work was formerly entitled ABSTRACTS FOR SOCIAL
WORKERS. Approximately five to ten articles are abstracted
each year which provide information on suicide.

Consult: Suicide

5.225   SOCIOLOGICAL ABSTRACTS. New York: 1953-- . Bimonthly, with
annual cumulated indexes.

Research articles from over four hundred journals in sociology
and related areas are abstracted and arranged under sixty
broad subject headings by this basic source for suicide information. A few books are abstracted, as are, on an irregular basis since 1968, papers presented at regional and
national sociological meetings. Approximately one-fourth
of the abstracted articles are prepared from foreign-language
periodicals. About 30 percent of the periodicals abstracted,
mostly foreign and regional, are not indexed by the SOCIAL
SCIENCES CITATION INDEX (5.134). On-line computer
searching is available from 1963 to date. These search
services are available at libraries or other information centers that provide computer facilities of this type. Approximately twenty to thirty articles on the social aspects of
suicide are abstracted each year.

Consult: Suicide

5.3 COMPUTERIZED SEARCHING

As mentioned in the descriptions of several of the indexing and abstracting services earlier in this chapter, computerized searches are available. These can be arranged for, or done, at large libraries or other information centers that provide facilities for this kind of searching. Some computerized searches may also be done directly through the publishers of the indexes and abstract journals. In many cases, the computerized files or bibliographic data bases are retrospective for only a limited number of years, although work may be in progress for completing these files. Assistance is recommended, and usually required, in using these services, particularly for formulating subject headings, or search terms, which must be tailored to the specific requirements of the searcher. This process, which may eliminate many useless citations, is important because fees are generally charged on the basis of the computer-connect time and the number of citations printed off-line.

Often there is a choice of direct on-line service or mail delivery service, that is, a query being called or mailed in and a print-out of citations being sent by mail. The on-line service takes place at a terminal which is often interactive. When the terminal is interactive, often within seconds the searcher can begin searching at the terminal by use of a telephone. After viewing the citations that are displayed on the terminal according to the search terms submitted, the searcher has a chance to review the search results, and revise the search with different combinations of search terms. The citations resulting can often be printed on-line, or if the search results in a long bibliography, the system can be ordered to print this, with the print-out being sent by airmail usually within twenty-four hours.

There are at least two major purveyors of computerized bibliographic search systems, who provide the service of connecting the searchers with a variety of electronic data bases when they use the search facilities at large libraries and information centers. It is helpful to get a broad view of these services. Various data bases that are of importance for suicide information can be accessed through them. Information about them, current through February 1979, is provided in items 5.301 and 5.302 below. Currency can be maintained by referring to the work cited in item 5.303 or by inquiring at the centers and libraries that provide computerized searching facilities. The data bases listed under the items below provide not only citations and often abstracts of journal articles, but also other types of data, such as books, dissertations, reports, and grant sources. All of these are brought together in this section so that the whole service, as applicable to suicide information, may be viewed broadly and then be referred to from other sections of this guide.

5.301   Lockheed Information Systems, Palo Alto, California.

Over seventy data bases, mostly in the sciences and technology, are made available for computerized searching through Lockheed's DIALOG information retrieval services. Those data bases relevant for information on suicide, largely in the format of periodical articles, but also in formats of books, reports, dissertations, and grant sources, are listed below. Cross-references to the sources as described in this guide are provided. Also provided for each data base is the year from which the computerized file or data base is presently available. Prior to the year indicated, in many cases, the search may still have to be done manually until the file is completed. For further description of the DIA-LOG services, refer to two Lockheed publications: (1) LOCKHEED INFORMATION SYSTEMS: A BRIEF GUIDE TO DIALOG SEARCHING, looseleaf, and (2) GUIDE TO DIA-LOG: DATA BASES, looseleaf.

BIOSIS (1969--). Represents BIOLOGICAL ABSTRACTS (5.205) and BIORESEARCH INDEX (5.104). Citations.

CDI (1861--). Represents COMPREHENSIVE DISSERTATION INDEX (6.103) and DISSERTATION ABSTRACTS INTERNATIONAL (6.104). Citations.

CONFERENCE PAPERS INDEX (1973--). See item (12.401). Citations.

ERIC. Represents CURRENT INDEX TO JOURNALS IN EDUCATION (1969--) (5.207) and RESOURCES IN EDUCATION (1966--) (6.302). Citations and abstracts.

EXCERPTA MEDICA (1975--). See item 5.209. Citations and abstracts.

FOUNDATION CENTER NATIONAL DATABASE (current year only). Represents current data supplementing the FOUNDATION DIRECTORY (12.204). Citations.

FOUNDATION DIRECTORY (current edition only). See item 12.204. Citations.

FOUNDATION GRANTS INDEX (1973--). See item 12. 205. Information on grants awarded. Citations and abstracts.

INTERNATIONAL PHARMACEUTICAL ABSTRACTS (1970--). See item 5.217. Citations and abstracts.

MAGAZINE INDEX (1976--). See item 5.127. Includes all magazines indexed by the READERS' GUIDE TO PERIODICAL LITERATURE (5.132). Citations.

NICEM (1964--). See item 11.203 ff. Citations and abstracts.

NTIS (1964--). Represents GOVERNMENT REPORTS ANNOUNCEMENTS (6.301), and WEEKLY GOVERNMENT ABSTRACTS. Citations and abstracts.

PAIS (1976--). Includes Public Affairs Information Service's BULLETIN (5.131). Citations.

PSYCHOLOGICAL ABSTRACTS (1967--). See item 5.219. Citations and abstracts.

SCISEARCH (1974--). Represents SCIENCE CITATION INDEX (5.133). Citations.

SOCIAL SCISEARCH (1972--). Represents SOCIAL SCIENCES CITATION INDEX (5.134). Citations.

SOCIOLOGICAL ABSTRACTS (1963--). See item 5.225. Citations and abstracts.

SSIE (latest two fiscal years). Represents Smithsonian Science Information Exchange (6.402). Citations and summaries.

5.302   SDC Search Service, a division of Systems Development Corporation, Santa Monica, California.

Since 1956, Systems Development Corporation has been designing and developing computer-related information systems for bibliographic information retrieval. Almost fifty data bases are available for computerized searching through their ORBIT system. Those data bases relevant for suicide information, largely in the format of periodical articles, but also in the formats of books, reports, dissertations, and grant sources, are listed below, with cross-references to the citations and descriptions of each source in this guide. Also provided for each is the year from which the data base is presently available. Prior to that year, in some cases the search may still have to be done manually until the source is completely computerized. For further description of the ORBIT services, refer to the following publications from SDC: (1) ORBIT QUICK-REFERENCE GUIDE, and (2) BASIC ORBIT USER MANUAL.

ASI (1973--). Represents AMERICAN STATISTICS INDEX (7.301), which includes selected coverage of U.S. documents issued during the 1960s. Citations and abstracts.

BIOSIS (1969--). Represents BIOLOGICAL ABSTRACTS (5.205) and BIORESEARCH INDEX (5.104). Citations.

CDI (1861--). Represents COMPREHENSIVE DISSERTATION INDEX (6.103) and DISSERTATION ABSTRACTS INTERNATIONAL (6.104). Citations.

CIS INDEX (1970--). Represents Congressional Information Service's INDEX TO PUBLICATIONS OF THE UNITED STATES CONGRESS (8.301). Citations and abstracts.

CONFERENCE PAPERS INDEX (1973--). See item 12.401. Citations.

CNI (1977--). Represents CANADIAN NEWSPAPER INDEX (10.102). Citations.

ERIC. Represents CURRENT INDEX TO JOURNALS IN EDU-
CATION (1969--) (5.207) and RESOURCES IN EDUCATION
(1966--) (6.302). Citations and abstracts.

GRANTS (current year only). Represents GRANT INFOR-
MATION SYSTEM (12.205). Citations and abstracts.

LIBCON (1968--). Covers monographs and some audiovisual
materials cataloged by the Library of Congress, including
records on MARC tapes. Citations.

NTIS (1970--). Represents GOVERNMENT REPORTS AN-
NOUNCEMENTS (6.301), and WEEKLY GOVERNMENT AB-
STRACTS (6.301). Citations and abstracts.

PSYCHOLOGICAL ABSTRACTS (1967--). See item 5.219.
Citations and abstracts.

SOCIAL SCISEARCH (1972--). Represents SOCIAL SCI-
ENCES CITATION INDEX (5.134). Citations.

SSIE (1974--). Represents Smithsonian Science Information
Exchange (6.402). Citations and summaries.

There are at least eight other suppliers of on-line multiple data bases, the most
notable of which are the rapidly growing Bibliographic Retrieval Services, Scotia,
N.Y.; the U.S. National Library of Medicine (5.103, 5.113, 5.115, 5.126,
5.137); and the Library of Congress. An important single on-line data base
supplier is the New York Times Information Bank (10.107).

Computer searching, as noted in various of the descriptions of the information
sources listed in this guide, is also offered off-line by the originating publisher
or agency itself. Notable among these are the U.S. National Technical Information Service (6.301), the U.S. Educational Resources Information Center
(6.302, 5.207), the Smithsonian Science Information Exchange (6.402), EX-
CERPTA MEDICA (5.209), DISSERTATION ABSTRACTS INTERNATIONAL (6.103,
6.104), Public Affairs Information Service (5.131), BioScience Information Service (5.205), American Psychological Association (5.219), and SOCIOLOGICAL
ABSTRACTS (5.225). Sources of grants also can be computer searched directly
from the Foundation Center (12.204, 12.205) and the GRANT INFORMATION
SYSTEM (12.206).

Computer searching of data bases is in a state of rapid change and development.
The suppliers of multiple data bases are adding new ones, expanding others, and
deleting still others. The electronic data bases themselves are growing retro-
spectively. One can keep current in regard to data bases and files of interest
by consulting with librarians at universities and other information centers that
provide computer searching facilities. Also the following sources may be consulted:

5.303   Capital Systems Group, Inc. DIRECTORY OF ON-LINE INFORMATION

RESOURCES: A GUIDE TO COMMERCIALLY AVAILABLE DATA BASES. Rockville, Md.: 1978-- . Semiannual. Title varies.

This is a compact, easy-to-use guide to on-line data bases supplied commercially from suppliers or from the originating agencies. A wide variety of subject areas are represented. The data bases are described according to number of records stored and time periods covered. A subject index and index of data bases by suppliers are also helpful.

5.304   DATABASE: THE MAGAZINE OF DATABASE REFERENCE AND REVIEW. Weston, Conn.: Online, 1978-- . Quarterly.

ONLINE: THE MAGAZINE OF ONLINE INFORMATION SYSTEMS. Weston, Conn.: Online, 1977-- . Quarterly.

These two journals keep one abreast of news and developments in the fast-moving field of data bases, and provide tips for more effective searching of them. Evaluations and comparisons are included. ONLINE, although also including information on the data bases themselves, has more emphasis on the management and innovative use of on-line systems.

Other sources for information on available computerized statistical data bases are found in items 7.210 and 7.213 to 7.217 of this information guide.

5.4 CURRENT AWARENESS SERVICES

Published current awareness services are specially prepared as a response to the need of clinicians, researchers, or educators for more rapid and efficient identification of relevant periodical articles in an area of interest, such as suicide. There is a time lag of only two to four weeks. Several effective services are described here.

5.401   CURRENT CONTENTS: ARTS AND HUMANITIES. Philadelphia: Institute for Scientific Information, 1979-- . Weekly.

Nearly one thousand journals in such areas as aesthetics, archaeology, art, classics, dance, film/radio/TV, folklore, history, literature, music, philosophy, religion, and theater are scanned and subject indexed according to significant words or phrases from the titles of every article of each journal as it appears. When using this type of index, the user must keep in mind alternative forms of the word under which he begins searching (suicide, suicidal) as well as synonyms (self-destruction) and related terms (overdose). Suicide, as a word, however, does not have many variant

forms and synonyms as have many other words. When a
title does not include significant words that adequately in-
form the user of the real content of the article, the in-
dexers supplement the original title with words which more
clearly describe the subject of the article. These supplementary words used in the subject index will lead the user
to the article in question. The main body of each issue
of this work is made up of reprints of the tables of contents
of the periodical issues that have been received and indexed each week. An Author Address Directory is provided
for requesting reprints. Also ISI has a rapid service by
which reprints of articles can be supplied. It can be an-
ticipated that between twenty-five and fifty articles on
suicide will be cited each year through this source.

Consult: The list of words suggested in item 5.133, and
any variation of these, remembering that additional ones may be used in the future.

5.402   CURRENT CONTENTS: LIFE SCIENCES. Philadelphia: Institute for
Scientific Information, 1958-- .   Weekly.

About twenty-seven hundred journals in the chemical, biological, and life sciences, as well as clinical practice, are
scanned and subject indexed according to significant words
or phrases from the titles of every article of each journal
received each week by the publisher. Refer to the description of item 5.401 above in regard to the use of this similar
work. This is a very good source for keeping up with articles on suicide according to the emphases of the source.

Consult: The list of words suggested in item 5.133, and
any variation of these, remembering that additional ones may be used in the future.

5.403   CURRENT CONTENTS: SOCIAL AND BEHAVIORAL SCIENCES. Philadelphia: Institute for Scientific Information, 1969-- .   Weekly.

Approximately fifteen hundred journals in the social, behavioral, and related sciences are scanned and subject indexed according to significant words or phrases from the
titles of every article of each journal received each week
by the publisher of this work. Refer to the description of
item 5.401 above in regard to the use of this similar work.
This is a very good source for keeping up with articles on
suicide.

Consult: The list of words suggested in item 5.133, and
any variation of these, remembering that additional ones may be used in the future.

Another rapid method for keeping abreast of the periodical and report literature related to suicide, as soon as it is published, is to establish an arrangement with one or more of the computer searching services mentioned throughout this chapter. Upon submission of a list of keywords or subject headings relevant to the investigator's interest, these services may supply citations, with or without abstracts, soon after they enter the data base, thus avoiding the time lag involved in waiting for the published issues of the indexes or abstract journals. The Institute for Scientific Information, for example, has an Automatic Subject Citation Alert which will scan fifty-two hundred journals as they are published and will mail weekly print-outs of the new citations. Also, some of the larger indexing and abstracting services publish newsletters which regularly list new items within specific subject categories for specialists in these areas. This can be determined from the services listed in this chapter. The NTIS (6.301) also publishes research report newsletters in twenty-six separate subject areas.

5.5 SCHOLARLY PERIODICALS ESPECIALLY USEFUL FOR SUICIDE INFORMATION

Articles on suicide appear annually in hundreds of journals. The articles are scattered among journals of many disciplines, with articles appearing only sporadically in many of the journals. Most of these articles may be found most efficiently by using the indexing and abstracting sources mentioned in prior sections of this chapter. There are only a few journals in English which have special emphases on suicide. These specialized journals are indexed by various of the indexing and abstracting services described in this chapter. The journals are listed below. The listing for each specialized journal also indicates which source indexes and abstracts articles from these journals. The person especially interested in keeping up with developments in suicidology may wish to peruse issues of these specialized journals as they appear.

5.501   OMEGA: THE JOURNAL OF DEATH AND DYING. Vol. 1, 1970-- . Farmingdale, N.Y.: Baywood Publishing Co., 1970-- . Quarterly.

> Articles on all aspects of death, including a fair number of articles on suicide, are published in this journal. It is indexed by BIOLOGICAL ABSTRACTS (5.205), PSYCHOLOGICAL ABSTRACTS (5.219), EXCERPTA MEDICA (5.209), SOCIAL SCIENCES CITATION INDEX (5.134), and CURRENT CONTENTS: SOCIAL AND BEHAVIORAL SCIENCES (5.403).

5.502   SUICIDE AND LIFE THREATENING BEHAVIOR. Vol. 1, 1971-- . New York: Human Sciences Press, 1971-- . Quarterly.

> An official publication of the American Association of Suicidology, this journal treats suicide and other self-destructive behavior, such as that associated with some automobile accidents. The journal was entitled LIFE THREATENING BEHAVIOR from 1971 to 1974, and SUICIDE in 1975. It is indexed by ABSTRACTS ON CRIMINOLOGY AND PENOLOGY (5.202), INDEX MEDICUS (5.115), PSYCHO-

LOGICAL ABSTRACTS (5.219), SOCIAL SCIENCES CITA-
TION INDEX (5.134), and CURRENT CONTENTS: SOCIAL
AND BEHAVIORAL SCIENCES (5.403). The American As-
sociation of Suicidology also publishes a newsletter, NEWS-
LINK, three times a year, starting in 1974.

A specialized journal on suicide, which has ceased publication, is noted here
because of its importance for the period prior to the publication of item 5.502.

5.503   BULLETIN OF SUICIDOLOGY. Chevy Chase, Md.: U.S. National
Clearinghouse for Mental Health Information, July 1967-Fall 1971.

Prepared by the clearinghouse jointly with the Center for
Studies of Suicide Prevention of the National Institute of
Mental Health, this periodical on suicide and suicide prevention ceased publication in 1971. A special supplement
entitled SUICIDE AMONG YOUTH, issued in December
1969, was written by Richard H. Seiden.

Chapter 6

DISSERTATIONS, THESES, AND OTHER "UNPUBLISHED" RESEARCH REPORTS ON SUICIDE

Research on suicide is reported in various ways. In addition to books and periodical articles, a significant amount of research on suicide is presented in dissertations, theses, and other "unpublished" research reports. These latter forms often present some difficulties both in identifying what research of this type is done on suicide, and then in securing copies of the research reports as needed. This chapter describes sources for identifying this type of materials and also, when possible, provides information on securing the materials themselves or copies of the same. For convenience, a checklist of doctoral dissertations on suicide is included.

6.1 LOCATING DISSERTATIONS AND THESES

In recent years, increasing numbers of doctoral dissertations and theses are being written on the topic of suicide. A typical dissertation on suicide tests a hypothesis by collecting empirical data. A good review of the previous literature on the particular aspect or issue being studied can also be helpful as an introduction and survey of the state of the art in the particular area. This, along with the findings and conclusions of the dissertation study, will often lead to further research. Consulting dissertation information is particularly important for the researcher in suicidology.

Some dissertations are published commercially as books and many therefore be located in the ways suggested in chapter 3 of this guide. Others may be published privately. However, many are considered "unpublished," being available only directly from the author or institution involved, or by securing photocopies or microform copies from a source which has been granted rights of reproduction by the authors or institutions. The best sources for locating completed dissertations are described below.

6.101   Aslib. INDEX TO THESES ACCEPTED FOR HIGHER DEGREES IN THE UNIVERSITIES OF GREAT BRITAIN AND IRELAND. London: 1950/51-- . Annual.

This listing of theses, prepared by the Association of Special Libraries and Information Bureaus, provides the author, title, name of university granting the degree, and the degree granted for each thesis cited. The theses are arranged by broad subject categories, and then by university within each category. No abstracts are provided, however. There is an author index and a subject index by broad categories. Also includes each university's rules for lending theses.

6.102   Black, Dorothy M. GUIDE TO LISTS OF MASTER'S THESES. Chicago: American Library Association, 1965. 144 p.

This work contains lists of master's theses arranged by institutions granting the degrees, and by subject or discipline. Unusually detailed annotations are provided for the items cited.

6.103   COMPREHENSIVE DISSERTATION INDEX, 1861-1972. 37 vols. Ann Arbor, Mich.: Xerox University Microfilm, 1973. Annual supplements.

This work, which indexes over 417,000 dissertations in the main set alone, in addition to about 36,000 more per year since 1973, is an attempt to be a complete inventory of the output of doctoral dissertations accepted by universities in the United States. Since 1970, many Canadian dissertations and some from other countries are included. This index in effect cumulates and supersedes the indexes to DISSERTA-TION ABSTRACTS INTERNATIONAL (6.104), including its RETROSPECTIVE INDEX, 1970, (29 vols.); the Library of Congress's LIST OF DOCTORAL DISSERTATIONS PRINTED in 1912-38; and DOCTORAL DISSERTATIONS ACCEPTED BY AMERICAN UNIVERSITIES, 1933/34-1954/55, by the Association of Research Libraries. Also included are disser-tations never before listed in other published lists. Each dissertation is cited under one of twenty-two major discipline areas. Most of the dissertations relating to suicide appear to be listed under psychology, sociology, education, social work, public health, religion, or literature. Within each discipline, the entries are listed by keyword-in-title. A computer-generated index by keyword and author leads the user to specific citations to dissertations. Care should be exercised, however, when the researcher uses the keyword index, to try to locate all of the dissertations on his specific area of concern. He must try to search under every possible related word, but may still miss a few pertinent dissertations. This makes the keyword type of index difficult to use ef-fectively for comprehensive searching, as there may be dis-sertations on suicide with titles containing words none of which are likely to come to mind. The citation for each dissertation provides the title, author, degree, institution,

date, pagination when available, the citation number by
which to locate the abstracts in the DISSERTATION AB-
STRACTS INTERNATIONAL or other listing, and the number
for ordering a microform copy or a photocopy of any dissertation held by Xerox University Microfilms. Computer
searching of the COMPREHENSIVE DISSERTATION INDEX
data base is available directly through the publisher's Datrix
service or at libraries and other information centers which
provide facilities for this. Refer to items 5.301 and 5.302.
A listing of search terms or keywords that may be useful in
locating dissertations on or related to suicide are suggested
below. This is only an initial listing; there may be other
terms that might be used.

Consult: Attempted suicide   Self-administered
          Crisis intervention   Self destruction
          Drowning   Self destructive
          Hanging   Self harm
          Hara-kiri   Self inflicted
          Kamikaze   Self mutilation
          Kill(ing) oneself   Self poisoning
          Life threatening behavior Suicidal
          Overdose   Suicide(s)
          Poisoning   Suicidology
          Psychiatric emergencies

6.104   DISSERTATION ABSTRACTS INTERNATIONAL. Ann Arbor, Mich.:
         Xerox University Microfilms, 1938-- . Monthly.

         This basic source of information on suicide research includes
         abstracts of doctoral dissertations which are submitted to
         Xerox University Microfilms by cooperating universities.
         These abstracts are arranged alphabetically within subject
         areas and then by the cooperating university. Each listing
         provides the dissertation author, title, university, date,
         name of supervisor, abstract, pagination, and the number
         for ordering microform copies or photocopies from Xerox
         University Microfilms. In 1966, with volume 27, this work
         was divided into two sections: (A) Humanities and Social
         Sciences and (B) Sciences and Engineering. Both sections
         should be consulted. Part 2 of issue number 12 each year
         is the annual subject and author index cumulated from the
         monthly indexes. Issue number 13, which started with
         volume 16, 1955/56, consists of an annual subject listing
         of essentially all dissertations accepted in the United States
         and Canada during that academic year, whether or not they
         have been submitted to Xerox University Microfilms. An
         author index is also provided. For volumes 1-11, 1938-51,
         this work was entitled MICROFILM ABSTRACTS. For volumes
         12-29, 1952 to June 1969, it was entitled DISSERTATION
         ABSTRACTS. After this date, as the present title indicates,

the publisher has been attempting to extend coverage to foreign dissertations. Also with volume 30, 1969/70, the indexes are now computer-generated on the basis of keywords-in-title, with separate indexes for the two sections, A and B. This basic work for information on suicide research is also indexed in the COMPREHENSIVE DISSERTATION INDEX, 1861-1972 (6.103). Computer searching is available at libraries and other information centers that have facilities for this. Refer to section 5.3. There is a time lag of six to nine months after a dissertation is completed until it appears in this work.

Consult: The keywords listed in item 6.103 above.

6.105   MASTERS ABSTRACTS: A CATALOG OF SELECTED MASTERS THESES ON MICROFILM. Ann Arbor, Mich.: Xerox University Microfilms, 1962-- . Quarterly, with annual cumulations.

Only a small proportion of the institutions granting master's degrees are represented in this index. The theses are arranged in broad subject areas with no other indexing. Very few theses on suicide are included in this work. Photocopies and microform copies of the theses are available from the publisher.

Consult: Sociology--Social problems

6.106   MASTER'S THESES IN EDUCATION, 1951/52-- . Cedar Falls, Iowa: Research Publications, 1953-- . Annual. Imprint varies.

As many as forty-five hundred master's theses each year from cooperating institutions in the United States and Canada are listed in this work. Information includes the name, title, institution, and the data of completion. The theses are available on interlibrary loan. Some of these have relevance for suicide information. There is no subject index.

Consult: Curriculum subjects--Psychology
Curriculum subjects--Sociology

6.107   Ottawa. Canadian Bibliographic Centre. CANADIAN GRADUATE THESES IN THE HUMANITIES AND SOCIAL SCIENCES, 1921-46. Ottawa: E. Cloutier, Printer to the King, 1951, 194 p.

This source lists over three thousand citations of master's theses and doctoral dissertations granted in Canada from 1921 through 1946. Entries contain the name of the author, title of the dissertation, the number of pages, the type of degree, the date granted, and professor directing the research. A brief abstract is sometimes included. The dissertations are arranged by discipline and subdivided by university, with an author index but no subject index other than by broad discipline.

6.108   Ottawa. National Library. CANADIAN THESES: A LIST OF THESES
ACCEPTED BY CANADIAN UNIVERSITIES. Ottawa: 1952-- . Annual.

This annual, with a time lag of four years, supplies the
author, title, degree, granting institution, and the year
granted for all master's theses and doctoral dissertations in
Canada. The theses are arranged by discipline, with an
author index but no subject index. Theses for the years
1947-60 are cumulated in a two-volume work.

6.109   RETROSPECTIVE INDEX TO THESES OF GREAT BRITAIN AND IRELAND,
1716-1950. Vol. 1: Social Sciences and Humanities. Vol. 3: Life
Sciences. Edited by Roger R. Bilboul; Francis L. Kent, assoc. ed.
Santa Barbara, Calif.: ABC-Clio, 1975-- .

This multivolume work attempts to list all of the theses
written prior to the Aslib annual (6.101).

Consult: Suicide

6.2 PRELIMINARY CHECKLIST OF DOCTORAL DISSERTATIONS ON SUICIDE: REPORTED 1861-JULY 1978

The following preliminary checklist of dissertations on suicide is submitted as a
convenience and aid to the researcher. It is the product of a search of the
COMPREHENSIVE DISSERTATION INDEX (6.103) through July 1978. Keywords
used in the search were suicide, suicidal, and self-destruction. The other keywords listed for consultation in item 6.103 could be used for searching in the
future, as well as other keywords that may have been overlooked in the list.
Therefore the checklist of dissertations cannot be considered entirely comprehensive. It is also referred to as a preliminary checklist because the other
sources listed in section 6.1, above, and which are not incorporated in the
COMPREHENSIVE DISSERTATION INDEX, have not as yet been searched in the
preparation of this checklist.

The dissertations below are listed in alphabetical order by author within broad
aspects pertaining to suicide. It should be noted that each dissertation appears
only once in the checklist, not being listed further under secondary aspects.
The author, title, and date of completion are given for each dissertation. When
the dissertation is abstracted in the DISSERTATION ABSTRACTS INTERNATIONAL
(DAI) (6.104) or its predecessors, the volume and page number is given for locating the abstract, followed by the order number for ordering microform or
photocopies of the dissertation from Xerox University Microfilms. The earlier
dissertations, that have not been abstracted in the above sources, simply indicate
the name of the university granting the degree.

Dissertations, Theses, Reports

6.201   ATTITUDES TOWARD SUICIDE

Bell, Don E. "Sex and Chronicity as Variables Affecting Attitudes of Undergraduates toward Peers with Suicidal Behaviors." University of Georgia, 1977. (DAI, 38/7B, p. 3380). 77-29742.

Leshem, Ariel, and Leshem, Yonina. "Attitudes of College Students toward Men and Women Who Commit Suicidal Acts." University of Northern Colorado, 1976, (DAI, 37/11A, p.7042). 77-11070.

Nichol, Diane S. "Factors Affecting the Negativity of Attitudes toward Suicide." York University, 1973. (DAI, 36/10B, p. 5235).

6.202   BLACK SUICIDE

Holmes, Christopher E. "An Ethnographic Look at Black Upward Mobility as It Relates to Internalization versus Externalization Factors in the Increase of Black Suicide." California School of Professional Psychology, 1976. (DAI, 38/2B, p. 902). 77-17177.

Kirk, Alton R. "Socio-psychological Factors in Attempted Suicide among Urban Black Males." Michigan State University, 1976. (DAI, 37/9B, p. 4757). 77-05839.

Salter, Dianne S. "Personality Differences between Suicidal and Non-suicidal Blacks." Adelphi University, 1977. (DAI, 38/7B, p. 3473). 77-30034.

6.203   THE CHILDHOODS OF SUICIDAL PEOPLE

Abraham, Yair. "Patterns of Communication and Rejection in Families of Suicidal Adolescents." Ohio State University, 1977. (DAI, 38/8A, p. 4669). 77-31810.

Hill, Mary N. "Suicidal Behavior in Adolescents and Its Relationship to the Lack of Parental Empathy." Smith College, 1969. (DAI, 31/1A, p. 472). 70-11497.

Jacobs, Jerry. "Adolescent Suicide Attempts: The Culmination of a Progressive Social Isolation." University of California, Los Angeles, 1967. (DAI, 28/2A, p. 801). 67-07394.

Windsor, James C. "An Analysis of the Childrearing Attitudes of the Parents of a Group of Adolescents Who Attempted Suicide." University of Virginia, 1972. (DAI, 33/3A, p. 1032). 72-23455.

6.204   CLIMATE AND SUICIDE

Milner, John R. "Suicide and Its Relations to Climatic and Other Factors." Johns Hopkins University, 1922.

6.205   CROSS-CULTURAL STUDIES OF SUICIDE

Krauss, Herbert H. "A Cross-cultural Study of Suicide." Northwestern University, 1966. (DAI, 27/11B, p. 4126). 67-04241.

Morgan, Marilyn W. "Navajo Suicide." Northwestern University, 1972. (DAI, 36/10B, p. 5235). 73-30669.

Rudestam, Kjell E. "Stockholm and Los Angeles: A Cross-cultural Study of the Communication of Suicidal Intent." University of Oregon, 1969. (DAI, 30/8B, p. 3875). 70-02537.

6.206   HISTORICAL STUDIES OF SUICIDE

Bouwman, Robert E. "Race Suicide: Some Aspects of Race Paranoia in the Progressive Era." Emory University, 1975. (DAI, 36/7A, p. 4706). 76-01611.

6.207   INTERPERSONAL RELATIONSHIPS OF SUICIDAL PEOPLE

Ganzler, Sidney. "Some Interpersonal and Social Dimensions of Suicidal Behavior." University of California, Los Angeles, 1967. (DAI, 28/3B, p. 1192). 67-11258.

Hattem, Jack V. "The Precipitating Role of Discordant Interpersonal Relationships in Suicidal Behavior." University of Houston, 1964. (DAI, 25/2, p. 1335). 64-06303.

Hoey, Henry P. "The Interpersonal Behavior of Suicidal Individuals." Ohio University, 1970. (DAI, 31/12B, p. 7598). 71-14497.

Huffine, Carol L. "Interpersonal Relations and Suicidal Behavior." University of California, Berkeley, 1972.

Peck, Michael L. "The Relation of Suicidal Behavior to Characteristics of the Significant Other." University of Portland, 1965.

Shagoury, Joan B. "A Study of Marital Communications and Attitudes toward Suicide in Suicidal and Non-suicidal Individuals." University of Florida, 1971. (DAI, 33/2B, p. 922). 72-21101.

Sutton, Wiley D. "Affiliative Behavior in the Interpersonal Relationships of Persons Prone to Suicide." California School of Professional Psychology, 1973. (DAI, 34/10B, 5212). 74-07942.

Dissertations, Theses, Reports

6.208   MISSING PERSONS

Weitzman, Lenore J. "Social Suicide: A Study of Missing
Persons." Columbia University, 1970. (DAI, 34/8A, p. 5356).
73-16360.

6.209   PHILOSOPHY OF SUICIDE

Novak, David. "Suicide and Morality in Plato, Aquinas and
Kant." Georgetown University, 1971. (DAI, 32/5A, p. 2748).
71-30355.

Whitehill, James D. "Homo Suicidens: An Envisionment of
Self-nihilation as a Human Way of Being." Drew University,
1970. (DAI, 31/4A, p. 1848). 70-17782.

6.210   PHYSIOLOGICAL STUDIES OF SUICIDE

Monck, Maurine F. "The Relationship between Bioelectric Potential Differences and Suicidal Behavior." New York University, 1968. (DAI, 29/2A, p. 415). 68-11802.

6.211   PREDICTION OF SUICIDE

Barnes, Thomas J. "Time Perception and Time Orientation as
Assessment Devices of Suicide Potential." De Paul University,
1977. (DAI, 38/1B, p. 343). 77-13719.

Brown, Timothy R. "The Judgment of Suicide Lethality: A
Comparison of Judgmental Models Obtained under Contrived
versus Natural Conditions." University of Oregon, 1970. (DAI,
31/5B, p. 2978). 70-21558.

Crasilneck, Harold B. "An Analysis of Differences between
Suicidal and Pseudo-suicidal Patients through the Use of Projective Techniques." University of Houston, 1954. (DAI, 14/9,
p. 1456). 00-08531.

Devries, Alcon G. "Methodological Problems in the Identification of Suicidal Behavior by Means of Two Personality Inven-
tories." University of Southern California, 1963. (DAI, 24/12,
p. 5541). 64-06237.

Durham, Thomas W. "A Probabilistic Approach to the Assessment of Suicidal Risk among Mental Hospital Patients." Florida
State University, 1977. (DAI, 38/8B, p. 3875). 77-31028.

Fleischer, Murray S. "Differential Rorschach Configurations of
Suicidal Psychiatric Patients." Yeshiva University, 1957. (DAI,
19/3, p. 568). 58-02823.

Furlong, Paul T. "Psychological Assessment of Potentially Suicidal Patients at the Community Mental Health Center, Salt
Lake City, Utah." University of Utah, 1970. (DAI, 31,11B,
p. 6899). 71-03012.

Jones, Ronald B. "Suicidal Out-patients: The MMPI and Case
File Data." University of Oregon, 1968. (DAI, 29/7B, p.
2635). 69-00029.

Kendra, John M. "Predicting Suicide from the Rorschach Ink-
blot Test." Temple University, 1974. (DAI, 36/6B, p. 3049).
75-28179.

Kinsinger, John R. "The Relationship between Lethality of Suicidal Intentions and Assertive, Aggressive and Hostile Traits."
University of Texas Health Science Center, Dallas, 1971. (DAI,
31/12B, p. 768). 71-16177.

Lemerond, John N. "Suicide Prediction for Psychiatric Patients:
A Comparison of the MMPI and Clinical Judgments." Marquette
University, 1977. (DAI, 38/10A, p. 5926). 78-01922.

Martin, Harry A. "A Rorschach Study of Suicide." University
of Kentucky, 1951. (DAI, 20/9, p. 3837). 60-00682.

Patterson, John E. "Student Lethality Form: A Guide to De-
termining the Potential Lethality of University Students' Suicide
Threats." Kent State University, 1974. (DAI, 35/10A, p. 6465).
75-07463.

Sakheim, George A. "Suicidal Responses on the Rorschach
Tests." Florida State University, 1954. (DAI, 14/8, p. 1253).
00-08259.

Salzberg, Norman. "The Development of a Composite Criminal
Suicide Attempt Scale." Utah State University, 1976. (DAI,
37/5B, p. 2527). 67-25630.

Smith, Vann A. "Perceived Value Deprivation as a Predictor of
Self-destructive Behavior." United States International University,
1975. (DAI, 36/3B, p. 1419). 75-19137.

Snavely, Harry R. "Factors Underlying Clinician Bias in Decisions about Suicide Potential." University of California, Los
Angeles, 1968. (DAI, 29/9B, p. 3496). 69-03934.

Steinkerchner, Raymond E. "Empirical Analysis of Suicidal Potential among Dialysis Patients." George Peabody College for
Teachers, 1974. (DAI, 36/4B, p. 1934). 75-21276.

6.212 PREVENTION OF SUICIDE

Amberg, William F. "A Cross-indexed Study of Suicide Intervention Programs and Analysis of Current Models." Brigham
Young University, 1970. (DAI, 31/11B, p. 6887). 71-12102.

Dissertations, Theses, Reports

Ansel, Edward L. "Correlates of Volunteer Performance in a Suicide Prevention/Crisis Intervention Service." University of Florida, 1972. (DAI, 34/1B, p. 402). 73-15561.

Belanger, Robert R. "CPI Predictors of Clinical Effectiveness of Volunteers in a Suicide and Crisis Intervention Service." University of Florida, 1972. (DAI, 33/7B, p. 3297). 73-00545.

Campagna, Jean-Louis. "Implementation and Evaluation of a Suicide Prevention Program in Quebec." California School of Professional Psychology, 1976. (DAI, 37/9B, p. 4666). 77-06290.

Egger, Norman L. "An Analysis of Suicides in San Francisco from 1939 to 1950 with an Educational Program for Prevention." University of California, 1954.

Fisher, Sheila A. "Suicide Prevention and/or Crisis Services: A National Survey." Case Western Reserve University, 1972. (DAI, 33/4A, p. 1835). 72-26153.

Franks, Ruth M. "The Pathogenesis and Prevention of Suicide." University of Toronto, 1936.

Jeuchter, Joanne K. "Guidelines for Suicide Prevention in New York State Colleges." Columbia University, 1971. (DAI, 32/5A, p. 2307). 71-28006.

Knickerbocker, David A. "Lay Volunteer and Professional Trainee Therapeutic Functioning and Outcomes in a Suicide and Crisis Intervention Service." University of Florida, 1972. (DAI, 34/1B, p. 416). 73-15510.

Praul, Edward J. "The Role of the College Counselor with Regard to the Problems of Suicide among Students." University of Toledo, 1971. (DAI, 32/11A, p. 6136). 72-16254.

Schwartz, Michael B. "Suicide Prevention and Suicidal Behavior." Tulane University, 1971. (DAI, 33/5A, p. 2506). 72-30073.

Slaikeu, Karl A. "Telephone Referral Calls to a Suicide Prevention and Crisis Intervention Service." State University of of New York at Buffalo, 1973. (DAI, 34/9B, p. 4677). 74-04448.

Thompson, Lois E.L. "Selection, Training, and Evaluation of Paraprofessionals in Suicide Prevention Telephone Work." California School of Professional Psychology, 1973. (DAI, 34/10B, p. 5213). 74-07920.

Welu, Thomas C. "Evaluating a Special Program for Suicide Attempters." University of Pittsburgh, 1973. (DAI 34/3B, p. 1171). 73-21341.

6.213 PSYCHOLOGICAL STUDIES OF SUICIDE

Berk, Norman. "A Personality Study of Suicidal Schizophrenics." New York University, 1949. (DAI, 10/2, p. 155). 00-01484.

Brown, Irving R. "Attempted Suicide: A Value-added Analysis." University of Missouri, 1976. (DAI, 37/9A, p. 6102). 77-04891.

Cabiles, Palma. "Impulsivity and Depression as Factors in Suicidal Males." Long Island University, 1976. (DAI, 37/4B, p. 1890). 76-23714.

Callender, Willard D. "A Socio-psychological Study of Suicide-related Behavior in a Student Population." University of Connecticut, 1967. (DAI, 28/9A, p. 3765). 68-01324.

Cohorn, Ronnie L. "Suicide Attempts; The Significance of Hope, Threat, Competence and Succorance." Texas Tech University, 1972. (DAI, 33/8B, p. 3932). 73-04048.

Darbonne, Allen R. "An Investigation into the Communication Style of Suicidal Individuals." University of Southern California, 1966. (DAI, 27/7B, p. 2504). 67-00399.

Elliott, Thomas B. "Conceptual Styles of Suicidal Psychiatric Patients." University of Missouri, 1972. (DAI, 34/3B, p. 1273). 73-21413.

Esler, Harold D. "An Investigation of the Causes of Suicide in Patients Diagnosed as Schizophrenic." Michigan State University, 1964. (DAI, 26/2, p. 1169). 64-09735.

Farberow, Norman L. "Personality Patterns of Suicidal Mental Hospital Patients." University of California, Los Angeles, 1950.

Flynn, Michael F. "Time Perspective in Suicidal Patients." Loyola University, Chicago, 1974. (DAI, 35/4B, p. 1907). 74-22425.

Geller, Andrew M. "Cognitive and Personality Factors in Suicidal Behavior." Yeshiva University, 1976. 77-05004.

Gibson, Gail S. "The Relationship between Certain Problem Areas and Suicidal Thoughts of Adolescents." George Peabody College for Teachers, 1974. (DAI, 35/10A, p. 6511). 74-29170.

Goldsmith, Lisa A. "Adaptive Regression, Humor and Suicide." City University of New York, 1973. (DAI, 34/3B, p. 1275). 73-21907.

Greth, David L. "Anomie, Suicidal Ideation, and Student Ecology in a College Population." Ohio State University, 1972. (DAI, 33/7B, p. 3305). 72-27015.

Haws, Ben F. "A Study of Personality Characteristics of Students Having a Suicidal History with Other Groups." Brigham Young University, 1972. (DAI, 33/5A, p. 2103). 72-28929.

Henderson, James T. "Competence, Threat, Hope and Self-destructive Behavior." University of Maryland, 1972. (DAI, 33/1B, p. 439). 72-20493.

Hynes, James J. "An Exploratory Study of the Affective Future Time Perspective of Adolescent Suicide Attempters." Catholic University of America, 1976. (DAI, 37/3A, p. 1404). 76-19973.

Jacobson, Hanna M. "An Investigation of the Relationship between Risk-taking Characteristics, Belief, in Internal-external Control, Emotional Reactivity, and the Lethality of the Suicide Plan in Women Who Have Attempted Suicide." New York University, 1973. (DAI, 34/6B, p. 2738). 73-30077.

Kilpatrick, Diane C. "Tendencies toward Suicide among College Students." University of Illinois, Urbana, 1976. (DAI, 37/5B, p. 2160). 76-24114.

Kochansky, Gerald E. "Risk-taking and Hedonic Mood Stimulation in Suicide Attempters." Boston University, 1970. (DAI, 31/6B, p. 3709). 70-22395.

Lee, Mercile J. "A Search for Meaning: A Study of Threatened, Attempted and Completed Suicides among Selected College Students." Hartford Seminary Foundation, 1969. (DAI, 30/11B, p. 5224). 70-07908.

Lester, David. "Suicidal Behavior: Aggression or Hostility in Social Relationships?" Brandeis University, 1968. (DAI, 29/1B, p. 391). 68-09937.

Lettieri, Dan J. "Affect, Attitude and Cognition in Suicidal Persons." University of Kansas, 1970. (DAI, 31/6A, p. 3039). 70-25369.

Levenson, Marvin. "Cognitive and Perceptual Factors in Suicidal Individuals." University of Kansas, 1972. (DAI, 33/11B, p. 5521). 73-11914.

McEvoy, Theodore L. "A Comparison of Suicidal and Nonsuicidal Patients by Means of the Thematic Apperception Test." University of California, Los Angeles, 1963. (DAI, 24/3, p. 1248). 63-06594.

McGrath, Marcia K.K. "Superego and Ego Factors in Suicidal Forms of Coping with Crisis." University of California, Berkeley, 1972.

Neuringer, Charles. "An Exploratory Study of Suicidal Thinking." University of Kansas, 1960. (DAI, 21/5, p. 1257). 60-04335.

Pearson, Nils S. "Identification of Psychological Variables Distinguishing Suicide-attempters Within a Sample of Depressive Individuals." Rutgers University, 1972. (DAI, 33/4B, p. 1803). 72-27582.

Perlman, Baron. "Suicide, Taxonomy and Behavior." Michigan State University, 1974. (DAI, 35/9B, p. 4660). 75-07232.

Politano, Paul M. "The Process Model of Suicidal Behavior." Indiana University, 1977. (DAI, 38/11B, p. 5588). 78-05641.

Ruby, Thomas M. "Rigidity in a Risk-taking Task among Serious Suicide Attempters and Nonsuicidal Psychiatric Patients." University of Missouri, 1973. (DAI, 35/2B, p. 1062). 74-18627.

Rutstein, Eleanor H. "The Effects of Aggressive Stimulation on Suicidal Patients." New York University, 1970. (DAI, 31/12B, p. 7611). 71-15424.

Scholz, James A. "Defense Styles in Suicide Attempters." Fordham University, 1972. (DAI, 33/1B, p. 452). 72-20583.

Sharon, Isaac. "A Study of Self-concept among Suicide Attempters." United States International University, 1975. (DAI, 36/5B, p. 2453). 75-25973.

Tapper, Bruce J. "A Behavioral Assessment of the Reinforcement Contingencies Associated with the Occurrence of Suicidal Behaviors." University of Southern California, 1975. (DAI, 36/3B, p. 1462). 75-19040.

Tauber, Ronald K. "Suicide Notes." University of California, Berkeley, 1969. (DAI, 31/4A, p. 1914). 70-17475.

Temoche, Abelardo. "Suicide and Known Mental Disease." Harvard University, 1961.

Viers, Lawrence A. "Dependency Features of High Risk for Suicide Groups." California School of Professional Psychology, 1977. (DAI, 38/11B, p. 5600). 78-04579.

Vogel, Roberta B. "A Projective Study of Dynamic Factors in Attempted Suicide." Michigan State University, 1967. (DAI, 28/10B, p. 4303). 68-04230.

Walker, Derald R. "A Study of the Characteristics of Individuals Treated for Attempted Suicide in Six Utah Hospital Emergency Rooms during 1975." Brigham Young University, 1976. (DAI, 37/9B, p. 4710). 77-04858.

Waugh, Douglas B. "Attempted Suicide and Aggression." United States International University, 1974. (DAI, 35/3B, p. 1398). 74-20554.

Wetzel, Richard D. "Suicide, Intent, Affect and Cognitive Style." St. Louis University, 1974. (DAI, 36/6B, p. 3080). 75-26341.

Wilson, Karl E. "Suicide Risk, Self-injury Risk, and Expected Intentionality for a Population and Its Component Sub-populations." University of Florida, 1976. (DAI, 37/10B, p. 5387). 77-06915.

6.214   SEX DIFFERENCES IN SUICIDE

Diamond, Harriet A. "Suicide by Women Professionals." California School of Professional Psychology, 1977. (DAI, 38/10B, p. 5009). 78-02823.

Linehan, Marsha M. "Sex Differences in Suicide and Attempted Suicide." Loyola University of Chicago, 1971. (DAI, 32/5B, p. 3036). 71-28130.

Miller, Marv. "Suicide among Older Men." University of Michigan, 1976. (DAI, 37/6B, 3156). 76-27546.

6.215   SOCIOLOGICAL STUDIES OF SUICIDE

Abbiati, David L. "Suicide in Maine." University of Connecticut, 1975. (DAI, 36/7B, p. 3668). 76-01646.

Andress, LaVern R. "An Epidemiological Study of the Psychosocial Characteristics of Suicidal Behavior in Riverside County between 1960 and 1974." United States International University, 1976. (DAI, 37/3B, p. 1481). 76-20945.

Black, Kimball D. "A Descriptive Survey of Student Suicide in Higher Education within the Southwestern Rocky Mountain States." University of Denver, 1971. (DAI, 32/6A, p. 3015). 72-01073.

Bradshaw, Alfred D. "The Social Construction of Suicide Rates." Syracuse University, 1973. (DAI, 34/10A, p. 6775). 74-08228.

Campion, Donald R. "Patterns of Suicide in Philadelphia." University of Pennsylvania, 1960. (DAI, 21/5, p. 1279). 60-03568.

Cavan, Ruth S. "Suicide." University of Chicago, 1926.

Davis, Robert. "A Statistical Analysis of the Current Reported Increase in the Black Suicide Rate." Washington State University, 1975. (DAI, 36/8A, p. 5573). 76-04350.

Demmer, Charles C. "A Study of Suicide among Active Officers of the United States Army for the Fiscal Years 1901 to 1932 Inclusive." Johns Hopkins University, 1934.

Frenay, Adolph D. "The Suicide Problem in the United States." Catholic University of America, 1927.

Gibbs, Jack P. "A Sociological Study of Suicide." University of Oregon, 1957. (DAI, 17/12 p. 3112). 00-24388.

Hartman, Joseph H. "Community Unemployment Conditions in Relation to Four Psycho-social Indices." Florida State University, 1976. (DAI, 37/6B, p. 3076). 76-28616.

Hutcherson, Karen P. "Temporal Aspects of Asphyxia Suicides in Greater Cleveland." Case Western Reserve University, 1978. (DAI, 38/12B, p. 6157). 78-09286.

MacKinnon, Douglas R. "Suicide, the Community and the Coroner's Office." University of Southern California, 1977. (DAI, 38/10A, p. 6340). 03-13267.

Marks, Alan H. "A Regional Comparison of Attitudes toward Suicide and Methods of Self-destruction." University of Georgia, 1973. (DAI, 34/9A, p. 6123). 74-04837.

Marshall, James R. "An Investigation of Longitudinal Variation in Suicide." University of California, Los Angeles, 1977. (DAI, 38/8A, p. 5085). 77-30939.

O'Connell, Martin T. "The Effect of Changing Age Distributions on Fertility and Suicide in Developed Countries." University of Pennsylvania, 1975. (DAI, 36/8A, p. 5575). 76-03206.

Schmid, Calvin F. "Suicide in Seattle, Washington, and Pittsburgh." University of Pittsburgh, 1930.

Vigderhous, Gideon. "Socio-demographic Determinants of Suicide and Homicide." University of Illinois, Urbana, 1975. (DAI, 36/5A, p. 3154). 75-24424.

Vincentnathan, Sugridnathan. "Patterns of 'Serious' Crimes and Suicide in San Francisco, Tokyo and Madras." University of California, Berkeley, 1973.

Wendling, Aubrey. "Suicide in the San Francisco Bay Region." University of Washington, 1954. (DAI, 14/12, p. 2430). 00-10017.

6.216 SOCIOLOGICAL THEORIES OF SUICIDE

Douglas, Jack D. "The Sociological Study of Suicide." Princeton University, 1965. (DAI, 28/2A, p. 799). 65-13137.

Ferguson, Charlotte G. "Social Factors in Suicidal Behavior." Boston University, 1975. (DAI, 36/3A, p. 1825). 75-20988.

Futrell, Richard H. "An Empirical Test of a Social Structural Model for the Prediction of Suicide and Homicide." University of Kansas, 1974. (DAI, 36/2A, p. 1105). 75-17603.

Geisel, Robert L. "Suicide in Missouri: An Empirical Test of Durkheim's Social Integration Theory." University of Iowa, 1972. (DAI, 33/4A, p. 1861). 72-26680.

Henry, Andy F. "The Nature of the Relation between Suicide and the Business Cycle." University of Chicago, 1951.

Humphrey, John A. "Homicide, Suicide and Role Relationships in New Hampshire." University of New Hampshire, 1973. (DAI, 34/5A, p. 2789). 73-25783.

Krohn, Marvin D. "Social Change and Social Disorganization."
Florida State University, 1974. (DAI, 36/9A, p. 6259). 75-06287.

Maris, Ronald W. "Suicide in Chicago: An Examination of
Emile Durkheim's Theory of Suicide." University of Illinois,
Urbana, 1965. (DAI, 26/12, p. 7487). 66-04232.

Miley, James D. "Structural Change and Suicide." Tulane
University, 1970. (DAI, 31/6A, p. 3059). 70-24536.

Miller, Dorothy H. "Suicidal Careers." University of California, Berkeley, 1967. (DAI, 28/11A, p. 4720). 68-05687.

Nelson, Zane P. "A Study of Suicide in Wyoming: A Durkheimian Analysis." Brigham Young University, 1969. (DAI,
30/9A, p. 4032). 70-04711.

Peck, Dennis L. "Social Integration, Goal Commitment, and
Fatalistic Suicide." Washington State University, 1976. (DAI,
37/8A, p. 5394). 77-02877.

Reinhart, George R. "Social Structure and Self-destructive Behavior." University of Georgia, 1977. (DAI, 38/7A, p. 4390).
77-29799.

Tennant, Donald A. "Revisions and Further Tests of the Theory
of Status Integration and Suicide." Washington State University,
1971. (DAI, 32/1A, p. 558). 71-18592.

Wenz, Frederich V. "Completed Suicide, Attempted Suicide
and Urban Social Structure." Wayne State University, 1975.
(DAI, 35/12A, p. 8037). 75-13408.

Whitt, Hugh P. "The Lethal Aggression Rate and the Suicide-
Murder Ratio." University of North Carolina, 1968. (DAI,
29/7B, p. 2624). 69-01697.

Whittemore, Kenneth R. "Role Failure and Suicide." Emory
University, 1971. (DAI, 32/7A, p. 4135). 72-03046.

6.217 SUICIDE AND LITERATURE

Cleary, James J. "Seneca, Suicide and English Renaissance
Tragedy." Temple University, 1969. (DAI, 30/4A, p. 1521).
69-16284.

Crane, Theodore. "The Imagery of Suicide in Lucan's 'De Bello
Civili.'" University of North Carolina, 1964. (DAI, 25/11,
p. 6604). 65-03999.

Davies, Mark I. "Studies on the Early Traditions of the Oresteia
Legend in Art and Literature with Related Studies on the Suicide
of Ajax." Princeton University, 1971. (DAI, 32/11A, p. 6321).
72-13736.

Faber, Melvin D. "Suicide in Shakespeare." University of California, Los Angeles, 1964. (DAI, 24/11, p. 4697). 64-07124.

Green, Paul D. "Long Lent Loathed Light: A Study of Suicide in Three English Nondramatic Writers of the Sixteenth Century." Harvard University, 1971.

Harmon, Alice I. "'Loci Communes' on Death and Suicide in the Literature of the English Renaissance." University of Minnesota, 1940.

Hicks, Cora E. "Suicide in English Tragedy, 1587-1622." University of Texas, 1968. (DAI, 29/6A, p. 1868). 68-16093.

Rolfs, Daniel J. "The Theme of Suicide in Italian Literature." University of California, Berkeley, 1972.

Sewell, Robert G. "The Theme of Suicide: A Study of Human Values in Japanese and Western Literature." University of Illinois, Urbana, 1976. (DAI, 37/10A, p. 6467). 77-09180.

Slavensky, Sonia W. "Suicide in the Plays of Arthur Miller." Loyola University of Chicago, 1973. (DAI, 34/4A, p. 1936). 73-23156.

6.218 SUICIDE AND RELIGION

Demopulos, Alexander. "Suicide and Church Canon Law." Claremont School of Theology, 1968. (DAI, 31/4A, p. 1876). 70-19082.

Pretzel, Paul W. "Suicide and Religion." Claremont Graduate School of Theology, 1966. (DAI, 34/6B, p. 2948). 73-28779.

6.219 SUICIDE IN CHILDREN AND ADOLESCENTS

Cantor, Pamela C. "Personality and Status Characteristics of the Female Youthful Suicide Attempter." Columbia University, 1972. (DAI, 37/1B, p. 452). 76-15532.

Doroff, David R. "Attempted and Gestured Suicide in Adolescent Girls." Rutgers University, 1968. (DAI, 29/7B, p. 2631). 69-01042.

Francis, Charles R. "Adolescent Suicide Attempts, Experienced Rejection and Personal Constructs." California School of Professional Psychology, 1976. (DAI, 38/9B, p. 4453). 77-32474.

Korella, Karl. "Teen-age Suicidal Gestures." University of Oregon, 1971. (DAI, 32/9A, p. 5039). 72-08561.

Mapes, Bruce E. "Suicidal versus Acting-out Adolescents." University of Pennsylvania, 1974. (DAI, 35/4B, p. 1919). 74-22875.

Motanky, Carl S. "The Role of Acting-out and Identification in Adolescent Suicidal Behavior." Illinois Institute of Technology, 1970. (DAI, 31/12B, p. 7606). 71-14051.

O'Reilly, Patricia J. "Youthful Suicide." Marquette University, 1973. (DAI, 35/5B, p. 2442). 74-18237.

Reese, Frederick D. "School-age Suicide." Ohio State University, 1966. (DAI, 27/9A, p. 2895). 67-02519.

Walch, Steven M. "Adolescent Attempted Suicide." California School of Professional Psychology, 1977. (DAI, 38/6B, p. 2892). 77-27616.

6.220 SURVIVORS OF SUICIDE

Demi, Alice M. "Adjustment to Widowhood after a Sudden Death." University of California, San Francisco, 1978. (DAI, 38/12B, p. 5847). 78-09192.

Stone, Howard W. "The Grief Responses of Middle-aged Spouses." Claremont School of Theology, 1971. (DAI, 31/12A, p. 6709). 71-15058.

6.221 THERAPY FOR SUICIDE

Bartman, Erwin R. "Assertive Training with Hospitalized Suicide Attempters." Catholic University of America, 1976. (DAI, 37/3B, p. 1425). 76-19363.

Billings, James H. "The Efficacy of Group Treatment with Depressed and Suicidal Individuals in Comparison with Other Treatment Settings as Regard the Prevention of Suicide." California School of Professional Psychology, San Francisco, 1974. (DAI, 36/12B, p. 6369). 76-11964.

Clanton, Elizabeth M. "Changes in the Level of Depression and Self-concept of Suicidal Clients Following Nursing Intervention in a Small Group Setting." Catholic University of America, 1975. (DAI, 36/10B, p. 4942). 76-08944.

Corte, Henry E. "The Use of Punishment in the Modification of Self-destructive Behavior of Retarded Children." University of Kansas, 1969. (DAI, 30/12B, p. 5685). 70-11010.

Cowgell, Virginia G. "Responding to Suicidal Communications." Duke University, 1974. (DAI, 35/2B, p. 1043). 74-16584.

Erickson, Gustave A. "Effects of Patient Selected Contingent Verbal Stimuli on Verbal Output of Hospitalized Suicidal Males." Arizona State University, 1965. (DAI, 26/4, p. 2319). 65-10374.

Lum, Doman. "Suicide: Theological Ethics and Pastoral Counseling." Claremont School of Theology, 1967. (DAI, 29/1B, p. 374). 68-09428.

Reubin, Richard H. "A Study of the Factors Involved in the Decision to Treat Suicidal Clients." University of California, Los Angeles, 1973. (DAI, 34/1B, p. 296). 73-16696.

White, Rosemary S. "The Effects of Specialized Group Techniques upon the Social Isolation and Depression of Suicidal Persons." California School of Professional Psychology, 1976. (DAI, 37/9B, p. 4714). 77-06317.

Selected dissertations are cited in the INTERNATIONAL NURSING INDEX (5.126) and PSYCHOLOGICAL ABSTRACTS (5.219).

6.3 UNPUBLISHED RESEARCH REPORTS

Most basic, applied, and evaluative research reporting is published in books and periodical articles. Research is also reported in dissertations and theses. There also exists, however, a growing body of literature which is often referred to as report literature, or, especially in the applied science areas, "technical reports." In the social sciences, the applied research reports are often in the form of program evaluation reports, for example, reports on the effectiveness of suicide prevention programs. Research reports of all types are being published less often in book form in recent years because the reports often do not require the lengthy and expensive format of books. Also, the time lag in regard to publishing research reports in book form, and even as articles in periodicals, is not considered tolerable by many researchers and sponsoring agencies. The U.S. government has taken the lead in establishing reporting services with less time lag, and which disseminate the reports in a nontraditional manner. The government solicits research reports through various clearinghouses and information centers, abstracts them, indexes these abstracts, publishes speedily the abstracts and indexes, and provides upon request photocopies or microform copies of the original reports. Thus the reports in a sense cannot really be considered unpublished and are sometimes referred to as "near-print" materials. Several of these government sources, of importance to research on suicide, are described here.

6.301   GOVERNMENT REPORTS ANNOUNCEMENTS AND INDEX. Springfield, Va.: National Technical Information Service, 1946-- . Semimonthly, with an annual cumulative index. C51.9/3/vol./no.

This extensive reporting service abstracts and indexes all newly released federally funded or sponsored research and development reports. Approximately fifty thousand reports

from 225 U.S. government agencies are abstracted annually.
Although it is heavily oriented toward the physical sciences,
some behavioral science research is reported. About three
to eight reports on suicide research appear each year. The
index has been issued concurrently with the announcement
volumes which include the abstracts. Annual cumulated
index volumes have been provided since 1965. Indexing is
done by subject, personal and corporate author (agency,
etc.), contract number, and the report number. Each abstract
includes the source and price of purchase for each report,
and also indicates whether the report can be obtained in
paper copy or in microform. Computerized searching is
available from the NTIS. The data base also can be searched
through the services described in items 5.301 and 5.302
available at large libraries and information centers which
have computer searching facilities of this type available.
From 1946 to 1964 the announcement volumes have been
variously known as BIBLIOGRAPHY OF SCIENTIFIC AND
INDUSTRIAL REPORTS; BIBLIOGRAPHY OF TECHNICAL RE-
PORTS; and U.S. GOVERNMENT RESEARCH REPORTS.
From 1965 to January 1971 they were entitled U.S. GOV-
ERNMENT RESEARCH AND DEVELOPMENT REPORTS. The
title of the index volumes also has varied since 1965 as
follows: GOVERNMENT-WIDE INDEX; U.S. GOVERN-
MENT RESEARCH AND DEVELOPMENT REPORTS; and since
1965, GOVERNMENT REPORTS INDEX. This abstracting
and indexing service is difficult to use.

Consult: Suicide

6.302   RESOURCES IN EDUCATION. Washington, D.C.: U.S. Educational
Resources Information Center, November 1966-- . Monthly, with annual cumulative indexes. HE19.210:vol./no.

Suicide information as related to education and allied fields
can be secured from this extensive source published by the
U.S. government through the sixteen clearinghouses of the
Educational Resources Information Center (ERIC) system. This
center acquires, selects, reviews, abstracts, indexes, and
disseminates research reports in educational and other fields
useful to educators. Most of the research is presented for
the first time. Individuals may submit unpublished research
for consideration. Each entry consists of an ERIC accession
number, the author(s) name, the title of the paper or report,
the organization and/or sponsoring body of the research,
pagination, cost of purchasing upon request a copy of the
report in paper copy or microfiche, descriptors and identifiers
of the subject of each report, and an abstract of the contents of the report. The entries are arranged by the ERIC
accession number under subject descriptors which are alphabetically arranged. By referring to the THESAURUS OF

ERIC DESCRIPTORS, searches can be performed more efficiently. In addition to the descriptors tagged to each entry
in the RIE, the authors of the abstracts assign other words
known as identifiers to the description of the report. These
identifiers thereby provide added information and access.
This is not the easiest work to use, even though the cross-
reference system is good, and separate author, subject, and
institution indexes are provided. Manual searches are faci-
litated by cumulations such as Prentice-Hall's COMPLETE
GUIDE AND INDEX TO ERIC REPORTS, THROUGH 1969,
published in 1970, and the ERIC EDUCATION DOCUMENTS
INDEX, 1966-69. Computer searches are available directly
by mail from ERIC. The data base also can be searched
through the services described in items 5.301 and 5.302
available at large libraries and information centers which
have computer searching facilities of this type available.
Computer tapes are also available for purchase, as well as
hard copy and microfiche copies of the reports, as indicated
above. Many universities hold complete files of the ERIC
reports on microfiche. Only two or three reports on suicide
currently appear each year. This work was previously entitled RESEARCH IN EDUCATION, 1966-74.

Consult: Suicide

6.4 RESEARCH IN PROGRESS

Research in progress on suicide is difficult to locate. Unfortunately, even though
it is especially important for the researcher to keep informed of dissertations and
other research announced and in progress, there is apparently no regularly published listing of "dissertations in progress" or "research in progress," specifically
on suicide research, in the scholarly literature. Several possible sources for
becoming aware of funded research in progress on suicide are described below.

6.401   THE FOUNDATION CENTER. Associates Program, 888 Seventh Avenue,
New York, N.Y. 10019.

The Foundation Center maintains a data bank on the research
that is supported by grants of $5,000 or more, donated by
private foundations and reported by the same. An index of
recipients and the corresponding subject categories can be
obtained. Computer searching of this index is available for
organizations associated with the Foundation Center. The
data base also can be searched through the service described
in item 5.301 available at large libraries and information
centers which have computer searching facilities of this type.
The center publishes FOUNDATION NEWS, the FOUNDA-
TION DIRECTORY (12.204), and the annual FOUNDATION
GRANTS INDEX, 1970/71-- (12.205).

6.402   The SMITHSONIAN SCIENCE INFORMATION EXCHANGE. Room 300,
        1730 M Street, N.W.   Washington, D.C.   20036.

The SSIE maintains a data bank for over thirteen hundred
state, local, and federal agencies that fund and/or conduct
research.   The file contains information on approximately
two hundred thousand ongoing or recently completed research
projects.   The information includes supporting agency, title
of the project, principal investigators, and an abstract of
the project.   A current awareness service is also available.
A fee is charged for these services.   The data base can be
computer searched.   Refer to section 5.3 for this.

Chapter 7
SUICIDE STATISTICS

Basic sources for locating suicide statistics are described and evaluated in this chapter. Often the very latest statistics on suicide are what is required. At other times retrospective statistics for specific time periods in the past are needed. In both cases, comparative statistics for various countries may also be important. In section 7.1, sources of brief or condensed statistical information of these types are described for the person who is interested in suicide data without extensive detail. In section 7.2 main sources of extensive and more detailed suicide statistics are described. A special section, 7.3, describes ways by which a researcher can keep abreast of newly published sources of suicide statistics.

Some of the statistics on suicide referred to in this chapter are available in published form and some also are stored in large computer data bases from which they can be retrieved as desired by the researcher. The computer data bases generally contain somewhat more detailed and more up-to-date data than do the published works. Many universities have some of these data available or can arrange computer searching of the data bases. Tapes and punched cards can also be procured directly from the data-gathering agencies.

Statistics on public opinion regarding suicide or related to suicide are discussed in section 10.4 of this information guide.

Throughout this chapter, the document number assigned by the staff of the Superintendent of Documents is given, where possible, after each volume or item for easier location of the material in libraries which arrange materials from the U.S. government by this system.

7.1 SUICIDE STATISTICS IN BRIEF

When reliable up-to-date and retrospective data are needed on suicide, a few basic annuals, which are described below, are referred to frequently. Although there is only a limited analysis of data on suicide in these works, they may be sufficient for the general user who requires brief, condensed, or summarized data of this nature.

7.101   CANADA YEAR BOOK, 1905-- . Ottawa: Statistics Canada, 1971-- .
         Annual. Charts, graphs, maps, tables, bibliography.

         This review of current social, economic, and political de-
         velopments in Canada contains a summary table which pro-
         vides the annual number of suicides, according to sex and
         age group. Sources of the data reported are cited. There
         is a time lag of two years in the publication of the data.
         Volumes for 1905-71 were issued under the agency's former
         name, Bureau of Statistics.

         Consult: Suicide

7.102   DEMOGRAPHIC YEARBOOK. New York: United Nations, 1948-- .
         Annual.

         This compendium of population data contains the official
         statistics from nearly 250 nations and territories of the world,
         with suicide data on 80 of these. Each year a table on the
         cause of death is provided which gives the number of sui-
         cides and suicide rate for these countries. Occasionally,
         a special topical report emphasizes mortality, including sui-
         cide. Data are then reported on the number and rate of
         suicides, by sex and by age groups. The last special report
         of this type appeared in the 1974 annual. This work is a
         basic source for U.S. as well as worldwide statistics on sui-
         cide. See also item 7.303.

7.103   Great Britain. Central Statistics Office. ANNUAL ABSTRACT OF
         STATISTICS. London: H.M. Stationery Office, 1935/36-- . Annual
         since 1948.

         This abstract of British statistics contains data on social,
         economic, and health conditions of the United Kingdom and
         Northern Ireland. It provides information on the number of
         suicides annually. There is a one-year time lag prior to
         publication of the data.

7.104   INFORMATION PLEASE ALMANAC. New York: Simon & Schuster,
         1947-- . Annual.

         Refer to item 4.201.

7.105   READER'S DIGEST ALMANAC AND YEARBOOK. Pleasantville, N.Y.:
         Reader's Digest Association, 1966-- . Annual.

         Refer to item 4.202.

7.106   U.S. Bureau of the Census. HISTORICAL ABSTRACTS OF THE UNITED
         STATES, COLONIAL TIMES TO 1970. Bicentennial ed. 2 pts. Wash-
         ington, D.C.: Government Printing Office, 1975. 1,232 p. C3.124/
         2:H62/1789-1970/pts.

For earlier U.S. statistics on suicide, this is the best quick reference work based on authoritative sources. It is essentially a supplement to the STATISTICAL ABSTRACT OF THE UNITED STATES (7.107) and presents historical statistics of the same type. The historical statistics include the following data on suicide in the United States from 1900 to 1970: suicide rates, number of suicides, number of males and females, whether by poisoning, hanging, firearms, or other means.

Consult: Suicides

7.107 _____. STATISTICAL ABSTRACT OF THE UNITED STATES. Washington, D.C.: Government Printing Office, 1878-- . Annual. C3.134:yr.

A quick, basic source of chiefly official government data on suicide, the annual volumes provide data on suicide rates in the United States by race and sex and by method, including firearms, poisoning, hanging, and strangulation. Also, for approximately twenty-five selected countries, data are provided on suicide by sex and age groups. There is a two- to three-year time lag in the publication of the data. Since the exact sources of the data are given below each table presented, this work also thereby serves as a guide to further information. The user can then go to these direct sources and find more current data that may appear throughout the present year or find more detailed data. A most useful tabulation for 1900 to 1970 is provided by the HISTORICAL ABSTRACTS OF THE UNITED STATES, CO-LONIAL TIMES TO 1970 (7.106). It should be noted that suicide statistics were first reported annually in 1910, and were retrospective to 1900. No national suicide and other death data were collected annually in the United States before 1900, except for decennial censuses (see section 7.2).

Consult: Suicides

7.108 Urquhart, M.C., and Buckley, K.A.H., eds. HISTORICAL STATISTICS OF CANADA. Toronto: Macmillan; London: Cambridge University Press, 1965. xv, 672 p.

Arranged like the HISTORICAL ABSTRACTS OF THE UNITED STATES, COLONIAL TIMES TO 1970 (7.106), this guide to Canadian historical statistics contains information on the number of suicides, male and female, for each province from 1921 to 1960. The sources of data are given.

Consult: Suicide

7.109 WORLD ALMANAC AND BOOK OF FACTS. New York: Newspaper
Enterprise Associates, 1868-- . Annual.

Refer to item 4.203.

7.110 WORLD HEALTH STATISTICS ANNUAL. Geneva: World Health Organization, 1962-- . Annual.

Refer to item 7.308. This is a very good source of worldwide suicide data.

Although not in itself a primary source of suicide information, the following
ongoing index offers a very quick way to locate precise and relevant statistics
on various aspects of suicide as needed.

7.111 AMERICAN STATISTICS INDEX: A COMPREHENSIVE GUIDE AND
INDEX TO THE STATISTICAL PUBLICATIONS OF THE UNITED STATES
GOVERNMENT, 1960-- . Washington, D.C.: Congressional Informa-
tion Service, 1973-- . Annual, with monthly supplements.

Refer to item 7.301.

7.2 DETAILED PUBLISHED AND COMPUTERIZED DATA FILES

In this section the basic sources of collected data on suicide in the United States and
Canada are presented and evaluated. These statistics may be found both in
printed sources and in computerized data bases. For world suicide statistics see
section 18.1. See also sections 16.1 and 16.2.

Census Reports—United States

Prior to the establishment of a nationwide system for collecting vital statistics,
data on mortality were collected along with the decennial censuses for the years
1850, 1860, 1870, 1880, 1890, and 1900. Each family head was asked whether
any family member had died between June 1 of the previous year and May 31
of the census year. Information was collected on all persons who died, including suicides, by name, age, sex, color, free or slave status (1850 and 1860
only), state and county of birth, month of death, cause, and occupation. All
of these census schedules are available for direct use, except the 1890 schedules
which were destroyed by fire, from the national archives, research or genea-
logical libraries that have microfilm copies. The tabulations on suicide that
were made in the census reports are described below.

7.201 U.S. Census Office. 7th census, 1850. MORTALITY STATISTICS OF
THE SEVENTH CENSUS OF THE UNITED STATES, 1850 . . . . By
J.D.B. DeBow, superintendent of the United States Census. Washington, D.C.: A.O.P. Nicholson, Printer, 1855. 306 p. (33d Cong.,
2d Sess., House Ex. doc. 98.) 18.5:2.

These data collected on suicides that occurred twelve months prior to the 1850 census are analyzed by age, race, sex, occupation, and slave or free status for various geographical areas and by month of occurrence.

7.202 _____. 8th Census, 1860. STATISTICS OF THE UNITED STATES, (INCLUDING MORTALITY, PROPERTY, ETC.). Washington, D.C.: Government Printing Office, 1866. lxvi, 584 p. 19.5:4.

The number of suicides by sex and the means of suicide are recorded for each state. Suicides by age groups, means, and months are given for the United States. Summaries on suicide by sex and means are located on page 253, and suicide by race on pages 282 and 283.

Consult: Suicide (in the Mortality Index)

7.203 _____. 9th Census, 1870. CENSUS REPORTS. 3 vols. Washington, D.C.: Government Printing Office, 1872. I10.5:2

_____. MORTALITY OF THE UNITED STATES. Washington, D.C.: Government Printing Office, 1870. 423 p. I10.5

Suicide statistics are analyzed by age, sex, means of suicide, nativity, and month of the year for states and the entire nation in this census. There are comparative suicide statistics given for the years 1850, 1860, and 1870.

7.204 _____. 10th Census, 1880. CENSUS REPORTS. 22 vols. Washington, D.C.: Government Printing Office, 1883-88. I11.5:11&12

"Mortality and Vital Statistics," in volumes 11 and 12, reports the number and rates of suicides for the twelve months prior to the 1880 census. These data are analyzed by age, sex, race, month of occurrence, and means of suicide for the nation, regions, states, and large cities. Volume 12 contains a useful summary article for these suicide data, including tables, graphs, and maps. Table 19 contains comparative data for suicide and the means of suicide for 1850, 1860, 1870, and 1880.

7.205 _____. 11th Census, 1890. CENSUS REPORTS. 25 vols. in 23. Washington, D.C.: Government Printing Office, 1892-97. I12.5:20-23.

Volume 4, VITAL AND SOCIAL STATISTICS, is divided into four parts. Part 1 contains a good summary article on the 1890 suicide data, while the succeeding parts contain information on suicide by the variables described below for cities, states, and rural-urban areas. The number and rates of suicide are presented by age, race, sex, marital status, occupation, and month of occurrence. The means of committing suicide are also included.

Suicide Statistics

7.206 _____. 12th Census, 1900. CENSUS REPORTS . . . TWELFTH
CENSUS OF THE UNITED STATES TAKEN IN THE YEAR 1900. 10
vols. Washington, D.C.: Government Printing Office, 1901-02.
I13.5:3&4.

"Vital Statistics" is found in volumes 3 and 4, which reports the suicides that occurred in the twelve months prior
to the 1900 census. Volume 3 contains a useful overview
article on suicide in the 1900 census. The suicide data
are analyzed by age, sex, nativity, marital status, and
rural-urban residence. There are extensive tables on suicide and occupation. Volume 4 contains suicide data for
cities and states.

Vital Statistics—United States and Canada

Since 1900 the data on suicide have been collected annually in the United
States. From 1850 to 1900 suicide data were collected just for the twelve
months preceeding the decennial census. The U.S. government collects monthly
reports on death, including suicides, for each state. These compilations of
vital statistics are published monthly (7.209) and annually as advanced final
reports, followed much later by annual final reports with more detail (7.212).
The characteristics of these reports and computer data bases are described below.

7.207 Canada. Statistics Canada. Vital Statistics Section. CAUSES OF
DEATH: PROVINCES BY SEX AND CANADA BY SEX AND AGE.
Ottawa: Information Canada, 1970-- . Annual.

This publication gives the number of Canadian suicides by
sex and the means of committing suicide for each province,
and the suicide data for Canada by age, sex, and methods
used.

7.208 U.S. Bureau of the Census. MORTALITY STATISTICS, (1900-1936).
37 vols. Washington, D.C.: Government Printing Office, 1906-38.
Maps, tables, diagrams, forms.

These annual reports were the forerunners of the current
VITAL STATISTICS OF THE UNITED STATES (7.212). The
number and rates of suicides by age, sex, race, and occupation, rural-urban residence are reported for states, cities,
and the nation. The means of committing suicide are also
given. These data were collected from the Death Registration Areas. In 1900 there were ten states, the District of
Columbia, and some large cities, comprising 40 percent of
the U.S. population, that cooperated in sending their death
statistics to the federal government. By 1933 all states cooperated in the death registration program.

7.209   U.S. National Center for Health Statistics. MONTHLY VITAL STA-
         TISTICS REPORT. Washington, D.C.: Government Printing Office,
         1952-- . Monthly. Graphs, tables. HE20.6009:vol./no.

         This publication reports the provisional number and rate of
         suicides occurring in the entire nation during the month and
         several preceeding months. There is a time lag of three to
         four months until these data are collected and disseminated.
         An advanced final report summary is published in March of
         the following year. The advanced report contains the num-
         ber and rate of suicides by age, sex, and race. A more
         detailed summary report (7.212) is issued several years later.
         This monthly report is the best source of the most current
         data on suicide in the United States.

7.210   _____. STANDARDIZED MICRO-DATA TAPE TRANSCRIPTS. Wash-
         ington, D.C.: Government Printing Office, 1978. 38 p. HE20.6202:
         T68/yr.

         Suicide data are contained in two surveys stored in this data
         base. This publication describes the information stored on
         these tapes, the cost, and other details. Information on
         suicide is supplied for the following variables in the 1966-
         68 Mortality Survey Data tape:

                   Age (35-84)   Place of death
                   Race   Family income
                   Marital status   Smoking habits
                   Number and age of children   Weight
                   Household composition   Value of estate
                   Cause of death

         Data from the 1968-75 Mortality Data tapes includes the
         following variables:

                   Date of death   Sex
                   Age   Residence
                   Race

         Future issues of this publication should be examined as ad-
         ditional data become available.

7.211   _____. VITAL AND HEALTH STATISTICS. DATA ON MORTALITY.
         Series 20. Washington, D.C.: Government Printing Office, 1965-- .
         FS2.85/2:20/no. changed to HE20:2210:20/no.

         This series of special analyses of vital statistics data and
         special surveys contains some data on suicide. One issue
         was devoted entirely to suicide: SUICIDE IN THE UNITED
         STATES, 1950-1964 (item 16.216). Another issue, MOR-
         TALITY FROM SELECTED CAUSES BY MARITAL STATUS--
         UNITED STATES, gives some data on suicide. Future issues
         in this series may contain additional information on suicide.

7.212 _____ . VITAL STATISTICS OF THE UNITED STATES, 1937-- . 3 vols. Washington, D.C.: Government Printing Office, 1939-- . Annual. Maps, tables. HE20.6210:yr./vol.

> This is the basic authoritative source for suicide statistics in the United States. It contains data on suicide by age, race, and sex for each state, county, Standard Metropolitan Statistical Area, specified urban areas, and the entire nation. The means of committing suicide are also included. There is a three- to four-year time lag in the publication of these data in this source which limits the usefulness of this publication. For more current but less detailed data, see item 7.209.

Most states publish their own vital statistics data, but a search of these documents indicated that little additional information on suicide can be obtained from the state sources.

With the advent of the electronic computer and more efficient methods of storing, handling, and searching large data files, the researcher must not overlook the information stored in these data bases. These bases contain the raw data from vital statistics and social surveys, many of which may have been gathered for other purposes but incidentally contain information on suicide. Various means of identifying appropriate data bases are described below.

7.213 Canada. Statistics Canada. STATISTICS CANADA CATALOGUE. Ottawa: 1954-- . Annual.

> This guide to the statistical publications of the Canadian government contains some information on data bases. It may eventually have data on suicide.
>
> Consult: Vital statistics

7.214 DIRECTORY OF COMPUTERIZED DATA FILES, SOFTWARE AND RELATED TECHNICAL REPORTS. Springfield, Va.: National Technical Information Service, 1974-- . Annual. Title varies. C51.11/2/yr.

> Over one thousand data files from hundreds of federal agencies and divisions are described in this volume. Agency, hardware, language, and subject indexes are included. A brief abstract of the file, the kinds of information included, and its availability and cost, and source of information are given for each computerized data base. A few data bases contain some suicide statistics.
>
> Consult: Death
> Vital statistics

7.215   Gerhan, David, and Walker, Loretta. "A Subject Approach to Social Science Data Archives." RQ (REFERENCE QUARTERLY) 15 (1975): 132-49.

> This article gives the name, address, telephone number, and person to be contacted in regard to forty ongoing governmental and private computerized data archives in the United States. It also provides information on the subject scope of the holdings, fee structure, restrictions on the data and user, available lists of holdings, output format, and hardware for these data bases. It may be beneficial to follow the development of these archives.

7.216   Sessions, Vivian S., ed. DIRECTORY OF DATA BASES IN THE SO-CIAL AND BEHAVIORAL SCIENCES. New York: Science Associates/International, 1974. xv, 300 p.

> This directory provides a description of data bases in some 550 data centers in the United States and over 130 centers in thirty-nine foreign countries. Each center has reported the following information: name, address, and telephone number of the center, the senior staff member, major subject field, file title, time frame, and geographic scope of the data, data sources and collecting agency, storage media, hardware, software, output media, data products, documentation, publications, and access. The contents are organized by the name of the center, and indexed by keywords and categories. Basically a source of nongovernmental data bases, this directory also includes some federal, state, and municipal bases as well as academic ones.

> Consult: Vital statistics

7.217   U.S. National Center for Health Statistics. STANDARDIZED MICRO-DATA TAPE TRANSCRIPTS. Washington, D.C.: Government Printing Office, 1978. 38 p. HE20.6202:T68.

> Refer to 7.210 for the description of the suicide data included in these data files.

Another ongoing source to be checked for on-line data bases which are becoming available publicly in the future is the DIRECTORY OF ON-LINE INFORMATION RESOURCES: A GUIDE TO COMMERCIALLY AVAILABLE DATA BASES (5.303). Two important new journals that should be watched are described in item 5.304.

WORLD SUICIDE STATISTICS

Refer to section 18.1.

7.3 IDENTIFYING NEW SOURCES OF SUICIDE STATISTICS

It is often of utmost importance for the researcher or investigator to locate the most up-to-date relevant statistics available. In this section sources and strategies are presented by which the researcher can systematically locate data as they become available. In earlier sections of this chapter and in chapters 2, 3, 4, 5, and 6, continuing works and series have been described. Many of these ongoing works can be identified in the chapters by noting which have been cited with the dates left "open," that is, with a dash following the date in the citation. These sources can be checked regularly, as appropriate, for new sources of data. At the same time, the investigator may keep abreast of new specific sources available to him in the libraries that he uses by checking periodically in the subject card catalog under such headings as "Suicide--U.S.--Statistics" and other subject headings, such as those listed in item 3.104 which may be similarly subdivided.

The sources described below are also good for identifying suicide statistics as they appear, either in printed form or as part of computerized data bases. Since significantly more statistical data are being stored in computer files, and only a portion of these data are tabulated and printed for general use, knowledge of the locations and types of data in this form is becoming increasingly important.

7.301   AMERICAN STATISTICS INDEX: A COMPREHENSIVE GUIDE AND INDEX TO THE STATISTICAL PUBLICATIONS OF THE UNITED STATES GOVERNMENT, 1960-- . Washington, D.C.: Congressional Information Service, 1973-- . Annual, with monthly supplements.

This excellent index to the statistical publications and statistics of the U.S. government, which is the result of searching nearly one million pages of reference materials annually, and which cites the specific tables within government publications, is a basic tool for identifying new data and data sources. It indexes and describes statistical publications having research significance from the early 1960s, and indexes and describes all statistical publications of the United States issued since 1970. The work contains a good subject index, a name index, a title index, and a category index containing extensive demographic variables. Each citation contains the name of the issuing agency, the title of the publication, the assigned Superintendent of Documents number, the source of publication, price, date of issue, an abstract, and the title and page locations of tables in the work. The ASI is somewhat difficult for the novice to use. Explanations for its use are found in the flyleaf. Microfiche files of the printed publications are available for purchase from the publisher of this index. Also, each document from the files is available from the publisher on an individual order basis. Large libraries and information centers may hold the complete ASI microfiche library and all of the publications identified in the ASI. The data file which is the basis of this index is now computerized, with a computer search service available in libraries and information centers that have these facilities. See item 5.302.

Consult: Suicide

7.302   Canada. Statistics Canada. STATISTICS CANADA CATALOGUE. Ottawa: 1954-- . Annual.

The statistical publications of the Canadian government are described in this work as they are issued. This is a basic guide to current Canadian statistics.

Consult: Suicide
            Vital statistics

7.303   DEMOGRAPHIC YEARBOOK. New York: United Nations, 1948-- . Annual.

This important compendium of population data contains the official statistics from nearly every nation and territory of the world. Information on the cause of death, including suicide, is reported from about eighty nations and territories annually, giving numbers and rates of suicides. An excellent discussion of the reliability of the data is given in the beginning of these volumes. In the 1951, 1957, 1961, 1966, 1967, and 1974 yearbooks special analyses were made of mortality, including suicide data, which gave the number of suicides by age and sex. This annual is a basic source of U.S. and worldwide statistics on suicide. There is a time lag of two to ten years until the data are published. This work is supplemented by the WORLD HEALTH STATISTICS ANNUAL (7.308).

7.304   Great Britain. Stationery Office. GOVERNMENT PUBLICATIONS. London: 1936-- . Monthly, with annual and quinquennial cumulations. Title varies.

This work is an index to the official documents published by the British government, including vital statistics publications. A very useful two-volume cumulative index covering the period 1922-72 was published in 1976 and contains subject, author, and title indexes. All of the documents for this fifty-year period are available on microfilm.

Consult: Suicide

7.305   U.S. Library of Congress. Division of Documents. MONTHLY CHECKLIST OF STATE PUBLICATIONS, 1910-- . Washington, D.C.: Government Printing Office, 1912-- . Monthly, with annual index. LC30. 9:vol./no.

By means of this source, it is possible to identify any special state government publications received by the Library of Congress which are likely to contain suicide statistics.

Consult: Suicide

7.306   U.S. National Center for Health Statistics. FACTS AT YOUR FINGER-TIPS: A GUIDE TO SOURCES OF STATISTICAL INFORMATION ON MAJOR HEALTH TOPICS. 3d ed. Washington, D.C.: Government Printing Office, 1978. HE20.6208:F11

This publication is good for citing the various numbers of series, such as the VITAL AND HEALTH STATISTICS series (7.211) and the specific parts and issues pertinent to suicide in the VITAL STATISTICS OF THE UNITED STATES (7.212) and the MONTHLY VITAL STATISTICS REPORT (7.209). Future editions should be watched for.

Consult: Suicide

7.307   U.S. Superintendent of Documents. MONTHLY CATALOG OF UNITED STATES GOVERNMENT PUBLICATIONS. Washington, D.C.: Government Printing Office, 1895-- . Monthly, with annual indexes. GP3.8:yr./no.

A monthly search of the subject index of this basic listing of the publications issued by all branches of the U.S. government enables the researcher to identify new publications which may contain suicide data. The AMERICAN STATIS-TICS INDEX (7.301) is a preferred source for finding statistics on suicide in U.S. government documents. For U.S. documents issued from 1900 to 1970, a fourteen-volume cumulative index is available for more rapid searching. See item 8.302.

Consult: Suicide
(Also, since July 1976, any of the subject headings listed in item 3.104 may be used.)

7.308   WORLD HEALTH STATISTICS ANNUAL. Geneva: World Health Organization, 1962-- . Annual.

This important compendium of health data reports the number and age-specific rates of suicide for fifty countries by sex and age groups. Availability of data bases for some countries are reported. This work supplements the DEMO-GRAPHIC YEARBOOK (7.303).

Chapter 8
SUICIDE ISSUES IN LEGAL LITERATURE

A suicidal death has various legal implications. Many questions arise: Is it in fact legal for a person to kill himself? What happens to him if he survives the attempt? When two persons make a pact to die together, what happens to them if one or both survive? What are the legal issues involved in assisting a person who wishes to commit suicide? These, and similar questions, are often addressed largely by the legislative and judicial branches of governments.

8.1 OVERVIEWS OF LEGAL ISSUES IN SUICIDE AND SUICIDE PREVENTION: SELECTED REFERENCES

The following articles have been selected to provide quick and well-balanced, as well as scholarly, reviews of the legal issues involved in regard to suicide.

8.101   Markson, D.S. "The Punishment of Suicide." VILLANOVA LAW RE-
         VIEW 14 (1969): 463-83.

> A review of laws and court cases dealing with the legality of completed suicide, attempted suicide, suicide pacts, and aiding and abetting suicidal persons. The author includes a proposal for how suicide should be dealt with in the model penal code.

8.102   Perr, Irwin N. "Liability of Hospital and Psychiatrist in Suicide."
         AMERICAN JOURNAL OF PSYCHIATRY 122 (1965): 631-38.

> A review of court cases on the responsibility of hospitals and psychiatrists in cases of suicide. The issues involved are delineated and discussed.

8.103   Schulman, R.E. "Suicide and Suicide Prevention." JOURNAL (American
         Bar Association) 54 (1968): 855-62.

> A review of legal issues concerned with suicidal behavior. In addition, attempted suicide in offenders as an admission

of guilt, the legal basis for intervening in acts of suicide,
and the right to refuse treatment are examined.

8.104   Slawson, Paul F.; Flinn, Don E.; and Schwartz, Donald A. "Legal
          Responsibility for Suicide." PSYCHIATRIC QUARTERLY 48 (Spring
          1974): 50-64.

          A review of recent court decisions on the responsibility of
          doctors and hospitals in the suicidal deaths of their patients.
          The trend is toward greater accountability.

8.105   Wright, Donald M. "Criminal Aspects of Suicide in the United States."
          NORTH CAROLINA CENTRAL LAW JOURNAL 7 (Fall 1975): 156-63.

          An excellent brief survey article on the legal treatment of
          suicide in English and American law, including attempted
          suicide and aiding a person to commit suicide.

8.2 LOCATING SUICIDE INFORMATION IN LEGAL LITERATURE

Since the legal literature is very complex, no attempt is made here to explain
in depth approaches and procedures for legal research. Only the most generally
useful sources for information on suicide from the legal perspective are described.
There are various good handbooks which provide basic nontechnical introductions
to the legal literature, among which are the following.

8.201   Cohen, Morris L. LEGAL RESEARCH IN A NUTSHELL. 3d ed. St.
          Paul, Minn.: West Publishing Co., 1978. ix, 415 p.

          A good explanation of the organization of U.S. statute law,
          case law, legislative history, and administrative law is pre-
          sented here as an aid to research in these areas. Important
          secondary sources are also discussed. Some British legal
          works are included.

8.202   Lloyd, David. FINDING THE LAW: A GUIDE TO LEGAL RESEARCH.
          Legal Almanac Series, no. 74. Dobbs Ferry, N.Y.: Oceana Publi-
          cations, 1974. v, 119 p.

          This basic introduction to searching the law explains the use
          of basic legal tools. It contains also a list of commonly
          used legal abbreviations.

8.203   Pollack, Ervin H. ERVIN H. POLLACK'S FUNDAMENTALS OF LEGAL
          RESEARCH. 4th ed. Edited by J. Myron Jacobstein and Roy M. Mersky.
          Mineola, N.Y.: Foundation Press, 1973. xxix, 565 p.

          Intended as an aid to students beginning the study of law,
          this work is somewhat more detailed than the above two sources.

It is recommended that the researcher with little or no legal training confer as closely as possible with librarians, especially law librarians, or with lawyers, when using the legal literature. A great deal of skill and practice in the literature is necessary for effective research in the area. The sources of legal information described in this chapter are those considered most useful for locating suicide information. There may be others not listed, either more limited or more specialized. These can be identified from one of the above handbooks or from the professional personnel indicated above.

8.3 LEGISLATIVE AND STATUTORY PUBLICATIONS: LAWS, STATUTES

There appears to be comparatively little treatment of suicide issues in the legislative literature, which includes bills, laws, statutes, and codes. The same is apparently true of the administrative or regulatory legal literature, which includes regulations, proclamations, and orders. Suicide issues are treated mostly in judicial publications which include court reports and digests. These are described in section 8.4. In this section, 8.3, several ongoing aids to identifying legislative publications related to suicide are described. Later sections of this chapter suggest other secondary publications by which laws can be identified.

8.301 Congressional Information Service. INDEX TO PUBLICATIONS OF THE UNITED STATES CONGRESS. Washington, D.C.: 1970-- . Monthly, with quarterly cumulative indexes, along with annual and quinquennial cumulations.

> Known as the CIS INDEX, this work indexes and also provides abstracts of committee hearings, House and Senate documents, reports, miscellaneous publications, and Senate executive reports and documents on pending bills. There is a good subject index and a personal name index, as well as an index by number of bills, reports, and documents. The annual volumes are known as the CIS/ANNUALS. Microfiche files of the printed publications are available for purchase from the publisher. Many large libraries and information centers have the complete microfiche collection of all the publications indexed. Computer searching is available for this data base from the publisher and at libraries and information centers who have arrangements to use the facilities of System Development Corporation search service (item 5.302).

> Consult: Suicide

8.302 CUMULATIVE SUBJECT INDEX TO THE MONTHLY CATALOG OF UNITED STATES GOVERNMENT PUBLICATIONS, 1900-1971. 14 vols. Compiled by William W. Buchanan and Edna M. Kanely. Washington, D.C.: Carrollton Press, 1973-75.

> The cumulative subject index provides indexing in one alpha-

bet, of over eight hundred thousand documents for the period. It cites the year and page or item number in the MONTHLY CATALOG (item 8.303) where the document description can be found. No assigned Superintendent of Documents numbers are provided.

Consult: Suicide

8.303   U.S. Superintendent of Documents. MONTHLY CATALOG OF UNITED STATES GOVERNMENT PUBLICATIONS. Washington, D.C.: Government Printing Office, 1895-- . Monthly, with monthly and annual cumulative indexes. GP 3.8:yr./no.

By using the subject index to this basic monthly listing of publications issued by all branches of the U.S. government, the researcher is able to identify congressional documents and reports, hearings, and public laws. For documents issued between 1900 and 1970, refer to item 8.302.

Consult: Suicide

Public, general, and permanent federal laws for the United States are compiled and arranged under fifty titles, subdivided into chapters, in the UNITED STATES CODE, published in Washington, D.C., by the Government Printing Office. This has annual cumulative supplements and a good subject index. To date very little on suicide has appeared in the code. The lawyers' edition of the UNITED STATES CODE SERVICE, published by Lawyers Co-operative Publishing Co., Rochester, New York, since 1972 has been providing full annotations of all federal laws of general and permanent nature, with references to court reports. This is arranged in the same manner as is the UNITED STATES CODE. Again, to date very little related to suicide is cited in this work.

8.4 JUDICIAL PUBLICATIONS: COURT REPORTS, DIGESTS

Compilations of the written court opinions and decisions in the United States, particularly resulting from courts of appeal and district courts, have some references relating to suicide. The major sources are described below.

8.401   AMERICAN LAW REPORTS. ALR FEDERAL: CASES AND ANNOTATIONS. Rochester, N.Y.: Lawyers Co-operative Publishing Co., 1969-- . Several annual volumes. Pocket supplements. FEDERAL QUICK INDEX. 2d ed., 1975. Pocketparts.

This work is a selective reporter of federal appellate court decisions which are thought to become "leading" cases. The annotations and further references are highly valued. Prior to 1969 the type of information included in this work was included in the AMERICAN LAW REPORTS: CASES AND ANNOTATIONS (8.402), but since 1969, as the federal litigation increased, the publishers decided to start this new

series. The FEDERAL QUICK INDEX (2d ed., 1975, with
pocketparts) is very useful for important references on the
judicial aspects of suicide, and should be one of the first
points of entry into this area. It leads the investigator
also to the AMERICAN LAW REPORTS. ALR 3d: CASES
AND ANNOTATIONS (8.402), the UNITED STATES CODE
SERVICE, the UNITED STATES SUPREME COURT REPORTS,
and AMERICAN JURISPRUDENCE, 2d series (8.601), as
well as to several other compilations.

Consult: Suicide (in the FEDERAL QUICK INDEX)

8.402 AMERICAN LAW REPORTS. ALR 3d: CASES AND ANNOTATIONS.
Rochester, N.Y.: Lawyers Co-operative Publishing Co., 1965-- .
Several annual volumes. Pocket supplements. QUICK INDEX, 2d ed.,
1975-- . Pocketparts.

This work is a selective reporter of appellate court decisions
which are considered significant. The annotations and further references are highly valued. The first series of this
set started in 1919. The QUICK INDEX is very useful in
much the same way as described in item 8.401. This is a
very important point of entry into the area of the judicial
aspects of suicide. There is a WORD INDEX for the second
series of this work which is also helpful.

Consult: Suicide (in the QUICK INDEX)

8.403 FEDERAL REPORTER. 2d series. St. Paul, Minn.: West Publishing
Co., 1880-- . FEDERAL SUPPLEMENT. St. Paul, Minn.: West Publishing Co., 1931-- .

These two works are part of West's National Reporter System,
which uses the American Digest System for locating court
opinions. This is a system of classifying each decision by
a key number and thus providing a DESCRIPTIVE WORD IN-
DEX arranged topically under each key number. Information
on suicide-related opinions is difficult to locate in these
sets.

8.404 GENERAL DIGEST. 5th series. COVERING STATE AND FEDERAL
COURTS. St. Paul, Minn.: West Publishing Co., 1976-- . Monthly.
2 to 4 cumulative vols. per year. Decennial indexes. DESCRIPTIVE
WORD INDEX.

As part of West's National Reporter System, this work has
good subject access. Since 1886, going back to 1650, the
West Publishing Company has been receiving and dividing
digests of all cases into seven main classes, and then into
subclasses, and then further into topics. There are now
435 topics, each corresponding to a legal concept, and

Suicide Issues in Legal Literature

each assigned a key number. Each month, all digests received are arranged and issued in the GENERAL DIGEST. These issues are cumulated several times a year, and later into cumulative decennial volumes. From 1966, each decennial cumulation, as well as all the issues, are called the GENERAL DIGEST. Since the coverage is so broad and the DESCRIPTIVE WORD INDEX, because of the key numbers, is so specific, the GENERAL DIGEST quickly provides references to suicide in various areas of the legal system.

Consult: Suicide (in the DESCRIPTIVE WORD INDEX)

8.405 MODERN FEDERAL PRACTICE DIGEST: ALL FEDERAL CASE LAW OF THE MODERN ERA. 58 vols. St. Paul, Minn.: West Publishing Co., 1960-62. Replacement volumes and pocket supplements. DESCRIPTIVE WORD INDEX.

Covering, since 1939, U.S. Supreme Court decisions and the material in the FEDERAL REPORTER and the FEDERAL SUPPLEMENT (8.403), this work is arranged under West's National Reporter System with topics and key numbers. Because of this, it provides good access to any information on suicide included. For federal case laws of historical significance, its predecessor, the FEDERAL DIGEST, is still referred to.

Consult: Suicide (in the DESCRIPTIVE WORD INDEX)

Selected court decisions are also cited in the BIBLIOGRAPHY OF BIOETHICS (5.103).

8.5 INDEXES TO LEGAL PERIODICALS

8.501 INDEX TO CANADIAN LEGAL PERIODICAL LITERATURE. Montreal: Canadian Association of Law Libraries, 1961-- . Bimonthly, with annual and decennial cumulations.

Over sixty Canadian law journals are indexed by author and subject in this publication. A table of cases and a book review index are also included. There is a time lag of about one year from the time the articles appear until they are indexed.

Consult: Suicide

8.502 INDEX TO LEGAL PERIODICAL LITERATURE, 1886-1937. Vols. 1 and 2, edited by Leonard A. Jones; vols. 3-6, edited by Frank E. Chipman. Boston: Boston Book Co., 1888-1919 (vols. 1-3); Chipman, 1924 (vol. 4); Indianapolis: Bobbs-Merrill, 1933 (vol. 5); Los Angeles: Parker and Baird, 1939 (vol. 6).

Materials indexed in this set include articles in legal periodicals, annotated cases, biographical notices, and papers
of bar associations from the United States, England, Ireland,
Scotland, and the English colonies. Up to 160 legal and
general periodicals were indexed in the various volumes.
A few sets of eighteenth-century periodicals were also included. Each volume has subject and author indexing, and
volumes 3-6 also have title indexing. This index is a good
source of information on suicide for the nineteenth century.

Consult: Suicide

8.503 INDEX TO LEGAL PERIODICALS, 1908-- . New York: H.W. Wilson
Co., in cooperation with the American Association of Law Libraries,
1908-- . Monthly (except September), with annual and triennial cumulations.

A basic author and subject index to nearly four hundred
legal and law-related periodicals published in the United
States, Canada, Great Britain, Northern Ireland, Australia,
and New Zealand, this work is a good source for legal
periodical articles on suicide. Book reviews, case notes,
yearbooks, annual institutes, and annual reviews are indexed in this work in addition to articles. A table of cases
is also included. Approximately four times as many legal
periodicals are indexed by this index than are indexed in
the SOCIAL SCIENCES CITATION INDEX (5.134). There
is a six- to eight-month time lag from the time the articles
appear until they are indexed. Approximately three articles
appear per year on suicide.

Consult: Suicide

8.504 INDEX TO U.S. GOVERNMENT PERIODICALS, 1970-- . Chicago:
Infordata International, 1975-- . Quarterly, with annual cumulative
indexing.

An index to over 140 U.S. government periodicals, many
of which are not indexed elsewhere, this publication is a
subject index based on a thesaurus of terms. This work is
also easy to use. Microfiche copies to the text of all periodical articles indexed are available as listed in CURRENT
U.S. GOVERNMENT PERIODICALS ON MICROFICHE (Sanford, N.C.: Microfilming Corporation of America).

Consult: Suicide

8.6 LEGAL ENCYCLOPEDIAS AND HANDBOOKS

Legal encyclopedias and handbooks are used as aids to legal research. They lack legal authority and cannot be cited as such, but they are helpful for the generalist looking for a broad summary treatment on a topic of interest. In this respect, they should be one of the first types of publications to be consulted when approaching a search in the legal literature. The main legal encyclopedias and handbooks for American, English, and Canadian law are described below.

8.601 AMERICAN JURISPRUDENCE: A MODERN COMPREHENSIVE TEXT STATEMENT OF AMERICAN LAW, STATE AND FEDERAL. 82 vols. 2d ed. Rochester, N.Y.: Lawyers Co-operative, 1962-76. Updated by replacement vols. and pocket supplements. Vol. and general indexes.

Arranged alphabetically by broad legal topics, this work is essentially on judicial law, although in this second edition more emphasis is on federal statutory and regulatory law and state statutory laws broadly viewed. It often refers the user to more detail in the AMERICAN LAW REPORTS (8.401 and 8.402), as well as to other sources.

Consult: Insurance--Suicide
Homicide--Suicide

8.602 CORPUS JURIS SECUNDUM: A COMPLETE RESTATEMENT OF THE ENTIRE AMERICAN LAW AS DEVELOPED BY ALL REPORTED CASES . . . 101 vols. in 136. St. Paul, Minn.: West Publishing Co., 1936-74. Updated by replacement vols. and annual cumulative pocket supplements. 5 vol. general index.

Essentially providing information on and citations to federal and state case law, this work also includes some information on federal and state statutory law. It also cites treatises and legal periodical articles. Through its cross-references, it connects with West's American Digest System for more specific information. This work continues the CORPUS JURIS, 1914-37, still often referred to. Both of these works are good sources for legal information on suicide.

Consult: Suicide (in the general index)

8.603 CURRENT LAW YEAR BOOK. London: Sweet and Maxwell, 1947-- . Monthly. Bound annually.

The preface of this work states: "This comprehensive research service includes a case digest and citator, statutory digest and citator, and a limited index to British legal periodicals and books. It is the most effective citator for English law." Separate editions are also published for Canada and Scotland.

Consult: Suicide

8.604   HALSBURY'S LAWS OF ENGLAND. 4th ed. London: Butterworth, 1973-- . Annual cumulative supplements and looseleaf service. Annual indexes.

A general legal encyclopedia with references to case laws, statutes, and administrative law, this is a good source for English suicide information. Each annual supplement is well indexed. For Canada, its CANADIAN CONVERTER, 1954-1973, provides information on Canadian federal and provincial statutes, excluding the province of Quebec.

Consult: Criminal law (in volume 11 which was written in 1976.)

Chapter 9
SUICIDE AND LITERATURE

Literature provides a rich source of information for the student of suicide. Two kinds of information may be derived. First, a number of authors have killed themselves and their works may be read in order to search for clues about suicidal persons. Second, literary works often contain characters who kill themselves and these works may be read in order to see whether the lives and deaths of the characters give clues about the motives of suicidal people.

9.1 AUTHORS WHO COMPLETED SUICIDE: A PRELIMINARY CHECKLIST

The following list of authors who killed themselves was compiled by Dr. Melvin D. Faber and is printed here with his permission.

Thomas Lovell Beddoes (1803-49)
Ambrose Bierce (1842-1914?) (he disappeared)
Thomas Chatterton (1752-70)
Hart Crane (1899-1932)
Osamu Dazai (1909-48)
Ramon Fernandez (1894-1944)
John Gould Fletcher (1886-1950)
Nikolai Gogol (1809-52) (probably a suicide)
Ernest Hemingway (1898-1961)
Randall Jarrell (1914-65)
Weldon Kees (1914-55)
Heinrich von Kleist (1777-1811)
Vachel Lindsay (1879-1931)
Ross F. Lockridge Jr. (1914-49)
Jack London (1876-1916)
Lucan (39-65 A.D.)
Francis O. Matthieson (1902-50)
Vladimir Mayakovski (1893-1930)
Grace Metalious (1924-64)
Yukio Mishima (1925-70)
Gerard de Nerval (1808-55)
Cesare Parvese (1908-50)
Sylvia Plath (1932-63)

Suicide and Literature

Grant Redford (1908-65)
Sappho (ca. 600 B.C.)
Seneca (4 B.C.-65 A.D.)
Sara Teasdale (1884-1933)
Ernst Toller (1893-1939)
George Trakl (1887-1914)
Kurt Tucholsky (1890-1935)
Virginia Woolf (1882-1941)
Stephan Zweig (1881-1942)

Few, if any, psychological studies of these authors have appeared, although many journal articles and books have been written by laymen on these authors. Consult with professional librarians to develop an initial strategy for effective searching for biographical and psychological materials on any of the above authors. See items 12.103 and 12.105.

9.2 SUICIDES IN LITERATURE: REFERENCES AND A PRELIMINARY CHECKLIST

For a general treatment of suicide in literature, refer to the work of Alvarez (1.101). Specific treatments of suicide in literature include analyses of the suicides in order to explore the motivations of people who kill themselves. Some examples of these analyses include the following.

9.201 Faber, Melvin D. "The Adolescent Suicides of Romeo and Juliet." PSYCHOANALYTIC REVEIW 59 (Summer 1972): 169-81.

An analysis of the motives behind the suicides of Romeo and Juliet in Shakespeare's play of the same name.

9.202 _____. SUICIDE AND GREEK TRAGEDY. New York: Sphinx Press, 1970. 280 p.

An analysis of the suicides in the plays of Sophocles and Euyripides, with a particularly useful discussion of altruistic suicides.

9.203 Lester, David. "Suicide in Ibsen's Plays." LIFE-THREATENING BE-HAVIOR 2 (Spring 1972): 35-41.

The motives behind the suicides in the plays of Henrik Ibsen are analyzed in order to see whether they are consistent with Herbert Hendin's assertions about the motives behind Scandinavian suicide. See item 18.208.

See also section 6.217, for further analyses of suicide and literature.

The following list of literary works that deal with suicidal characters was compiled by Dr. Melvin D. Faber and is printed here with his permission.

114

9.204   SUICIDES IN LITERATURE: A PRELIMINARY CHECKLIST--Melvin D. Faber

This checklist serves as an aid to the individual who investigates suicide in literature. No claims of comprehensiveness are made in regard to the checklist. As the heading indicates, only a preliminary checklist is offered, to which additions can be made in the future. The list includes the author and title of the work, the work's genre, and the work's date. The works listed are classified into three categories: (1) items that are not starred contain only intentional suicidal behaviors which result in death; (2) items that are starred once (*) contain suicidal behaviors some of which do and some of which do not result in death. The suicidal behaviors which do not result in death are in some instances intentioned and in some instances subintentional. The suicidal behaviors which do result in death are, in this category, subintentioned; and (3) items that are starred twice (**) contain meditation on suicide, and/or discussion of suicide, and/or threat of suicide, and/or preoccupation with suicide. There are no suicidal or self-destructive behaviors, per se, in this category.

Evaluative judgments on the role of suicide, or on the importance of suicide, in any and in all works cited have been rigorously avoided. What one investigator may be looking for may not be what another investigator is looking for. Likewise, what is of significance for one investigator may not be of significance for another.

AUTHOR	TITLE	GENRE	DATE
*Aeschylus	THE SEVEN AGAINST THEBES	Drama	5th Cent. B.C.
**Aiken, Conrad	COLLECTED POEMS	Poem	1953
Ainsworth, William H.	JACK SHEPPARD	Fiction	1839
*Albee, Edward	WHO'S AFRAID OF VIRGINIA WOOLF?	Drama	1963
Albee, Edward	ZOO STORY	Drama	1959
Aldington, Richard	DEATH OF A HERO	Fiction	1929
Aleman, Mateo	GUZMAN DE ALFARACHE	Fiction	1604
*Amicis, Edmondo de	THE ROMANCE OF A SCHOOLMASTER	Fiction	1876
*Amis, Kingsley	THAT UNCERTAIN FEELING	Fiction	1955
Anderson, Maxwell	WINTERSET	Drama	1935
**Anderson, Sherwood	DARK LAUGHTER	Fiction	1925
*Andric, Ivo	THE BRIDGE ON THE DRINA	Fiction	1945
Annunzio, Gabriele d'	THE TRIUMPH OF DEATH	Fiction	1894
*Anonymous	THE BATTLE OF MALDON	Poem	1100
Anonymous	BEVIS OF HAMPTON	Poem	1200

AUTHOR	TITLE	GENRE	DATE
**Anonymous	KING HORN	Poem	1226
*Anonymous	MANKIND	Drama	1475
Anonymous	APPIUS AND VIRGINIA	Drama	1575
Arnold, Matthew	EMPEDOCLES ON ETNA	Poem	1852
Artsybashev, Mikhail	SANINE	Fiction	1907
*Asturias, Miguel	EL SENOR PRESIDENTE	Fiction	1946
Auden, W(ytan) H. and Isherwood, Christopher	THE ASCENT OF F6	Drama	1936
Azuela, Mariano	THE UNDER DOGS	Fiction	1915
Baldwin, James	GO TELL IT ON THE MOUNTAIN	Fiction	1953
Baldwin, James	ANOTHER COUNTRY	Fiction	1964
*Balzac, Honore de	THE WILD ASS'S SKIN	Fiction	1830
Balzac, Honore de	EUGENIE GRANDET	Fiction	1833
**Balzac, Honore de	LOST ILLUSIONS	Fiction	1837
Balzac, Honore de	COUSIN BETTE	Fiction	1847
**Barbier, Auguste	SPLEEN	Poem	1830
Barclay, John	ARGENIS	Fiction	1621
*Barrie, James M.	THE LITTLE MINISTER	Fiction	1891
*Barrios, Eduardo	BROTHER ASS	Fiction	1922
**Barth, John	THE FLOATING OPERA	Fiction	1960
Bax, Clifford	THE VENETIAN	Drama	1931
Beaumont, Francis and Fletcher, John	THE MAID'S TRAGEDY	Drama	1610
*Beckett, Samuel	ENDGAME	Drama	1958
**Beckett, Samuel	WAITING FOR GODOT	Drama	1952
**Beddoes, Thomas L.	THE BRIDES' TRAGEDY	Drama	1822
*Beddoes, Thomas L.	DEATH'S JEST BOOK	Drama	1850
Beerbohm, Max	ZULEIKA DOBSON	Fiction	1911
Behn, Aphra	OROONOKO	Fiction	1688
*Bellow, Saul	THE VICTIM	Fiction	1947
Bennett, Arnold	ANNA OF THE FIVE TOWNS	Fiction	1902
**Bernanos, Georges	THE DIARY OF A COUNTRY PRIEST	Fiction	1937
Bernard, William Bayle	A LIFE'S TRIAL	Drama	1857

AUTHOR	TITLE	GENRE	DATE
*Beyle, Marie Henri (Stendhal)	THE RED AND THE BLACK	Fiction	1830
Bjornson, Bjornstjerne	BEYOND HUMAN POWER, II	Drama	1895
**Blok, Aleksandr	DANSES MACABRES	Poem	1911
Boccaccio, Giovanni	THE DECAMERON (TANCRED AND THE GOLDEN CUP)	Fiction	1313
*Boccaccio, Giovanni	IL FILOSTRATO	Poem	1335
*Boccaccio, Giovanni	L'AMOROSA FIAMETTA	Fiction	1340
Bourget, Paul	LE DISCIPLE	Fiction	1889
Bowen, Elizabeth	THE HOUSE IN PARIS	Fiction	1936
*Bowen, Elizabeth	THE HEAT OF THE DAY	Fiction	1949
*Braine, John	ROOM AT THE TOP	Fiction	1957
Brecht, Bertolt	BAAL	Drama	1918
Brecht, Bertolt	THE PRIVATE LIFE OF THE MASTER RACE	Drama	1938
*Bronte, Anne	THE TENANT OF WILDFELL HALL	Fiction	1848
**Bronte, Emily	POEMS	Poem	1846
Bronte, Emily	WUTHERING HEIGHTS	Fiction	1847
Broke, Arthur	ROMEUS AND JULIET	Poem	1562
Brown, Charles Brockden	WIELAND	Fiction	1798
Brown, George Douglas (Douglas, George	THE HOUSE WITH THE GREEN SHUTTERS	Fiction	1901
Browning, Robert	A BLOT IN THE 'SCUTCHEON	Drama	1843
*Buchner, Georg	WOZZECK	Drama	1879
*Bunin, Ivan	THE VILLAGE	Fiction	1910
**Burney, Fanny	CECILIA	Fiction	1782
*Byron, George Gordon	MANFRED	Poem	1817
Cable, George W.	THE GRANDISSIMES	Fiction	1880
*Camus, Albert	THE STRANGER	Fiction	1942
*Camus, Albert	THE PLAGUE	Fiction	1947
Camus, Albert	THE FALL	Fiction	1956
*Cary, Joyce	TO BE A PILGRIM	Fiction	1942

AUTHOR	TITLE	GENRE	DATE
Cather, Willa	MY ANTONIA	Fiction	1918
*Cather, Willa	THE PROFESSOR'S HOUSE	Fiction	1925
Chapman, George	BUSSY D'AMBOIS	Drama	1604
Chapman, George	THE REVENGE OF BUSSY D'AMBOIS	Drama	1610
Chapman, George	CEASAR AND POMPEY	Drama	1631
Chatterton, Thomas	ELLA	Poem	1777
Chaucer, Geoffrey	THE LEGEND OF GOOD WOMEN	Poem	1380
Chateaubriand, Francois de	ATALA	Fiction	1801
Cheever, John	THE WAPSHOT CHRONICLE	Fiction	1957
Cheever, John	THE WAPSHOT SCANDAL	Fiction	1963
Chekhov, Anton	THE SEAGULL	Drama	1896
Chesterton, G(ilbert) K.	THE NAPOLEON OF NOTTING HILL	Fiction	1904
Chikamatsu, Monzaemon	SONEZAKI SHINJU	Drama	1703
Clark, Walter Van Tilburg	THE OX-BOW INCIDENT	Fiction	1940
*Clark, Walter Van Tilburg	THE TRACK OF THE CAT	Fiction	1949
Cocteau, Jean	THE HOLY TERRORS (LES ENFANTS TERRIBLES)	Fiction	1929
Compton-Burnett, Ivy	BULLIVANT AND THE LAMBS	Fiction	1947
*Conrad, Joseph	THE NIGGER OF THE NARCISSUS	Fiction	1897
*Conrad, Joseph	LORD JIM	Fiction	1900
Conrad, Joseph	NOSTROMO	Fiction	1904
Conrad, Joseph	THE SECRET AGENT	Fiction	1907
Cooper, James Fenimore	THE PRAIRIE	Fiction	1827
**Corbiere, Tristan	LES AMOURS JAUNES	Poem	1873
*Corneille, Pierre	HORACE	Drama	1640
*Corneille, Pierre	POLYEUCTE	Drama	1643
Coward, Noel	POST-MORTEM	Drama	1933
Coward, Noel	THE ASTONISHED HEART	Drama	1935
**Cozzens, John Gould	GUARD OF HONOR	Fiction	1948
Crane, Stephen	MAGGIE: A GIRL OF THE STREETS	Fiction	1893

AUTHOR	TITLE	GENRE	DATE
*Craik, Dinah (Mulock, Dinah)	JOHN HALIFAX, GENTLE-MEN	Fiction	1857
Daniel, Samuel	THE COMPLAINT OF ROSAMOND	Poem	1592
Daniel, Samuel	THE TRAGEDY OF CLEOPATRA	Drama	1594
**Dante, Alighiere	THE DIVINE COMEDY (SEVENTH CIRCLE OF HELL)	Poem	1307
**Daudet, Alphonse	KINGS IN EXILE	Fiction	1879
Davis, Andre	FOUR MEN	Drama	1958
**Defoe, Daniel	CAPTAIN SINGLETON	Fiction	1720
Defoe, Daniel	COLONEL JACK	Fiction	1720
Dekker, Edward D. (Multatuli)	MAX HAVELAAR	Fiction	1860
**Dekker, Thomas	SATIRO-MASTIX	Drama	1601
**de la Mare, Walter	THE RETURN	Fiction	1910
de la Mare, Walter	MEMOIRS OF A MIDGET	Fiction	1921
Dennis, Nigel	AUGUST FOR THE PEOPLE	Drama	1961
Dickens, Charles	NICHOLAS NICKLEBY	Fiction	1838
*Dickens, Charles	THE OLD CURIOSITY SHOP	Fiction	1840
Dickens, Charles	BARNABY RUDGE	Fiction	1841
Dickens, Charles	MARTIN CHUZZLEWIT	Fiction	1843
*Dickens, Charles	DOMBEY AND SON	Fiction	1846
Dickens, Charles	A TALE OF TWO CITIES	Fiction	1859
*Dickens, Charles	THE MYSTERY OF EDWIN HOOD	Fiction	1870
Dos Passos, John	THREE SOLDIERS	Fiction	1921
Dos Passos, John	MANHATTAN TRANSFER	Fiction	1925
Dos Passos, John	U.S.A.	Fiction	1930
**Dostoyevsky, Fyodor	NOTES FROM THE UNDER-GROUND	Fiction	1864
Dostoyevsky, Fyodor	CRIME AND PUNISHMENT	Fiction	1866
Dostoyevsky, Fyodor	THE POSSESSED	Fiction	1867
Dostoyevsky, Fyodor	THE BROTHERS KARAMAZOV	Fiction	1880
*Dreiser, Theodore	THE TITAN	Fiction	1914

AUTHOR	TITLE	GENRE	DATE
Dreiser, Theodore	THE BULWARK	Fiction	1946
Dryden, John	ALL FOR LOVE	Drama	1677
Dumas, Alexandre	THE COUNT OF MONTE CRISTO	Fiction	1844
Dumas, Alexandre	MEMOIRS OF A PHYSICIAN	Fiction	1846
*Dumas, Alexandre	THE VICOMTE DE BRAGELONNE	Fiction	1848
Du Maurier, Daphne	REBECCA	Fiction	1938
Duranty, Louis Edmond	MALHEUR d'HENRIETTE GERARD	Fiction	1860
Durrell, Lawrence	THE ALEXANDRIA QUARTET	Fiction	1957, 1961
Dunn, Olav	THE PEOPLE OF JUVIK	Fiction	1918
**Eliot, George	ADAM BEDE	Fiction	1859
*Eliot, George	THE MILL ON THE FLOSS	Fiction	1860
*Eliot, George	DANIEL DERONDA	Fiction	1876
*Esenin, Sergei	MOSCOW OF THE TAVERNS	Poem	1922
Euripides	ALCESTIS	Drama	5 B.C.
*Euripides	ANDROMACHE	Drama	5 B.C.
Euripides	HECUBA	Drama	5 B.C.
Euripides	THE HERACLEIDAE	Drama	5 B.C.
Euripides	HIPPOLYTUS	Drama	5 B.C.
*Euripides	IPHIGENIA IN AULIS	Drama	5 B.C.
Euripides	THE PHOENISSAE	Drama	5 B.C.
Euripides	THE SUPPLIANTS	Drama	5 B.C.
*Faulkner, William	SARTORIS	Fiction	1929
Faulkner, William	THE SOUND AND THE FURY	Fiction	1929
Faulkner, William	ABSALOM, ABSALOM!	Fiction	1936
Faulkner, William	INTRUDER IN THE DUST	Fiction	1948
Faulkner, William	A FABLE	Fiction	1954
Faulkner, William	THE TOWN	Fiction	1957
Feuchtwanger, Lion	POWER	Fiction	1925
Fielding, Henry	TOM THUMB THE GREAT	Drama	1730
Fitzgerald, F(rancis) Scott	THE GREAT GATSBY	Fiction	1925

AUTHOR	TITLE	GENRE	DATE
*Fitzgerald, F(rancis) Scott	TENDER IS THE NIGHT	Fiction	1934
Fitzgerald, F(rancis) Scott	THE LAST TYCOON	Fiction	1941
Flaubert, Gustave	MADAME BOVARY	Fiction	1857
Flaubert, Gustave	SALAMMBO	Fiction	1862
*Fletcher, John	THE FAITHFUL SHEPHERDESS	Drama	1609
Fletcher, John Massinger, Philip	THE TRAGEDY OF SIR JOHN VAN OLDEN BARNAVELT	Drama	1619
**Ford, Ford Madox	PARADE'S END	Fiction	1924
*Forster, E(dward) M.	THE LONGEST JOURNEY	Fiction	1907
*Forster, E(dward) M.	PASSAGE TO INDIA	Fiction	1924
*Frederic, Harold	THE DAMNATION OF THERON WARE	Fiction	1896
*Freytag, Gustav	DEBIT AND CREDIT	Fiction	1855
*Fromentin, Eugene	DOMINIQUE	Fiction	1862
*Fry, Christopher	THE LADY'S NOT FOR BURNING	Drama	1948
*Gaboriau, Emile	MONSIEUR LECOQ	Fiction	1869
*Galsworthy, John	THE MAN OF PROPERTY	Fiction	1906
Galsworthy, John	JUSTICE	Drama	1910
Galsworthy, John	THE PIGEON	Drama	1912
Galsworthy, John	THE FUGITIVE	Drama	1913
Galsworthy, John	THE SKIN-GAME	Drama	1915
Galsworthy, John	THE LOYALTIES	Drama	1922
*Galsworthy, John	A MODERN COMEDY	Fiction	1924
Galsworthy, John	THE SHOW	Drama	1925
Galsworthy, John	THE FIRST AND THE LAST	Drama	1927
Garnier, Robert	ANTONIUS	Drama	1592
*Gautier, Theophile	DEATH IN LIFE	Poem	1838
Gibson, Wilfried	ON THE THRESHOLD	Drama	1907
*Gide, Andre	THE COUNTERFEITERS	Fiction	1925
**Giraudoux, Jean	AMPHITRYON 38	Drama	1929
*Giraudoux, Jean	THE MADWOMAN OF CHAILLOT	Drama	1945
**Gissing, George	THE PRIVATE PAPERS OF HENRY RYECROFT	Fiction	1903

Suicide and Literature

AUTHOR	TITLE	GENRE	DATE
Goethe, Johann Wolfgang von	THE SORROWS OF YOUNG WERTHER	Fiction	1774
Goethe, Johann Wolfgang von	EGMONT	Drama	1788
*Goethe, Johann Wolfgang von	WILHELM MEISTER'S APPRENTICESHIP	Fiction	1795
Goethe, Johann Wolfgang von	ELECTIVE AFFINITIES	Fiction	1808
*Gogol, Nikolai	THE OVERCOAT	Fiction	1842
Golding, William	THE INHERITORS	Fiction	1955
*Goncharov, Ivan	OBLOMOV	Fiction	1858
Goncourt, Jules de and Edmond de	SISTER PHILOMENE	Fiction	1861
*Goncourt, Jules de and Edmond de	RENEE MAUPERIN	Fiction	1864
*Goncourt, Jules de and Edmond de	GERMINIE LACERTEUX	Fiction	1865
Gorky, Maxim	THE LOWER DEPTHS	Fiction	1902
*Gorky, Maxim	THE ARTAMONOV BUSINESS	Fiction	1925
Gourmont, Remy de	A NIGHT IN THE LUXEMBOURG	Fiction	1906
Granville-Barker, Harley	WASTE	Drama	1907
Grass, Gunter	THE TIN DRUM	Fiction	1959
Graves, Robert	I, CLAUDIUS	Fiction	1934
Green, Julien	DARK JOURNEY	Fiction	1929
*Greene, Graham	THE POWER AND THE GLORY	Fiction	1940
Greene, Graham	THE MINISTRY OF FEAR	Fiction	1943
Greene, Graham	THE HEART OF THE MATTER	Fiction	1948
Greene, Graham	A BURNT-OUT CASE	Fiction	1961
Greene, Graham	BRIGHTON ROCK	Fiction	1938
Greene, Graham	THE COMEDIANS	Fiction	1966
Greene, Graham	THE CONFIDENTIAL AGENT	Fiction	1939
Grillparzer, Franz	SAPPHO	Drama	1818
**Gunnarsson, Gunnar	GUEST THE ONE-EYED	Fiction	1920

AUTHOR	TITLE	GENRE	DATE
Hardy, Thomas	THE RETURN OF THE NATIVE	Fiction	1878
*Hardy, Thomas	THE MAYOR OF CASTER- BRIDGE	Fiction	1886
Hardy, Thomas	THE WOODLANDERS	Fiction	1887
*Hardy, Thomas	TESS OF THE D'URBERVILLES	Fiction	1891
Hardy, Thomas	JUDE THE OBSCURE	Fiction	1894
*Hartmann von Aue	DER ARME HEINRICH	Poetry	1192
*Hauptmann, Gerhart	THE SUNKEN BELL	Drama	1897
Hawkes, John	THE CANNIBAL	Fiction	1949
Hawthorne, Nathaniel	ETHAN BRAND	Fiction	1851
*Hawthorne, Nathaniel	THE SCARLET LETTER	Fiction	1850
Hawthorne, Nathaniel	THE BLITHEDALE ROMANCE	Fiction	1852
Hearn, Lafcadio	YOUMA	Fiction	1890
Hebbel, Friedrich	MARIA MAGDALENA	Drama	1844
Heller, Joseph	CATCH-22	Fiction	1961
**Hemingway, Ernest	A CLEAN WELL-LIGHTED PLACE	Fiction	1924
*Hemingway, Ernest	THE SUN ALSO RISES	Fiction	1926
Hergesheimer, Joseph	JAVA HEAD	Fiction	1919
Herlihy, James L.	ALL FALL DOWN	Fiction	1960
**Hesse, Hermann	STEPPENWOLF	Fiction	1927
Holderlin (Johann) Frederich	THE DEATH OF EMPEDOCLES	Poem	1800
Howe, Edgar W.	THE STORY OF A COUNTRY TOWN	Fiction	1883
Hughes, Langston	MULATTO	Drama	1935
Hugo, Victor	LES MISERABLES	Fiction	1862
Hugo, Victor	THE TOILERS OF THE SEA	Fiction	1866
Hutchinson, A(rthur) S.M.	IF WINTER COMES	Fiction	1920
**Huxley, Aldous	CHROME YELLOW	Fiction	1922
Huxley, Aldous	POINT COUNTER POINT	Fiction	1928
Huxley, Aldous	BRAVE NEW WORLD	Fiction	1932
*Huysmans, Joris Karl	AGAINST THE GRAIN	Fiction	1884
**Ibsen, Henrik	GHOSTS	Drama	1881
Ibsen, Henrik	THE WILD DUCK	Drama	1884

AUTHOR	TITLE	GENRE	DATE
Ibsen, Henrik	ROSMERSHOLM	Drama	1887
**Ibsen, Henrik	THE LADY FROM THE SEA	Drama	1889
Ibsen, Henrik	HEDDA GABLER	Drama	1890
*Ibsen, Henrik	THE MASTER BUILDER	Drama	1892
**Ibsen, Henrik	WHEN WE DEAD AWAKEN	Drama	1899
*Icaza, Jorge	HUASIPUNGO	Fiction	1934
Ihara, Saikaku	FIVE WOMEN WHO LOVED LOVE	Fiction	1685
*Jackson, Charles	THE LOST WEEKEND	Fiction	1944
*James, Henry	THE TURN OF THE SCREW	Fiction	1898
James, Henry	THE PRINCESS CASAMASSIMA	Fiction	1886
**Jarrell, Randall	THE STATE	Poetry	1945
*Jeffers, Robinson	TAMAR	Poem	1924
Jeffers, Robinson	CAWDOR	Poem	1928
Jellicoe, Ann	THE SPORT OF MY MAD MOTHER	Drama	1958
Jensen, Johannes V.	THE LONG JOURNEY	Fiction	1923
*Johnson, Uwe	SPECULATIONS ABOUT JACOB	Fiction	1963
Jokai, Maurus (Mor)	A MODERN MIDAS	Fiction	1872
*Jones, Henry Arthur	THE DANCING GIRL	Drama	1907
Jonson, Ben	SEJANUS	Drama	1603
*Jonson, Ben	VOLPONE	Drama	1605
**Jonson, Ben	THE SILENT WOMAN	Drama	1609
Joyce, James	ULYSSES***	Fiction	1922
*Kazantzakes, Nikos	THE GREEK PASSION	Fiction	1953
Kazantzakes, Nikos	FREEDOM OR DEATH	Fiction	1956
Kennedy, Adrienne	FUNNYHOUSE OF A NEGRO	Drama	1964
Kesey, Ken	ONE FLEW OVER THE CUCKOO'S NEST	Fiction	1962
Kyd, Thomas	THE SPANISH TRAGEDY	Drama	1586
*Lawrence, D(avid) H.	SONS AND LOVERS	Fiction	1913
*Lawrence, D(avid) H.	THE RAINBOW	Fiction	1915

***Bloom's father was a suicide

AUTHOR	TITLE	GENRE	DATE
Lawrence, D(avid) H.	WOMEN IN LOVE	Fiction	1920
*Lawrence, D(avid) H.	THE PLUMED SERPENT	Fiction	1926
Le Fanu, Joseph S.	UNCLE SILAS	Fiction	1864
*Lermontov, Mikhail	A HERO OF OUR TIME	Fiction	1839
Le Sage, Alain-Rene	LE DIABLE BOITEUX	Fiction	1707
*Lewis, Sinclair	CASS TIMBERLANE	Fiction	1945
Lewis, Wyndham	TARR	Fiction	1918
Li, Hsing-Tao	THE CIRCLE OF CHALK	Drama	1300
*Lie, Jonas	THE FAMILY AT GILJE	Fiction	1883
Llewellyn, Richard	HOW GREEN WAS MY VALLEY	Fiction	1940
*Lockridge, Ross F.	RAINTREE COUNTY	Fiction	1948
*Lowry, Malcom	UNDER THE VOLCANO	Fiction	1947
Machen, Arthur	THE HILL OF DREAMS	Fiction	1907
McCoy, Horace	THEY SHOOT HORSES, DON'T THEY?	Fiction	1935
McCullers, Carson	THE HEART IS A LONELY HUNTER	Fiction	1940
*Mackenzie, Henry	THE MAN OF FEELING	Fiction	1771
MacKintosh, Elizabeth (Daviot, Gordon)	RECKONING	Drama	1954
*Maeterlinck, Maurice	PELLEAS AND MELISANDE	Drama	1893
Malraux, Andre	MAN'S FATE	Fiction	1933
*Mann, Thomas	DEATH IN VENICE	Fiction	1912
Mann, Thomas	THE MAGIC MOUNTAIN	Fiction	1924
Mann, Thomas	DOCTOR FAUSTUS	Fiction	1947
*Mann, Thomas	THE BLACK SWAN	Fiction	1953
Mann, Thomas	CONFESSIONS OF FELIX KRULL	Fiction	1954
*Marie de France	THE LAIS OF MARIE DE FRANCE (THE TWO LOVERS)	Poem	1175
Masters, Edgar L.	SPOON RIVER ANTHOLOGY	Poetry	1915
*Maturin, Charles	MELMOTH THE WANDERER	Fiction	1820
Maugham, W(illiam) Somerset	THE MOON AND SIXPENCE	Fiction	1919

AUTHOR	TITLE	GENRE	DATE
Maugham, W(illiam) Somerset	EAST OF SUEZ	Drama	1931
*Maupassant, Guy de	A WOMAN'S LIFE	Fiction	1883
*Mayakovsky, Vladimir	TO SERGEI ETENIN	Poetry	1926
Melville, Herman	REDBURN	Fiction	1849
*Melville, Herman	MOBY DICK	Fiction	1851
Melville, Herman	PIERRE	Fiction	1852
Mercer, David	THE BIRTH OF A PRIVATE	Drama	1964
Middleton, Thomas	WOMEN BEWARE WOMEN	Drama	1621
Middleton, Thomas & Rowley, William	THE CHANGELING	Drama	1622
*Middleton, Thomas & Rowley, William	THE SPANISH GIPSY	Drama	1623
Miller, Arthur	DEATH OF A SALESMAN	Drama	1949
Miller, Henry	TROPIC OF CAPRICORN	Fiction	1939
**Milton, John	PARADISE LOST (Esp. Book X)	Poem	1667
Molnar, Ferenc	LILIOM	Drama	1909
*Monkhouse, Allan	PAUL FELICE	Drama	1930
Munro, H(ector) H. (Saki)	KARL LUDWIG'S WINDOW	Drama	1933
Murdoch, Iris	THE BELL	Fiction	1958
Musset, Alfred de	ROLLA	Poem	1833
**Nabokov, Vladimir	PALE FIRE	Fiction	1962
*Narayan, R.K.	THE GUIDE	Fiction	1958
Nash, Thomas	THE UNFORTUNATE TRAVELER	Fiction	1594
Norris, Frank	THE PIT	Fiction	1903
*O'Connor, Flannery	WISE BLOOD	Fiction	1952
O'Hara, John	APPOINTMENT IN SAMARRA	Fiction	1934
O'Neill, Eugene	THE HAIRY APE	Drama	1925
*O'Neill, Eugene	THE EMPEROR JONES	Drama	1920
*O'Neill, Eugene	DESIRE UNDER THE ELMS	Drama	1924
O'Neill, Eugene	MOURNING BECOMES ELECTRA	Drama	1931
Osborne, John	A PATRIOT FOR ME	Drama	1965
Otway, Thomas	THE ORPHAN	Drama	1680
Otway, Thomas	VENICE PRESERVED	Drama	1682

AUTHOR	TITLE	GENRE	DATE
Pasternak, Boris	DOCTOR ZHIVAGO	Fiction	1958
*Pater, Walter	MARIUS THE EPICUREAN	Fiction	1885
*Perada, Jose Maria de	SOTILEZA	Fiction	1884
Pilnyak, Boris	THE NAKED YEAR	Fiction	1922
Pincherle, Alberto (Moravia, Alberto)	THE WOMAN OF ROME	Fiction	1947
Pinero, Arthur W.	THE SECOND MRS. TANQUERAY	Drama	1893
Pinero, Arthur W.	MID-CHANNEL	Drama	1909
**Pirandello, Luigi	THE LATE MATTIA PASCAL	Fiction	1904
Pirandello, Luigi	THE OLD AND THE YOUNG	Fiction	1913
Pirandello, Luigi	SIX CHARACTERS IN SEARCH OF AN AUTHOR	Drama	1921
*Poe, Edgar Allan	LIGEIA	Fiction	1838
*Poe, Edgar Allan	THE FALL OF THE HOUSE OF USHER	Fiction	1839
Porter, Katherine Anne	NOON WINE	Fiction	1939
**Porter, Katherine Anne	OLD MORTALITY	Fiction	1939
*Porter, Katherine Anne	SHIP OF FOOLS	Fiction	1962
Powell, Anthony	CASSANOVA'S CHINESE RESTAURANT	Fiction	1960
Powys, Llewelyn	EBONY AND IVORY	Fiction	1923
Powys, T(heodore) F.	MR. WESTON'S GOOD WINE	Fiction	1927
Priestley, J(ohn) B.	CORNELIUS	Drama	1935
Priestley, J(ohn) B.	DESERT HIGHWAY	Drama	1944
Priestley, J(ohn) B.	PEOPLE AT SEA	Drama	1937
Prokosch, Frederic	THE SEVEN WHO FLED	Fiction	1937
*Purdy, James	MALCOLM	Fiction	1959
Pushkin, Alexander	BORIS GODUNOV	Drama	1831
Pushkin, Alexander	THE BRONZE HORSEMAN	Poem	1841
Racine, Jean Baptiste	ANDROMACHE	Drama	1667
**Racine, Jean Baptiste	BERENICE	Drama	1670
Racine, Jean Baptiste	MITHRIDATE	Drama	1673
Radcliffe, Ann	THE ITALIAN	Fiction	1797

AUTHOR	TITLE	GENRE	DATE
*Rattigan, Terence	THE DEEP BLUE SEA	Drama	1952
Rego, Jose Lins do	DEAD FIRES	Fiction	1943
*Rego, Jose Lins do	PLANTATION BOY	Fiction	1932
Reid, Forrest	THE BRACKNELS	Fiction	1911
Reid, Forrest	PETER WARING	Fiction	1936
*Reymont, Wladyslaw	THE PEASANTS	Fiction	1902
*Richardson, Henry H.	THE FORTUNES OF RICHARD MAHONY	Fiction	1917
*Richardson, Samuel	CLARISSA HARLOWE	Fiction	1747
**Richepin, Jean	LE JOYEUX PENDU	Poetry	1876
Richter, Conrad	THE TOWN	Fiction	1950
Roberts, Elizabeth Madox	THE TIME OF MAN	Fiction	1926
Rojas, Fernando de	CELENTINE	Fiction	1502
Rolland, Romain	JEAN-CHRISTOPHE	Fiction	1904-12
*Rolvaag, O(le) E.	GIANTS IN THE EARTH	Fiction	1924
**Rolvaag, O(le) E.	PEDER VICTORIOUS	Fiction	1929
Rostand, Edmond	L'AIGLON	Drama	1900
*Roth, Henry	CALL IT SLEEP	Fiction	1934
**Rousseau, Jean Jacques	THE NEW HELOISE	Fiction	1760
Rydberg, Viktor	THE LAST ATHENIAN	Fiction	1859
**Sainte-Beuve, Charles	VOLUPTE	Fiction	1832
Salinger, J(erome) D.	FRANNY AND ZOOEY	Fiction	1961
Sand, George	INDIANA	Fiction	1832
Santayana, George	THE LAST PURITAN	Fiction	1936
Santo, Kyoden	INAZUMA-BYOSHI	Fiction	1806
*Sassoon, Siegfried	MEMOIRS OF AN INFANTRY OFFICER	Fiction	1930
*Schreiner, Olive	THE STORY OF AN AFRICAN FARM	Fiction	1883
Scott, Sir Walter	GUY MANNERING	Fiction	1815
Scott, Sir Walter	KENILWORTH	Fiction	1821
*Scott, Sir Walter	THE TALISMAN	Fiction	1825
Scudery, Madeleine de	ARTAMENES	Fiction	1646
**Seneca, Lucius	MAD HERCULES	Drama	1st Cent.

AUTHOR	TITLE	GENRE	DATE
*Seneca, Lucius	THE TROJAN WOMEN	Drama	1st Cent.
Seneca, Lucius	HERCULES ON OEATA	Drama	1st Cent.
Seneca, Lucius	OEDIPUS	Drama	1st Cent.
Seneca, Lucius	PHAEDRA	Drama	1st Cent.
Shakespeare, William	A MIDSUMMER NIGHT'S DREAM	Drama	1594
Shakespeare, William	THE RAPE OF LUCRECE	Poetry	1594
Shakespeare, William	ROMEO AND JULIET	Drama	1594
Shakespeare, William	JULIUS CAESAR	Drama	1599
Shakespeare, William	HAMLET	Drama	1601
Shakespeare, William	OTHELLO	Drama	1604
Shakespeare, William	KING LEAR	Drama	1606
Shakespeare, William	MACBETH	Drama	1608
Shakespeare, William	ANTONY AND CLEOPATRA	Drama	1611
*Shaw, George Bernard	ST. JOAN	Drama	1923
Shih, Nai-an	ALL MEN ARE BROTHERS	Fiction	1300
**Shirley, James	THE TRAITOR	Drama	1631
Shirley, James	HYDE PARK	Drama	1632
Sholokhov, Mikhail	THE DON FLOWS HOME TO THE SEA	Fiction	1933
*Sidney, Sir Philip	ARCADIA	Fiction	1590
*Sienkiewicz, Henryk	WITH FIRE AND SWORD	Fiction	1883
Sienkiewicz, Henryk	QUO VADIS	Fiction	1895
*Skelton, John	MAGNIFICENCE	Drama	1504
*Smith, Betty	A TREE GROWS IN BROOKLYN	Fiction	1943
**Snow, C(harles) P.	THE AFFAIR	Fiction	1960
Sophocles	AJAX	Drama	5th Cent.
Sophocles	ANTIGONE	Drama	5th Cent.
Sophocles	THE TRACHINIAE	Drama	5th Cent.
Sophocles	OEDIPUS REX	Drama	5th Cent.
*Spark, Muriel	THE BACHELORS	Fiction	1961
Spenser, Edmund	THE FAERIE QUEENE (Esp. Books I and II)	Poem	1590

Suicide and Literature

AUTHOR	TITLE	GENRE	DATE
Stael-Holstein, Anna Louise Germaine (Necker) de (Madame de Stael)	DELPHINE	Fiction	1802
**Steinbeck, John	EAST OF EDEN	Fiction	1952
*Stephens, James	DEIRDRE	Fiction	1923
Stevenson, Robert Louis	DR. JEKYLL AND MR. HYDE	Fiction	1886
Strindberg, August	THE RED ROOM	Fiction	1879
**Strindberg, August	THE FATHER	Drama	1887
*Strindberg, August	MISS JULIE	Drama	1888
Styron, William	LIE DOWN IN DARKNESS	Fiction	1952
*Styron, William	SET THIS HOUSE ON FIRE	Fiction	1960
*Sudermann, Hermann	THE SONG OF SONGS	Fiction	1909
Sue, Eugene	THE MYSTERIES OF PARIS	Fiction	1842
Sue, Eugene	THE WANDERING JEW	Fiction	1844
Sutro, Alfred	MAGGIE	Drama	1905
**Swift, Jonathan	A TALE OF A TUB	Fiction	1704
Synge, J(ohn) M.	DEIRDRE OF THE SORROWS	Drama	1910
*Tennyson, Alfred	THE LADY OF SHALOTT	Poem	1842
*Tennyson, Alfred	THE LOTOS-EATERS	Poem	1842
**Tennyson, Alfred	THE TWO VOICES	Poem	1842
**Tennyson, Alfred	IN MEMORIAM	Poem	1850
Tolstoy, Leo	ANNA KARENINA	Fiction	1875
**Tolstoy, Leo	THE POWER OF DARKNESS	Fiction	1886
*Tolstoy, Leo	THE KREUTZER SONATA	Fiction	1889
Traven, B.	THE DEATH SHIP	Fiction	1926
*Trollope, Anthony	DOCTOR THORNE	Fiction	1858
Trollope, Anthony	THE LAST CHRONICLE OF BARSET	Fiction	1867
Tsao, Chan (Hsueh-Chin)	DREAM OF THE RED CHAMBER	Fiction	1792
Turgenev, Ivan	VIRGIN SOIL	Fiction	1872
*Twain, Mark	THE GILDED AGE	Fiction	1873
Undset, Sigrid	KRISTIN LAVRANSDATTER	Fiction	1920-22

AUTHOR	TITLE	GENRE	DATE
Van Druten, John	DIVERSION	Drama	1937
Van Druten, John	GERTIE MAUDE	Drama	1937
Van Druten, John	LEAVE HER TO HEAVEN	Drama	1937
**Vega Carpio, Lope de	THE KING, THE GREATEST ALCALDE	Drama	1635
Vigny, Alfred de	STELLO	Drama	1834
Virgil	THE AENEID	Poem	19 B.C.
Virgil	ECLOGUES (eighth poem)	Poem	48 B.C.
Voltaire, Francois Marie Arouet	ZAIRE	Drama	1732
Wallant, Edward	THE PAWNBROKER	Fiction	1961
Wallant, Edward	THE TENANTS OF MOONBLOOM	Fiction	1963
Walpole, Hugh	JUDITH PARIS	Fiction	1931
Walpole, Hugh	THE FORTRESS	Fiction	1932
Warren, Robert Penn	ALL THE KING'S MEN	Fiction	1946
Warren, Robert Penn	WORLD ENOUGH AND TIME	Fiction	1950
Warton, Thomas	THE SUICIDE	Poem	1750
Waugh, Evelyn	VILE BODIES	Fiction	1930
Waugh, Evelyn	BRIDESHEAD REVISITED	Fiction	1945
*Waugh, Evelyn	THE ORDEAL OF GILBERT PINFOLD	Fiction	1957
Webb, Mary	PRECIOUS BANE	Fiction	1924
*Webster, John	THE DUCHESS OF MALFI	Drama	1612
Webster, John	THE DEVIL'S LAW CASE	Drama	1617
Wedekind, Frank	THE AWAKENING OF SPRING	Drama	1891
*Wells, H(erbert) G.	THE HISTORY OF MR. POLLY	Fiction	1909
Welty, Eudora	CLYTIE	Fiction	1936
Welty, Eudora	THE GOLDEN APPLES	Fiction	1949
**Werfel, Franz	GOAT SONG	Drama	1921
**West, Nathanael	MISS LONELYHEARTS	Fiction	1933
Wharton, Edith	THE HOUSE OF MIRTH	Fiction	1905

AUTHOR	TITLE	GENRE	DATE
*Wharton, Edith	ETHAN FROME	Fiction	1911
Wharton, Edith	THE CUSTOM OF THE COUNTRY	Fiction	1913
White, Patrick	THE TREE OF MAN	Fiction	1955
White, Patrick	RIDERS IN THE CHARIOT	Fiction	1961
Whiting, John	MARCHING SONG	Drama	1958
Wilde, Oscar	THE DUCHESS OF PADUA	Drama	1891
Wilde, Oscar	THE PICTURE OF DORIAN GRAY	Fiction	1891
*Wilde, Oscar	SALOME	Drama	1893
Wilder, Thornton	THE CABALA	Fiction	1926
Wilder, Thornton	OUR TOWN	Drama	1938
Williams, Charles	DESCENT INTO HELL	Fiction	1937
Williams, Charles	ALL HALLOWS EVE	Fiction	1945
*Williams, Tennessee	CAT ON A HOT TIN ROOF	Drama	1955
Woolf, Virginia	MRS. DALLOWAY	Fiction	1925
Woolf, Virginia	THE WAVES	Fiction	1931
**Woolf, Virginia	THE YEARS	Fiction	1937
Wu, Ch'eng-en	HSI YU CHI (MONKEY)	Fiction	1500
Wylie, Elinor	THE VENETIAN GLASS NEPHEW	Fiction	1925
Zeromski, Stefan	ASHES	Fiction	1904
Zola, Emile	NANA	Fiction	1880

Editors' note:

In the author list above, the names of the authors are in the form in which they are generally found in library card catalogs and many standard bibliographies. Note that fiction may be short stories that have not been published as separate works but in anthologies or periodicals. In this case consult the SHORT STORY INDEX (9.402) or the FICTION INDEX (9.304) to locate them. Likewise dramas may not have been published as separate works but rather in anthologies. Consulting the PLAY INDEX (9.506), the INDEX TO FULL LENGTH PLAYS (9.504 and 9.507), Dean H. Keller's INDEX TO PLAYS IN PERIODICALS and its supplement, and John H. Ottemiller's OTTEMILLER'S INDEX TO PLAYS IN COLLECTIONS helps to locate them. Poetry can be located by using GRANGER'S INDEX TO POETRY (9.604). In some instances the contents notes on the catalog card may indicate the contents of an anthology. Many more contemporary literary works on suicide can be found by searching items 9.301 through 9.703.

As can be seen from sections 9.1 and 9.2 of this chapter, suicide has been the theme of many novels, short stories, plays, essays, and poems. To locate literary works on suicide as they are being published, the following subject headings should be consulted in library card catalogs and in several of the bibliographies indicated in chapter 3:

> Suicide in literature
> Suicide in literature--Bibliography

The remaining sections of this chapter suggest sources to use for identifying literature having suicide as a theme, according to the various forms of the literature.

9.3 LOCATING NOVELS RELATED TO SUICIDE

It is difficult to identify fiction relating to a particular subject, including suicide, because not many literary bibliographies provide subject indexes. The following bibliographic sources, however, can be used to identify suicide novels because they offer indexing which includes suicide.

9.301   BOOK REVIEW DIGEST. New York: H.W. Wilson Co., 1905-- .
Monthly (except February and July), with annual cumulations and five-year cumulative indexes.

> Refer to item 3.501
>
> Consult: Fiction--Suicide
> Novels--Suicide
> Suicide

9.302   CUMULATIVE BOOK INDEX: A WORLD LIST OF BOOKS IN THE ENGLISH LANGUAGE. New York: H.W. Wilson Co., 1898-- .
Monthly (except August). Cumulated quarterly, annually since 1969, and at least biennially since 1957.

> Refer to item 3.203
>
> Consult: Suicide--Fiction

9.303   FICTION CATALOG. Edited by Estelle A. Fidell. New York: H.W. Wilson Co., 1908-- . Annual, with quinquennial cumulations.

> Experienced librarians select novels suitable for public libraries for inclusion in this work. Works of fiction on all subjects are included. Annotated entries are arranged by author, and since 1960 a title and subject index has been included.
>
> Consult: Suicide

9.304   FICTION INDEX. Compiled by Gerald B. Cotton, Raymond F. Smith, and Anthony J. Gordon. London: Association of Assistant Librarians, 1953-- . Cumulations.

Often referred to as the CUMULATED FICTION INDEX, this valuable work is a subject listing of works of fiction, including short story collections, written in English since 1945. There are no annotations but the works are described under some three thousand subject headings. The first cumulation, covering the period 1945-60, contains twenty-five thousand titles; the second cumulation, for the years 1961-69, contains eighteen thousand titles; and the third cumulation, for the years 1970-74, has over ten thousand titles. While this work essentially has the same coverage as the FICTION CATALOG (9.303), it also includes materials not in that work.

Consult: Suicide

Lists of novels may be identified in the future, as published, by periodically checking subject headings such as the following in library card catalogs. These listings may or may not be indexed by suicide as a subject, however.

American fiction--Bibliography
American fiction--20th century--Bibliography
Canadian fiction--Bibliography--Catalogs

9.4 LOCATING SHORT STORIES RELATED TO SUICIDE

The most useful sources for identifying short stories on suicide are listed below.

9.401   CANADIAN ESSAY AND LITERATURE INDEX, 1973-- . Toronto and Buffalo: University of Toronto Press, 1975-- . Annual.

Refer to item 9.702.

9.402   Cook, Dorothy Elizabeth. SHORT STORY INDEX: AN INDEX TO 60,000 STORIES IN 4,320 COLLECTIONS. New York: H.W. Wilson Co., 1953. Quinquennial supplements.

An index to short stories of less than 150 pages from the latter part of the nineteenth century to the present, this work contains more short stories than the title indicates. This good source for short stories on suicide also includes a list of the collections indexed. This work supersedes the INDEX TO SHORT STORIES, compiled by Ina Ten Eyck (Firkins) in 1923, and its supplements.

Consult: Suicide

To locate new listings of collections of short stories as they are published, sub-ject headings such as the following should be consulted periodically in library card catalogs. These listings, however, may not be indexed by suicide as a subject.

>Short stories--Bibliography
>Short stories, American--Bibliography
>Short stories, English--Bibliography

9.5 LOCATING DRAMATIC WORKS RELATED TO SUICIDE

Sources for finding dramatic works on suicide are described in this section.

9.501 CANADIAN ESSAY AND LITERATURE INDEX, 1973-- . Toronto and Buffalo: University of Toronto Press, 1975-- . Annual.

>Refer to item 9.702.

9.502 CUMULATED DRAMATIC INDEX, 1909-1949: A CUMULATION OF THE F.W. FAXON COMPANY'S DRAMATIC INDEX. Edited by Fred-erick W. Faxon, Mary E. Bates, and Anne C. Sutherland. 2 vols. Boston: G.K. Hall, 1965.

>A marginal source.

>Consult: Suicide

9.503 Firkins, Ina Ten Eyck, comp. INDEX TO PLAYS, 1800-1926. New York: H.W. Wilson Co., 1927. 307 p. Supplements.

>A selective list of over eleven thousand plays that have received public recognition, this work has an author index and a title-subject index which is somewhat inadequate for a subject approach. A list of periodicals consulted and collections indexed is included.

>Consult: Suicide

9.504 Ireland, Norma (Olin). INDEX TO FULL LENGTH PLAYS, 1944 TO 1964. Boston: F.W. Faxon, 1965. 328 p.

>Nearly twelve hundred plays published in English for the period are indexed in this work by author, title, and sub-ject in a single alphabet. This work continues Ruth Thomson's index (9.507).

>Consult: Suicide

9.505 Logasa, Hannah, and Ver Noy, Winifred, comps. AN INDEX TO ONE-ACT PLAYS FOR STAGE, RADIO, AND TELEVISION. Boston: F.W. Faxon, 1924-- . Irregular.

Over twenty-five thousand one-act plays published in English since 1900 are indexed in this work. It contains separate title, author, and subject indexes. The work was formerly entitled AN INDEX TO ONE-ACT PLAYS.

Consult: Suicide

9.506   PLAY INDEX, 1949/52-- . New York: H.W. Wilson Co., 1953-- . Irregular.

This index lists single plays and collections of plays published since 1949. Many pre-1949 plays are included in these collections. There is an author-title-subject index to all plays.

Consult: Suicide

9.507   Thomson, Ruth G. INDEX TO FULL LENGTH PLAYS, 1895 TO 1925. Boston: F.W. Faxon, 1956. xi, 172 p.

This work indexes 562 English-language plays for the period and includes separate title, author, and subject indexes.

To keep up with new listings and indexes to plays as they are published, consult periodically library card catalogs under subject headings such as the following:

American drama--Bibliography
English drama--Bibliography--Catalogs
Drama--Bibliography--Catalogs
Drama--Indexes
Drama--20th century--Indexes

9.6 LOCATING POETRY RELATED TO SUICIDE

Although locating poems on a specific subject is somewhat difficult, a number of indexes contain references to poetry on suicide. These are described below.

9.601   American Library Association. SUBJECT INDEX TO POETRY FOR CHILDREN AND YOUNG PEOPLE. Compiled by Violet Sell and others. Chicago: American Library Association, 1957. 582 p.

This subject index to 157 anthologies of children's poetry contains about twenty poems on suicide.

Consult: Humor--suicide
              Suicide

9.602   Bruncken, Herbert, comp. and ed. SUBJECT INDEX TO POETRY: A GUIDE FOR ADULT READERS. Chicago: American Library Association, 1940. xix, 201 p.

About ten poems on suicide are cited in this source.

Consult: Suicide

9.603 CANADIAN ESSAY AND LITERATURE INDEX, 1973-- . Toronto and Buffalo: University of Toronto Press, 1975-- . Annual.

Canadian poetry is indexed by subject in this work.

Refer to item 9.702.

9.604 Granger, Edith. GRANGER'S INDEX TO POETRY. Edited by William James Smith. 6th ed. New York: Columbia University Press, 1973. 2,260 p. SUPPLEMENT, 1970-77.

About fifty poems on suicide are indexed in the latest edition and supplement. Previous editions should also be consulted as there are additional suicide poems indexed although there is some overlap between editions.

Consult: Suicide

9.605 INDEX TO POETRY FOR CHILDREN AND YOUNG PEOPLE, 1964-1969. New York: H.W. Wilson, 1972. xxx, 575 p.

9.606 INDEX TO POETRY FOR CHILDREN AND YOUNG PEOPLE, 1970-1975. New York: H.W. Wilson, 1978. xxxii, 472 p.

These two volumes together index more than twenty-three thousand poems in 225 anthologies of poetry for children. Each volume contains an author, title, first line, and subject index. More than twenty suicide poems for children are indexed in these two volumes.

Consult: Suicide

9.607 Shaw, John MacKay. CHILDHOOD IN POETRY: A CATALOGUE, WITH BIOGRAPHICAL AND CRITICAL ANNOTATIONS OF THE BOOKS OF ENGLISH AND AMERICAN POETS. 5 vols. Detroit: Gale Research Co., 1967. Supplements.

The extensive children's poetry collection in the Robert Manning Strozier Library at the Florida State University, Tallahassee, is indexed in these volumes. Very few poems specifically on suicide are included to date.

Consult: Suicide

9.608 Smith, Dorothy B.F., and Andrews, Eva L. SUBJECT INDEX TO POETRY FOR CHILDREN AND YOUNG PEOPLE, 1957-1975. Chicago: American Library Association, 1977. xiv, 1035 p.

This subject index to children's poetry indexes 263 new anthologies since the 1957 volume (see 9.601). About fifty
poems on suicide are indexed in this work.

Consult: Humor--Suicide
Satire--Suicide
Suicide

To keep up with any new listings or indexes to poetry that may appear in the
future, consult periodically library card catalogs under the subject headings such
as the following:

American poetry--Indexes
Canadian poetry--20th century--Bibliography
Poetry--Bibliography
Poetry--Indexes

9.7 LOCATING ESSAYS ON SUICIDE

Sources for identifying essays on suicide are described in this section. They
may also be identified by consulting periodically library card catalogs under
such headings as the following:

Suicide--Addresses, Essays, Lectures
Suicide--United States--Addresses, Essays, Lectures

9.701   American Library Association. THE "A.L.A." INDEX: AN INDEX TO
GENERAL LITERATURE, BIOGRAPHICAL, HISTORICAL, AND LITERARY
ESSAYS AND SKETCHES. By William Isaac Fletcher. 2d ed. Boston:
1905. Reprint. Freeport, N.Y.: Books for Libraries Press, 1971.
Supplement, 1900-1910.

Selected English-language essays, historical works, and other
works from the last half of the nineteenth and the early
twentieth century are indexed in this work. The most commonly held works are analyzed. There is little overlap with
the ESSAY AND GENERAL LITERATURE INDEX (9.703) for
the period.

Consult: Suicide

9.702   CANADIAN ESSAY AND LITERATURE INDEX, 1973-- . Toronto and
Buffalo: University of Toronto Press, 1975-- . Annual.

This recent work is an author, title, and subject index to
essays, book reviews, poems, plays, and short stories published in Canada, in magazines, anthologies, and collections not already indexed.

Consult: Suicide

9.703   ESSAY AND GENERAL LITERATURE INDEX, 1900-- . New York:
         H.W. Wilson Co., 1934-- . Semiannual, with annual and quinquen-
         nial cumulations.

         This work indexes collections of essays and chapters in com-
         posite books in the humanities and social sciences, and to
         a lesser degree in the sciences. The disciplines of philosophy,
         religion, political science, economics, law, education, the
         arts, literature, and history are included. A good author
         and subject index is provided. Only two or three essays
         on suicide appear per year.

         Consult: Suicide

9.8 LOCATING JUVENILE LITERATURE ON SUICIDE

The best sources for finding juvenile literature with suicide themes or related to
suicide are described in this section.

9.801   CHILDREN'S BOOKS IN PRINT. SUBJECT GUIDE. New York: R.R.
         Bowker Co., 1970-- . Annual.

         Over thirty-nine thousand titles of children's books currently
         in print are listed under at least eight thousand subject cate-
         gories annually. This work should be used with care, as
         the lists are compiled from publishers' catalogs and not from
         an examination of the works themselves. This work was pre-
         ceded by CHILDREN'S BOOKS FOR SCHOOLS AND LI-
         BRARIES. To date there are few titles relating specifically
         to suicide.

         Consult: Suicide

9.802   JUNIOR HIGH SCHOOL LIBRARY CATALOG. 3d ed. H.W. Wilson
         Co., 1975. xii, 991 p. Annual, with quinquennial cumulations.

         The third edition of this catalog contains an analysis of
         nearly thirty-eight hundred books that were judged by spe-
         cialists to be suitable for grades seven through nine. This
         edition contains only a few references to books on the theme
         of suicide. Future editions should be consulted.

         Consult: Suicide

For children's poetry on suicide consult items 9.601 and 9.605-9.608.

9.9 SUICIDE IN BIBLICAL, PHILOSOPHICAL, MYTHOLOGICAL, AND FOLKLORE LITERATURE

Concern, opinion, and reflection on suicide have continued through the centuries. The Bible says very little about suicide specifically. Most of the references treat suicide or allude to suicide in a simple factual manner. Several passages which are often presumed to address suicide are subject to various interpretations. It is difficult to use Bible concordances to locate passages referring to suicide or suicidal behaviors, since the word "suicide" itself is seldom, if ever, used in the various versions of the Bible. Instead, various allusions, euphemisms, or other descriptive phrases, such as "falling on his sword," are used. Much searching in the concordances under many such descriptive words would be required. A very helpful and quick reference source is provided in the following item:

9.901   GREAT BOOKS OF THE WESTERN WORLD. Edited by Robert Maynard Hutchins. 54 vols. Chicago: Encyclopaedia Britannica, 1952.

In volume 2 of this set, which is volume 1 of the SYN-TOPICON, chapter 48 (Life and Death), section 8b (The desire for death; the death instinct; the problem of suicide) on page 1029, almost forty references to Old Testament texts or passages are given regarding suicide, five references to New Testament texts or passages are given, and about a dozen references to the Apocryphal literature are provided.

Philosophers through the centuries have also meditated and reflected upon suicide and suicidal tendencies and behavior. In addition to items 1.110, 1.114, 1.116, 1.202, 1.207, 4.107 and 5.218 of this information guide, the same source as above is also very helpful for references to suicide in the works of major philosophers:

9.902   GREAT BOOKS OF THE WESTERN WORLD. Edited by Robert Maynard Hutchins. 54 vols. Chicago: Encyclopaedia Britannica, 1952.

In volume 2 of the set, which is volume 1 of the SYN-TOPICON, chapter 48 (Life and Death), section 8b (The desire for death; the death instinct; the problem of suicide) on pages 1029 and 1030, specific references are provided to portions of the works of the following philosophers. This is very handy because the works cited are parts of the fifty-four-volume set. Philosophers and other great thinkers and essayists with references to suicide in their works include Sophocles, Euripides, Herodotus, Plato, Aristotle, Lucretius, Epictetus, Aurelius, Virgil, Plutarch, Tacitus, Plotinus, Augustine, Dante, Chaucer, Hobbes, Montaigne, Shakespeare, Spinoza, Milton, Pascal, Locke, Swift, Fielding, Montesquieu, Rousseau, Gibbon, Kant, Boswell, Hegel, Goethe, Melville, Tolstoy, James, and Freud.

A fair number of references to suicide and suicidal behavior appear in the my-thology of early and primitive cultures. Although these myths have been recounted and analyzed through the years, with a fairly extensive body of literature re-sulting, it is very difficult to identify specific myths that involve suicide. This is a result of the lack of subject indexing in the standard reference works on mythology. In addition to the ENCYCLOPEDIA OF RELIGION AND ETHICS (4.108), the following standard work is the best source for easy identification of myths incorporating suicide or suicidal behavior with various racial and cultural groupings:

9.903   MYTHOLOGY OF ALL RACES. 13 vols. Vols. 1, 3, 6, 9-12 edited by Louis Herbert Gray; vols. 2, 4-5, 7-8, 13 edited by John Arnott Macculloch and G.F. Moore. Boston: Archaeological Institute of America, 1916-32.

This extensive and important set provides references and information on suicide in the mythology of the Eddic, Slavic, Indian, Armenian, Japanese, Siberian, and Oceanic peoples.

Consult: Suicide (in the general index)

Using a standard work on Greek mythology, a special listing has been prepared for this information guide by Dr. Melvin D. Faber. The listing below cites the Greek myths included in the work which incorporate suicide and suicidal behavior:

9.904   Graves, Robert. THE GREEK MYTHS. Rev. ed. 2 vols. Baltimore: Penguin Books, 1960. 370 p. 412 p.

Describing and analyzing, with full references to classical sources, 171 Greek myths, this work has assembled scat-tered elements of each myth as well as recorded many vari-ants. A thorough page-by-page examination of the volumes by Dr. Melvin D. Faber reveals that thirty of the myths do incorporate suicide and suicidal behaviors. These are listed below with the myth numbers assigned to them by Graves in his work, for handy reference.

Alcestis, 69
The Rival Twins, 74
The Calydonian Boar, 80
Telamon and Peleus, 81
Midas, 83
Narcissus, 85
The Loves of Minos, 89
Daedalus and Talos, 92
Catreus and Althaemenes, 93
Theseus in Crete, 98
Phaedra and Hippolytus, 101
Oedipus, 105
The Seven Against Thebes, 106
The Children of Pelops, 110

The Trial of Orestes, 114
Iphigenia Among the Taurian, 116
Erginus, 121
The Ninth Labour: Hippolyte's Girdle, 131
Omphale, 136
Iole, 144
The Apotheosis of Heracles, 145
The Children of Heracles, 146
The Lemnian Women and King Cyzicus, 149
The "Argo" Returns to Greece, 154
The Death of Pelias, 155
Medea in Exile, 157
The First Gathering at Aulis, 160
The Second Gathering at Aulis, 161
The Nine Years War, 162
The Death of Achilles, 164
The Madness of Ajax, 165
The Oracles of Troy, 166
The Sack of Troy, 168
The Returns, 169
Odysseus's Wanderings, 170

There are occasional references to suicide in the literature of folklore. These references are difficult to locate because of inadequate subject indexing. Several sources which indicate materials relating suicide to folklore are described here.

9.905   Frazer, Sir James George. THE GOLDEN BOUGH: A STUDY IN MAGIC AND RELIGION. 3d ed. 8 pts. in 12 vols. London: Macmillan, 1907-15. In later reprintings, a 13th vol., AFTERMATH, is added.

Essentially on primitive religions, this work has a wealth of information on the folklore of many cultures and areas throughout the world.

Consult: Suicide (in the general index)

9.906   Haywood, Charles. A BIBLIOGRAPHY OF NORTH AMERICAN FOLKLORE AND FOLKSONG. 2d rev. ed. 2 vols. New York: Dover, 1961.

Including materials on folklore and legends from areas north of Mexico, this work provides a few references related to suicide. A subject index is provided.

Consult: Suicide

Chapter 10

SUICIDE AND THE NEWS MEDIA

This chapter presents various approaches to finding information or opinions on suicide as they are reported, transmitted, or otherwise treated in the news media. Published and on-line indexes to current, large daily newspapers are listed and described. Other indexing services to the news are also reported, as are checklists of newspapers, past and present. Finally, sources of opinion polls on suicide are considered.

10.1 MAJOR INDEXES TO CURRENT NEWSPAPERS: PUBLISHED AND ON-LINE

Since newspapers report facts and opinions on all facets of social life, news articles are a good source of general information in regard to current events and opinion on suicide.

10.101 CALIFORNIA NEWS INDEX. Claremont, Calif.: Claremont College, Center for Public Affairs, July 1970-- . Quarterly. Looseleaf.

> This multiple newspaper index selectively indexes a number of newspapers in one consolidated index. All significant state and regional news of research value is indexed from the LOS ANGELES TIMES and the SACRAMENTO BEE. Four other newspapers are indexed more selectively: the SAN DIEGO UNION, the SAN FRANCISCO EXAMINER, the SAN FRANCISCO CHRONICLE, and the SAN JOSE MERCURY. The NEWSPAPER INDEX series (10.105) does more thorough indexing of the LOS ANGELES TIMES and the SAN FRANCISCO CHRONICLE. Sunday supplements, editorials, and seven California magazines are also included in each volume. There is a fifteen-month lag in the indexing and also no cumulations of the index.

> Consult: Suicide

10.102 CANADIAN NEWSPAPER INDEX. Toronto: Information Access, 1977-- . Monthly, with annual cumulations.

This work selectively indexes the MONTREAL STAR, TO-
RONTO GLOBE AND MAIL, TORONTO STAR, VAN-
COUVER SUN, and the WINNIPEG FREE PRESS. The articles are listed in chronological order under subjects. A
subject index and a name index are provided. On-line
computer searching of this index is available at libraries
and other information centers which have facilities for this.
Refer to item 5.302 for this service. Approximately forty
articles on suicide per year are cited by this index.

Consult: Suicide

10.103 INDEX TO BLACK NEWSPAPERS. Wooster, Ohio: Bell and Howell,
1977-- . Quarterly.

This multiple newspaper index includes selective indexing
of the following black newspapers: NEW YORK AMSTER-
DAM NEWS, ATLANTA DAILY WORLD, BALTIMORE AFRO-
AMERICAN, BIRACIAL NEWS, CHICAGO DEFENDER,
CLEVELAND CALL AND POST, LOS ANGELES SENTINEL,
MICHIGAN CHRONICLE, and the NEW PITTSBURGH COU-
RIER. Subject and name indexes are provided. About
twenty citations on suicide appear annually.

Consult: Suicide

10.104 NEWSBANK. Greenwich, Conn.: 1970-- . Monthly, with cumulated
annual index. Looseleaf index. Articles on microfiche.

Over 100,000 news articles from nearly 200 U.S. daily
newspapers are indexed and reproduced on microfiche each
year by this unique index. In addition to selectively indexing nearly all of the 150 largest newspapers in the United
States, one newspaper from each state capital as well as
minority newspapers are also indexed. The index is arranged
in thirteen broad subject categories. It is a good source
of nationwide news articles on suicide.

Consult: Mental health (general)--Suicide
          Law and order--Correctional systems(inmates)--Suicide
          (Also consult the guide to the index for other possible
          headings that may be added in the future.)

10.105 NEWSPAPER INDEX (series). Wooster, Ohio: Bell and Howell, 1972-- .
Monthly, with annual cumulations.

In this important newspaper index series a number of individual newspapers are indexed separately using one standardized format. Nine separate, computerized, standardized
indexes provide access to nine large metropolitan daily newspapers. Comprehensive indexing is attempted for each paper.
The newspapers, with the date of the beginning of each

index, are indicated below:

CHICAGO SUN TIMES, 1979--
CHICAGO TRIBUNE, 1972--
DENVER POST, 1979--
DETROIT NEWS, 1976--
HOUSTON POST, 1976--
LOS ANGELES TIMES, 1972--
NEW ORLEANS TIMES-PICAYUNE, 1972--
SAN FRANCISCO CHRONICLE, 1976--
WASHINGTON (D.C.) POST, 1971--

All local, state, regional, national, and international news
is indexed by means of a subject index and a name index.
The supplements of the papers are indexed as well. PA-
RADE MAGAZINE is indexed in the WASHINGTON POST
index. The indexes are published within two months after
the news appears in the newspapers. The SAN FRANCISCO
CHRONICLE appears to have more articles on suicide than
any of the others listed above.

Consult: Suicide

10.106 NEW YORK TIMES. INDEXES. Sanford, N.C.: Microfilming Corporation of America, 1851-- . Bimonthly, with annual cumulations.
Imprint varies.

This basic newspaper index presents a brief summary of news
articles in addition to extensive indexing of news from the
local to the international levels. There is good coverage
of news relating to suicide and suicidal behavior. Book
reviews and the Sunday supplements are also indexed. There
is about a six-week time lag until the articles are indexed.
Computer searching is available from 1969. Refer to item
10.107.

Consult: Suicide

10.107 NEW YORK TIMES INFORMATION BANK. Parsippany, N.J.: 1973-- .
Weekly updates, forming continuous cumulated on-line files.

Known as the INFORMATION BANK, this on-line computerized system selectively indexes and abstracts news articles in at least seventy-two current magazines and newspapers. Twenty-seven of these are unique to this index,
not even being indexed in popular periodical indexes. At
the same time, twelve of these twenty-seven are newspapers
which have their own indexes, except for the MIAMI HER-
ALD and the MANCHESTER GUARDIAN. The newspapers
are ATLANTA CONSTITUTION, CHICAGO TRIBUNE,
CHRISTIAN SCIENCE MONITOR, HOUSTON CHRONICLE,
LOS ANGELES TIMES, MANCHESTER GUARDIAN, MIAMI
HERALD, NATIONAL OBSERVER, SAN FRANCISCO

CHRONICLE, TIMES of London, WASHINGTON POST, and the NEW YORK TIMES back to 1969. The magazines include various popular, financial, and economic titles, as well as CURRENT BIOGRAPHY. For a more detailed listing of the titles in this system, refer to the article "Indexing of Popular Periodicals: The State of the Art" by Brian Aveney and Rod Slade, in the LIBRARY JOURNAL (1 October 1978), pages 1915-23. The abstracts provided by the INFORMATION BANK are very informative and detailed. The service, which is very rapid, is marketed at a substantial fee and is also available at centers such as large public libraries which have facilities for this type of searching.

Consult: Suicide (in combination with other keywords as needed)

10.108   TIMES, London. INDEX TO THE TIMES. Reading, Engl.: Newspaper Archives Developments Unlimited, 1906-- . Quarterly.

This index to one of the world's leading newspapers has indexing by personal name and subject in one alphabet. Book reviews and the various supplements are also indexed. Former titles of this index were INDEX TO THE TIMES 1906-13, and the OFFICIAL INDEX TO THE TIMES 1914-57. There is about a one-year time lag in publishing this index. PALMER'S INDEX TO THE TIMES NEWSPAPER, 1790-1941, covers the earlier years of the TIMES.

Consult: Suicide
          Suicide attempts

10.109   WALL STREET JOURNAL. INDEXES. Princeton, N.J.: Dow Jones Books, 1955-- . Monthly, with annual cumulations.

This daily financial paper carries articles that relate to insurance, and other financial aspects related to suicide, but it also includes good general articles on suicide. The index is divided into two parts: (1) corporate news, and (2) general news. It is important that the user consult the second part. Book reviews are also indexed. There is a one-month time lag in this indexing.

Consult: Death

Other published indexes to individual newspapers are treated in section 10.3

10.2 SPECIAL NEWS MEDIA INDEXES

10.201   ALTERNATIVE PRESS INDEX. Baltimore: Alternative Press Center, 1969-- . Quarterly.

Over 110 alternative and underground journals and newspapers are indexed in this work, which is the only access
to publications of many social movements of this type in
the United States. A subject index is included along with
a list of alternative publications and their addresses. There
is an eighteen-month time lag between appearance of the
articles and the indexing. About ten to fifteen articles
on suicide per year are cited in this index.

Consult: Suicide

10.202 FACTS ON FILE: WEEKLY NEWS DIGEST. New York: Facts on
File, 1941-- . Weekly, with bimonthly and annual cumulated indexes. Looseleaf.

This pamphlet news service provides a weekly summary of
U.S. and world news. Suicide information is limited to
news of the suicides of well-known personalities. News
appears in this digest several weeks after its occurrence.

Consult: Suicides

10.203 INDEX TO BLACK NEWSPAPERS. Wooster, Ohio: Bell and Howell,
1977-- . Quarterly.

Refer to item 10.103.

10.204 TELEVISION NEWS INDEX AND ABSTRACTS. Nashville, Tenn.: Van-
derbilt Television News Archives, Joint University Libraries, 1972-- .
Monthly, with annual cumulations.

The evening-news broadcasts of ABC, CBS, and NBC are
completely indexed in this work. The index contains a
time-ordered abstract of each day's broadcast, with the
names of the commentators and reporters included. From
the index one can ascertain how the topic of suicide has
been interpreted in the evening television news. Videotapes of the news have been preserved at the archive since
5 August 1968, and may be viewed at the archive or rented
in a variety of videotape formats. About an eight-month
time lag exists in this indexing.

Consult: Suicide

Also the BIBLIOGRAPHY OF BIOETHICS (5.103) selectively cites articles from
various newspapers on suicide as it relates to bioethics.

10.3 INDIVIDUAL NEWSPAPER INDEXES

Sources of information on identifying published and unpublished indexes to individual newspapers in the United States and Canada are presented here. Following these, checklists of newspapers in the United States and other countries, whether indexed or not, are also described.

10.301   Sell, Kenneth D. "A Checklist of Published Indexes to Current American Daily Newspapers." RQ (REFERENCE QUARTERLY) 17 (Fall 1977): 13-16.

> A checklist of published indexes to newspapers in the United States with daily circulation in excess of 100,000 is presented here for quick reference. For the states that do not have newspapers of this size, the index to the newspaper in the state with the largest circulation is included. This checklist was a result of a special survey of the 150 largest newspapers in the United States by the author in 1976. No attempt was made to find or locate the unpublished indexes. Nor was any attempt made to locate indexes that were once published but have ceased publication. All indexes are available from the publishers in the format indicated.

For a more comprehensive and detailed list, with descriptions, of all known published and unpublished newspaper indexes in the United States, consult the following source:

10.302   LATHROP REPORT ON NEWSPAPER INDEXES. Wooster, Ohio: Norman Lathrop Enterprises, 1979-- . Core collection with annual update service.

> Detailed descriptions and sample illustrations of all known (over 500) published and unpublished newspaper indexes in the United States and Canada are provided by this service. Special subject cross-references will be provided.

Several standard listings of newspapers, past and present, are described here for both the United States and other countries, regardless of whether these newspapers have published indexes or not. When a newspaper of interest has not been indexed, finding information in it on suicide is a very tedious undertaking.

10.303   AYER DIRECTORY OF PUBLICATIONS. Philadelphia: Ayer, 1880-- . Annual. Title varies.

> This standard listing of U.S. and Canadian daily, weekly, monthly, and quarterly newspapers is arranged by cities within states or provinces. The information on each is very complete as to editions, circulation, and so forth. However, it does not indicate whether or not published indexes exist for these newspapers. In addition to newspapers, various other types of publications are included.

10.304   U.S. Library of Congress.   Catalog Publication Division.   NEWSPAPERS
IN MICROFORM: FOREIGN COUNTRIES, 1948-1972.   Washington,
D.C.:   1973.   xix, 269 p.   Annual supplements.

> This guide to foreign newspapers in microform is a good
> source for locating newspapers both past and present outside
> of the United States.   The newspaper titles are arranged
> alphabetically by state, then alphabetically by city within
> the state, with a general title index.

10.305   _____.   NEWSPAPERS IN MICROFORM: UNITED STATES, 1948-
1972.   7th ed.   Washington, D.C.:   1973.   xxiii, 1,056 p.   Annual
supplements.   Quinquennial cumulations.

> This valuable work cites the location of over thirty-four
> thousand newspaper titles published in the United States,
> from the eighteenth century to the present time, which are
> available in microform.   The newspapers are arranged as in
> item 10.304 above.

10.4 OPINION POLLS

Surveys and polls of public attitudes and opinions on a vast number of subjects
have been researched since the 1930s.   The results of these are often summarized and reported by the news media, although they may also be reported and
published in various other ways.   The large-scale opinion polls are taken usually
by special organizations, although many are done on a smaller scale by other
researchers or by the news media itself.   The major sources for locating information on these polls are described below.   For further information on poll
data, the researcher is advised to write to the following:

> Editor, Current Opinion
> Roper Public Opinion Research Center
> Williams College
> Williamstown, Mass.   01267

10.401   CURRENT OPINION.   Williamstown, Mass.:   Roper Public Opinion
Research Center, Williams College, 1973-- .   Monthly.

> This bulletin presents the results of current surveys con-
> ducted by the leading national and international opinion
> research organizations.   Data from approximately ten to
> twenty-five surveys are described each month.   Only a
> few surveys on suicide have been reported to date.   The
> source and date of each survey are indicated.   There is
> usually a time lag of three to six months before the poll
> results are reported here.   This bulletin is a good source
> for suicide information of this type.

> Consult: Suicide

10.402 Gallup, George H. THE GALLUP POLL: PUBLIC OPINION, 1972-
1977. 2 vols. Wilmington, Del.: Scholarly Resources, 1978.

This compendium of data from Gallup's poll includes only
two surveys about suicide in regard to the right to end
one's own life under certain conditions. Polls from 1935
to 1971 did not include any surveys on suicide.

Consult: Euthanasia

Chapter 11

SUICIDE IN NONPRINT MEDIA

The previous chapters of this information guide deal with sources of printed materials on suicide in formats such as books, journals, reports, newspapers, microfiche, and microfilm. This chapter deals with sources of materials on suicide in essentially nonprint formats such as motion pictures, filmstrips, slides, and sound and videotapes. Sources for reviews of these materials are also treated.

11.1 MOTION PICTURES FOR ENTERTAINMENT

Suicide has been used as a theme for motion pictures since the early days of filmmaking. Motion pictures have been produced since the early 1890s, and produced for commercial viewing since 1913. The Copyright Office has been granting rights to filmmakers since the early days of filmmaking. These lists of copyrighted films, without descriptions of the contents or subject access, are available. However, some of these early films have been lost, discarded, or have deteriorated. Until recently no adequate description of these films has existed. In the past decade projects have been initiated in both the United States and Great Britain to describe the film heritage of these nations.

11.101　The American Film Institute. THE AMERICAN FILM INSTITUTE CATA-LOG OF MOTION PICTURES PRODUCED IN THE UNITED STATES. Kenneth W. Munden, executive editor. New York and London: R.R. Bowker, 1971-- . In progress.

> When completed, this nineteen-volume set will be the most comprehensive description of American film production in existence. It contains an excellent subject index, and short but adequate descriptions of the plots of each film. Additional details are included with regard to the date produced, physical description of the film, the producer, the cast, and the type of film. The films are arranged in alphabetical order within each decade. The institute plans to describe all American feature films, short films, and newsreels up to 1970. Feature films will be described

151

and annotated for the period 1893-1910, with one volume
per decade thereafter. Volumes for the decades of the
1920s and 1960s have already been published. Approximately 6,600 films are described in each volume. About
250 films on suicide were produced in the 1920s and nearly
500 on suicide or attempted suicide were made in the 1960s.

Consult: Hara-kiri
           Suicide

11.102   Gifford, Denis. THE BRITISH FILM CATALOGUE 1895-1970: A REF-
         ERENCE GUIDE. New York: McGraw-Hill Book Co., 1973. 967 p.

         This volume has done, in a brief way, for British film pro-
         duction what the AMERICAN FILM INSTITUTE CATALOG
         (11.101) plans to do for American films. This work con-
         tains information on over 14,000 British films produced for
         public entertainment. There are one-sentence summaries
         of the plots. No subject index is included, which lessens
         the value of this work for finding British films on suicide.
         Film titles are arranged in chronological order together
         with a description of the physical features of the film, the
         cast, producer, director, and story source. The films are
         classified within twenty-three broad categories.

11.103   Niver, Kemp R. MOTION PICTURES FROM THE LIBRARY OF CON-
         GRESS PAPER PRINT COLLECTION, 1894-1912. Edited by Bebe
         Bergsten. Berkeley and Los Angeles: University of California Press,
         1967. xxii, 402 p.

         About three thousand silent, paper-positive print films held
         by the Library of Congress are described in this important
         work. Excellent but brief summaries of the plot of each
         film are included. There is no subject index but the films
         are in twelve subject categories in alphabetical order. Ad-
         ditional data included are the copyright date, the producer,
         length, and condition of the film. Prints of these films
         may be ordered from the Library of Congress. There are
         some films on suicide.

11.2 NONPRINT MEDIA FOR EDUCATIONAL PURPOSES

In this section the sources for identifying educational films, filmstrips, slide
series, and audio and video tapes on suicide are described. Refer also to
items 5.103 and 5.110.

11.201   CANADIANA: PUBLICATIONS OF INTEREST RECEIVED BY THE NA-
         TIONAL LIBRARY, 1950-- . Ottawa: National Library, 1951-- .
         Monthly, with annual cumulations.

         See item 3.103 for this source of Canadian nonprint media.

11.202 EDUCATIONAL FILM LOCATOR. Compiled and edited by the Consortium of University Film Centers and R.R. Bowker Co. 1st ed. New York: R.R. Bowker, 1978.

This excellent basic bibliographic source for location of educational films in the United States is a selective compilation of approximately 37,000 film titles. It provides locations of appropriate films on various topics and at all levels. Subject, title, and audience index, an alphabetical list of film descriptions, a series index, and a foreign title index are included. The descriptions are very informative, including physical characteristics and length of the films as well as abstracts of the contents. This is a good source for educational films on suicide. The subject headings in the subject index, however, are not specific enough, so that a number of more general subject areas must be scanned to identify films on suicide and suicide prevention.

Consult in the subject index: Death
Guidance, personal
Psychology
Social adjustments
Psychiatry
Public health

Also refer to "Suicide" in the title listing.

11.203 National Information Center for Educational Media (NICEM). NICEM MEDIA INDEXES. Los Angeles: University of Southern California, 1967. Periodic revision of each index. Supplements. Microfiche editions.

This series of indexes provides access to a wide range of educational audiovisual materials. A short summary of the contents of each item is provided in the description of the material. Each volume contains a subject-heading outline, an index to subject headings, and a subject guide, followed by an alphabetical listing of the materials. The indexes are revised biennially, and supplements are issued periodically. On-line computer searching is available. Refer to item 5.301.

Current NICEM index volumes relevant to suicide are listed below.

Consult: Sociology--Suicide

11.204 National Information Center for Educational Media (NICEM). INDEX TO EDUCATIONAL AUDIO TAPES. 4th ed. 1977-78.

Twenty-three tapes related to suicide are described.

11.205 _____. INDEX TO EDUCATIONAL OVERHEAD TRANSPARENCIES. 5th ed. 1977-78.

Twelve overhead transparencies on suicide are listed.

11.206 _____. INDEX TO EDUCATIONAL RECORDS. 4th ed. 1977-78.

One record on suicide is included in this section.

11.207 _____. INDEX TO EDUCATIONAL VIDEOTAPES. 4th ed. 1977-78.

Five videotapes are described containing information on suicide.

11.208 _____. INDEX TO 16MM EDUCATIONAL FILMS. 6th ed. 1977-78.

Thirteen educational films on suicide are listed in this section.

11.209 _____. INDEX TO 35MM EDUCATIONAL FILMSTRIPS. 6th ed. 1977-78.

Four filmstrips on suicide are described here.

11.210 U.S. Library of Congress. LIBRARY OF CONGRESS CATALOGS: FILMS AND OTHER MATERIALS FOR PROJECTION. Washington, D.C.: 1974-- . Three quarterly issues, with annual and quinquennial cumulations.

This useful index attempts to catalog all educational films, filmstrips, and since 1973, slide sets produced in the United States and Canada from over six hundred publishers. A useful subject index, a short summary of the contents of the material, a physical description, an author-title index, and a list of producers and distributors with addresses are included. This work has appeared under various titles since 1948, with subject access since 1953. The time lag for listing materials in this index is from one to three years. Several suicide films are listed each year.

Consult: Suicide
Suicide prevention
Youth--Suicidal behavior

11.3 LOCATING NONPRINT MEDIA REVIEWS

For current reviews on entertainment films, consult the following ongoing indexes, under the subject heading indicated.

ACCESS: THE SUPPLEMENTARY INDEX TO PERIODICALS:
Moving pictures (5.101)
CANADIAN PERIODICAL INDEX: Moving picture reviews (5.107)
HUMANITIES INDEX: Motion pictures--Reviews (5.114)
NEW YORK TIMES INDEX: Motion pictures--Reviews (10.106)
READERS' GUIDE: Moving picture plays--Criticisms, plots, etc.
(5.132)
SOCIAL SCIENCES INDEX: Moving pictures--Criticism (5.135)

Special indexes to film reviewers are described below:

11.301 Bowles, Stephen E. INDEX TO CRITICAL FILM REVIEWS IN BRITISH
AND AMERICAN FILM PERIODICALS, TOGETHER WITH: INDEX TO
CRITICAL REVIEWS ABOUT FILM, 1930-1972. 3 vols. New York:
B. Franklin, 1974-75.

Locations of reviews in thirty scholarly film periodicals from
the 1940s to 1971 are given in this index. There is no
separate subject index.

11.302 Educational Film Library Association. FILM EVALUATION GUIDE. New
Haven, Conn.: 1965-- . Looseleaf. Two five-year cumulations to date.

This card service evaluates educational films, giving the
following information on each film: a physical description,
an evaluation, a synopsis, the uses, the intended audience,
technical comments, ratings, and awards won. There is
about a one-year time lag between production and evaluation. A cumulated subject index is available.

Consult: Death

11.303 THE NEW YORK TIMES FILM REVIEWS, 1913-1968. 6 vols. New
York: New York Times, 1970. Biennial supplements.

The complete text of sixteen thousand motion picture reviews
published in the NEW YORK TIMES are reprinted in this work.
There are title, personal name, and corporate name indexes,
but no subject index. The indexes are located in volume 6.

11.304 Salem, James M. A GUIDE TO CRITICAL REVIEWS. Part IV: THE
SCREEN PLAY FROM THE JAZZ SINGER TO DR. STRANGELOVE.
Metuchen, N.J.: Scarecrow Press, 1971.

Film reviews of twelve thousand American and foreign films
that appeared in U.S. and Canadian periodicals from 1927 to
1963 are indexed in this work. Reviews that appeared in the
NEW YORK TIMES are also included, as are critical reviews
from scholarly journals. The reviews are arranged alphabetically by title with no subject index.

Chapter 12
SPECIAL RESOURCES

This chapter is devoted to consideration of information on special resources for the facilitation of suicide research. In section 12.1, resources such as suicide research centers, clearinghouses, and special collections of materials are considered. In section 12.2, special resources such as grants-in-aid and other special funding of suicide research are considered. In section 12.3, primary and secondary organizations concerned with suicide research and prevention are considered.

12.1 SPECIAL COLLECTIONS, CLEARINGHOUSES, AND RESEARCH CENTERS

As this information guide reveals, information on suicide, both retrospective and current, is scattered throughout the literatures of numerous diverse disciplines. It is also available in a great variety of types of materials, including books, parts of books, published and unpublished research reports, articles, literary works, legal literature, and news media. Each type may be found also in a variety of formats, such as print materials, including paper copy, microfiche, microfilm, computer output microfiche, and nonprint media, such as films, filmstrips, and audiocassettes, as well as in several types of computerized data bases. All of this makes it difficult for a researcher to attain and maintain a firm grasp on the field. This information guide is a preliminary attempt to overcome these difficulties.

One of the chief functions of research centers, clearinghouses, and special collections is to gather together and organize all relevant informational materials on a subject such as suicide so that in-depth study and analysis of the subject can be undertaken. To date, at least in the United States, it appears that special resources of this type for suicide research barely exist, except for those resources mentioned in items 12.101 and 12.102. Some large libraries such as the national libraries mentioned in chapter 2 of this guide, and such as the National Library of Medicine (5.115), may also provide comparatively large quantities of materials and data on suicide.

The following research centers, clearinghouses, and special collections of importance for suicide and suicide prevention research are described below.

12.101 SUICIDE PREVENTION CENTER OF LOS ANGELES AND INSTITUTE FOR STUDIES OF SELF-DESTRUCTIVE BEHAVIORS. 1041 S. Menlo Ave., Los Angeles, Calif. 90006. Founded in 1958.

Directed by Norman L. Farberow and Robert E. Litman, this separately incorporated research center, with its own Board of Directors, is affiliated with the School of Medicine at the University of Southern California. It is well staffed with research professionals, supporting professionals, and technicians. Principal fields of research include suicide and its prevention, including psychological, sociological, and medical studies of suicidal phenomena and expressions of self-destruction, also with efficacy of training programs in suicide prevention. It acts as a training and educational center in suicide prevention for professionals and nonprofessionals, through institutes, workshops, and publications. It also acts as a clearinghouse for data and information on suicide prevention. It maintains a library of over five hundred volumes on suicide and self-destruction. It answers queries and provides consulting services and referrals. For more information, consult items 12.104, 12.106, and 12.107. This is a major resource for suicide and suicide prevention information.

12.102 U.S. NATIONAL CLEARING HOUSE FOR MENTAL HEALTH INFORMATION. 5600 Fishers Ln., Rockville, Md. 20857.

A part of the National Institute of Mental Health, this clearinghouse provides information on a wide area of subjects, including suicide, related to mental health. Its broad information/education services include: publications of all types; handling of requests for information; computer services for the scientific and academic communities, including bibliographies and abstracts of mental health literature, as well as audiovisual materials, tailored to meet specific requests; and provision of exhibit and film information.

To locate new research centers, clearinghouses, and special collections in the future, the following sources are provided and described here. Various on-going reference works are available. Although these reference works contained few special resources that were specifically on suicide, future editions of these works should be watched for, as they may provide more specific references for suicide research in the future.

12.103 Ash, Lee, comp. SUBJECT COLLECTIONS, A GUIDE TO SPECIAL BOOK COLLECTIONS AND SUBJECT EMPHASES AS REPORTED BY

UNIVERSITY, COLLEGE, PUBLIC, AND SPECIAL LIBRARIES AND MUSEUMS IN THE UNITED STATES AND CANADA. 5th ed., rev. and enl. New York: R.R. Bowker Co., 1978. x, 1184 p.

Over seventy thousand special collections are listed in this directory. The addresses, number of volumes, budget, and brief description of each collection is provided. Only one suicide special collection is mentioned in this edition, and that erroneously. This work also cites special collections of materials about prominent persons. A number of authors who have committed suicide are mentioned as having special collections by and about them located at one or more centers. Those authors cited (see section 9.1) are Crane, Fletcher, Hemingway, Jarrell, Kees, Lindsay, London, Woolf, and Zweig. Knowing this, work could well be undertaken on the psychological aspects of the lives and works of these persons who ended their lives by suicide.

Consult: Suicide

12.104   ENCYCLOPEDIA OF ASSOCIATIONS. Edited by Nancy Yakes and Denise Akey. 13th ed. 3 vols. Detroit: Gale Research Co., 1979. Annual, with quarterly supplements.

Five local, national, and international organizations concerned with suicide and suicide prevention are listed in this latest edition. It may be possible, by querying the associations, to locate any special collections of materials that these organizations may have. See also item 12.309.

Consult: Suicide

12.105   NATIONAL UNION CATALOG OF MANUSCRIPT COLLECTIONS: BASED ON REPORTS FROM AMERICAN REPOSITORIES OF MANU-SCRIPTS, 1959/61-- . Washington, D.C.: Library of Congress, 1962-- . Annual. Publisher varies. Good subject index, with triennial cumulative indexes.

Nearly forty thousand collections of manuscripts in over one thousand repositories in the United States are described by this work, as of 1977. The number and nature of the manuscripts, the time span, the location, and public accessibility to the materials is given for each collection. A good subject index is included. While there are no collections specifically on suicide, a large number of collections are described that contain materials on seventeen authors who committed suicide (see section 9.1). The authors are Bierce, Crane, Fletcher, Gogol, Hemingway, Jarrell, Kees, Lindsay, London, Matthieson, Mishima, Gerard de Nerval, Plath, Teasdale, Toller, Woolf, and Zweig. Since new collections are formed continually and/or expanded, each triennial index must be searched for new materials.

Consult: Individual authors by name

12.106 RESEARCH CENTERS DIRECTORY. Edited by Archie M. Palmer. 6th ed. Detroit: Gale Research Co., 1979. xi, 1,121 p. Supplements between editions are entitled NEW RESEARCH CENTERS.

A guide to over six thousand university-related and other permanent nonprofit research organizations in nearly all branches of learning in the United States and Canada, this directory has three indexes: an institutional or sponsor index, a title index, and a subject index. The information provided in each listing includes the following: sponsor, address, telephone number, director, date of founding, current status, sources of support, staff, dollar value of research, principal fields of activity, special research facilities, publications, educational activities of the center, and any special library facilities of the center. One suicide research center (12.101) is described. Future editions and supplements of this work should be consulted.

Consult: Suicide

12.107 U.S. Library of Congress. National Referral Center. A DIRECTORY OF INFORMATION RESOURCES IN THE UNITED STATES: SOCIAL SCIENCES. Rev. ed. Washington, D.C.: Government Printing Office, 1973. iv, 700 p. LC1.31:D62/2/1973.

This guide to nearly twenty-five hundred professional societies, historical societies, university and research bureaus and institutes, federal and state agencies, special collections in museums, and individual experts, as well as to technical libraries, information and documents centers, and indexing and abstracting services is arranged alphabetically by agency. Each organization is described briefly, with addresses and telephone numbers, areas of interest, holdings, publications, and information services provided. Only one suicide research center (12.101) was mentioned. Future editions should be watched for.

Consult: Suicide

To keep up with new editions of the above reference works, as well as identifying new similar works as they are acquired in libraries, consult library subject card catalogs under headings such as the following, using the United States as an example:

Associations, Institutions, etc.--United States--Directories
Data libraries--United States--Directories
Information services--United States--Directories
Library resources--United States--Directories

Research--United States--Directories
United States--Learned institutions and societies--Directories

12.2 SOURCES FOR FUNDING OF SUICIDE RESEARCH

Although much needed, it is very difficult to identify sources, either governmental or private, for obtaining grants-in-aid specifically for support of suicide
research or for establishing the types of resources needed which were considered
in section 12.1. The works listed below are the ones which are most widely
used for locating sources of funding for research and demonstration programs in
many fields. However, "suicide" as a specific subject listing in these works
is virtually nonexistent. Therefore one must search under related listings, and
actually must examine carefully and individually the organizations, foundations,
and agencies listed as offering funds in terms of their possible interest in funding research on suicide and suicide prevention. In future editions of the works
described below, it is hoped there will be more interest indicated for funding
in this area. To find future new editions of these works, as well as new similar
works, consult, in the subject card catalog of large libraries, headings such
as those listed below, using the United States as an example:

Endowments--U.S.--Directories
Grants-in-aid--U.S.--Directories
Research grants--U.S.--Directories

12.201   ANNUAL REGISTER OF GRANT SUPPORT. 12th ed. Chicago: Mar-
quis Academic Media, 1978-79. xxiii, 736 p.

> This work contains data on sources of support for research,
> travel and exchange programs, and publication support in
> a variety of fields, from government agencies, public and
> private foundations, and business, professional, and special
> interest organizations throughout the world. Information is
> arranged by disciplines with a subject index, an organiza-
> tion and program index, a geographic index, and a per-
> sonnel index. The following information on each grant-
> making organization is provided: address, telephone num-
> ber, date of founding, major field of interest, nature of
> support, qualifications required of individuals, amount or
> range of funds, total funding, cost-sharing stipulations,
> number of applicants and recipients, application require-
> ments and procedures, closing dates for application, names
> of principal personnel, and other information.
>
> Consult: Mental health

12.202   Charities Aid Foundation. DIRECTORY OF GRANT MAKING TRUSTS.
4th comp. Tonbridge, Engl.: 1975. xv, 1030 p.

> This directory is an official listing of registered charities
> and foundations of Great Britain. Publisher varies.

Special Resources

12.203   Fondazione Giovanni Angelli. GUIDE TO EUROPEAN FOUNDATIONS.
Milan, Italy: Prepared by the Giovanni Angelli Foundation, distributed by Columbia University Press, 1973. 401 p.

Listing foundations in the United Kingdom and the conti-
nent, this work contains information on the founding, purpose, activities, as well as reports on spheres of activities,
finances, and organization of each foundation. Arranged
by county, it includes indexes with references to fields of
activity, persons, and foundation names.

Consult: Mental health
Psychology
Social sciences
Social welfare
Sociology

12.204   FOUNDATION DIRECTORY. Edited by Marianno O. Lewis. 6th ed.
New York: Compiled by the Foundation Center, distributed by Columbia
University Press, 1977. xxix, 661 p. Supplements.

This guide to over twenty-five hundred foundations in the
United States includes the address, date of founding, donor(s),
purpose and activities, assets and expenditures, officers
and directors, for each foundation listed. The directory is
arranged by states, with a subject index, a city and state
index, and personnel and title indexes. Additional information includes a list of regional libraries that have individual foundation reports and also suggestions on how to
write a proposal. A computer search of recent grants in
excess of $5,000 can be made for the associate members.
On-line computer searching is available at libraries and
other information centers with facilities for this. See item
5.301. See also 6.401.

12.205   FOUNDATION GRANTS INDEX, 1970/71--: A CUMULATIVE LIST-
ING OF FOUNDATION GRANTS. New York: Compiled by the
Foundation Center, distributed by Columbia University Press, 1972-- .
Annual.

A computer-generated (see item 5.301) alphabetical listing
of donating foundations by state, this work gives for each
listing the amount granted, the recipient, the purpose of
the grant, and the duration of the grant. There is also a
recipients index, a foundation index, and a subject index
by keyword. This index is cumulated from the Foundation
Center's newsletter, FOUNDATION NEWS, a bimonthly
publication. For computerized searching of this source see
5.301 and 6.401.

12.206   GRANT INFORMATION SYSTEM. Compiled by William K. Wilson;

edited by Betty L. Wilson. Scottsdale, Ariz.: Oryx Press, 1975-- .
4 cumulative quarterly updates per year. Looseleaf. Monthly FACULTY
ALERT BULLETIN.

> This extensive and well-organized system for grant infor-
> mation covers quarterly over fourteen hundred grants in
> eighty-eight academic disciplines. Entries include full de-
> scriptive information about each grant and its sponsoring
> organization, total dollar value, restrictions, special re-
> quirements for applicants, including student or faculty
> status, number of grants available each year with their
> deadline dates; and renewability. All programs are in-
> dexed by grant name and sponsoring organization. The
> grants are listed by deadline within each academic disci-
> pline. See 5.302 for computerized searching of this source.
> See also 12.211.

> Consult: Mental health
> Social sciences
> Social services

12.207 GRANTS REGISTER, 1977-1979. 5th ed. London: St. James Press;
New York: St. Martin's Press, 1976. xxv, 764 p. Biennial.

> Information on financial assistance for advanced training
> for graduate students and postgraduate scholars in the United
> States, Canada, and the United Kingdom, is provided by
> this source. Included are data on scholarships, fellowships,
> research grants, funding for research, grants-in-aid, and
> prizes. Information on each award includes the eligibility
> requirements. Besides a subject index, there is an index
> of awards and one by awarding body.

12.208 INTERNATIONAL FOUNDATION DIRECTORY. Consulting editor,
H.V. Hodson. Detroit: Gale Research Co.; London: Europa Publications, 1974. viii, 396 p.

> Worldwide information on foundations is provided by this
> directory. An index of activities is included.

12.209 U.S. Office of Education. CATALOG OF FEDERAL EDUCATION AS-
SISTANCE PROGRAMS: AN INDEXED GUIDE TO THE FEDERAL GOV-
ERNMENT'S PROGRAMS OFFERING EDUCATIONAL BENEFITS TO THE
AMERICAN PEOPLE. Washington, D.C.: Government Printing Office,
1972-- . Annual. HE19.127:978.

> This directory is difficult to use. Access is by keyword
> index for program grants. Although there is nothing speci-
> fically on suicide in this work at present, it is worth checking
> future editions. Some years there is a small amount of infor-
> mation on suicide research or suicide prevention training grants.

> Consult: Suicide

Special Resources

12.210 U.S. Office of Management and Budget. CATALOG OF FEDERAL
DOMESTIC ASSISTANCE. Washington, D.C.: Government Printing
Office, 1978. Annual with periodic updates. PrEx2.20:978.

> This directory is easier to use than item 12.209 above,
> because of its good subject index. One type of small
> grant for suicide research, in section 13.242 of the cata-
> log, is described, but searching under related subjects in
> the mental health fields may provide other possible sources
> to contact. Future annual editions of this work should be
> consulted.

> Consult: Suicide

12.211 Wilson, William K., and Wilson, Betty L. DIRECTORY OF RESEARCH
GRANTS, 1979. Scottsdale, Ariz.: Oryx Press, 1979. xviii. 334 p.
Annual.

> This is a well-organized and concise directory of over
> twenty-two hundred grant support programs, organized much
> as the GRANT INFORMATION SYSTEM (12.206). Infor-
> mation is provided on grants, contracted fellowships, and
> support programs available from federal and state govern-
> ments, private donors, private foundations and associations,
> and corporations for research, training, and innovative or
> demonstration efforts. Indexing is by grant name, sponsor-
> ing organization, and subject.

> Consult: Mental health
>   Social sciences
>   Social services

12.3 ORGANIZATIONS FOR THE STUDY AND PREVENTION OF SUICIDE: NATIONAL AND INTERNATIONAL

Only a few organizations at the national and international levels whose main
purposes are for the study and prevention of suicide have been identified.

12.301 AMERICAN ASSOCIATION OF SUICIDOLOGY. P.O. Box 3264,
Houston, Tex. 77001.

> Founded in 1967, the membership of this association con-
> sists of over 550 professionals from many helping services,
> such as psychologists, psychiatrists, social workers, nurses,
> health educators, clergy, physicians, directors of suicide
> prevention centers, and others. The association's aim is
> to encourage the study of suicide, suicide prevention and
> related self-destructive behavior, through education, pro-
> grams, and publications. Publications include the quarterly
> SUICIDE AND LIFE THREATENING BEHAVIOR (5.502) and
> its newsletter NEWSLINK (5.502), as well as the proceed-
> ings of its annual conference. A list of suicide prevention

centers is being prepared by the association. The association is affiliated with the INTERNATIONAL ASSOCIATION
FOR SUICIDE PREVENTION (12.302). For more information consult item 12.309 under the title of the association.

12.302 INTERNATIONAL ASSOCIATION FOR SUICIDE PREVENTION. Vienna,
Austria. Charlotte P. Ross, Secretary-General, Suicide Prevention and
Crisis Center, 1811 Trousdale Dr., Burlingame, Calif. 94010.

Founded in 1961, this association has a present membership
of over 850 individuals and societies which further suicide
research and/or participate in prevention programs and activities. It serves somewhat as a clearinghouse for inter-
change of information, literature, and experience on suicide research and prevention programs. It is active in research and training programs, especially in cases requiring
international cooperation. It also convenes international
conferences every two years, and publishes a newsletter entitled VITA. For more information, consult items 12.309
and 12.310.

12.303 SAMARITANS. 17 Uxbridge Road, Slough, Brookshire, England SLI ISN.

This British national organization, with more than 18,500
members, was founded in 1953, with the goal of helping
suicidal and despondent people by befriending them. An
annual report is published. This organization is affiliated
with the INTERNATIONAL ASSOCIATION FOR SUICIDE
PREVENTION (12.302) and TELEPHONIC EMERGENCY HELP
SERVICES (12.305). See item 24.105 for more information
on the Samaritans.

Other national and international organizations, not exclusively concerned with
suicide and suicide prevention, although very much interested in suicide and
suicide prevention, are listed below.

12.304 CONTACT TELEMINISTRIES U.S.A. 900 S. Arlington Ave., Room 125,
Harrisburg, Pa. 17109. Formerly NATIONAL COUNCIL FOR TELE-
PHONE MINISTRIES.

Founded in 1968, this association is a federation of over
eighty-five local centers throughout the nation, and is supported by individuals, foundations, and churches. The
local centers provide assistance by having trained lay persons communicate by telephone with distressed persons. Publications include a newsletter, CONTACT PAPER, semiannually the LIFE LINE INTERNATIONAL NEWSLETTER,
and an annual DIRECTORY OF CENTERS AND SERVICES.
For further information refer to 12.309. See also 24.103
for further information on this type of service.

12.305 TELEPHONIC EMERGENCY HELP SERVICES. 20, Rue du Marche,
CH-1204 Geneva, Switzerland. Formerly INTERNATIONAL FEDERA-
TION FOR SERVICES OF EMERGENCY TELEPHONIC HELP.

This international federation of national associations of
telephone-help services was founded in 1960. It coordi-
nates and disseminates information on help services by
telephone. It sponsors international conferences every three
years. For further information, refer to 12.309 and 12.310.
See also item 24.103 for a summary of this type of service.

12.306 WORLD FEDERATION FOR MENTAL HEALTH. 2075 Westbrook Cres-
cent, University of British Columbia, Vancouver, B.C., Canada V6T
1WS. Formerly INTERNATIONAL COMMITTEE FOR MENTAL HYGIENE.

Founded in 1948, this organization is a federation of almost
150 associations concerned with mental health, including
suicide prevention. The federation engages in charitable,
scientific, literary, and educational activities in these areas.
It publishes a quarterly newsletter. Congresses are convened biennially.

The WORLD HEALTH ORGANIZATION, Geneva, Switzerland, is another international association which has made contributions toward suicide prevention.
It publishes quinquennial bibliographies of its publications. The NATIONAL
INSTITUTE OF MENTAL HEALTH, Rockville, Maryland, has made contributions
toward suicide research and development of suicide prevention programs.

To identify national and international organizations concerned with suicide,
various standard directories should be consulted. These are updated at regular
intervals. Most of these have very few references at the moment, but should
be watched for new associations in the future.

12.307 DIRECTORY OF ASSOCIATIONS IN CANADA. Prepared under the
direction of Brian Land. Toronto and Buffalo: University of Toronto
Press, 1978. 675 p.

This book describes over eleven thousand associations, from
the local level to international groups, functioning in Canada
in the arts, business, trades, labor, and the professions.
The associations are listed alphabetically together with their
addresses and telephone numbers but with no descriptions of
their activities or publications. This work has a subject
index. Although at present no association specifically for
suicide research and prevention is listed, this directory should
be kept in mind for future editions.

12.308 DIRECTORY OF BRITISH ASSOCIATIONS AND ASSOCIATIONS IN
IRELAND. Edited by G.P. Henderson and S.P.A. Henderson. 5th ed.
Beckenham, Kent, Engl.: C.B.D. Research, 1977. xiv, 457 p.

This list of national organizations contains the address, date of formation, telephone number, number of branches, type of organization, activities, membership, titles and cost of publications, and previous name of each organization. At present, only one suicide organization is listed.

Consult: Suicide prevention

12.309 ENCYCLOPEDIA OF ASSOCIATIONS. Edited by Nancy Yakes and Denise Akey. 13th ed. 3 vols. Detroit: Gale Research Co., 1979. Annual, with quarterly supplements.

This guide lists nearly fourteen thousand national and international organizations operating in the United States, including trade, business, legal, governmental, educational, cultural, welfare, public affairs, religious, and citizen groups. Data on each association includes the name, acronym, address, telephone number, chief official, founding date, number of members, staff, the number of state and local affiliates, a description of the purposes and activities of the organization, publications, name changes, time and place of future meetings. Organizations are grouped alphabetically by type of group. There is good subject access through keyword indexes. Keywords are provided in cases where the activity is not indicated in the title. Mostly nonprofit organizations are included. Some regional and local associations are listed when these groups may be of national interest. This is a basic reference work of American associations.

Consult: Suicide
Suicide prevention
Suicidology

12.310 YEARBOOK OF INTERNATIONAL ORGANIZATIONS. Brussels: Union of International Associations, 1948-- . Biennial.

International associations and organizations are surveyed and described in great detail. Dates and places of conferences are given, as are lists of publications. Good indexes are provided. This is a basic source for information on international organizations.

Consult: Suicide

As noted in this section, many professional associations and organizations publish newsletters for their constituencies. The following source is basic for identifying these.

12.311 NATIONAL DIRECTORY OF NEWSLETTERS AND REPORTING SERVICES. Edited by Robert C. Thomas. 2d ed. Detroit: Gale Research Co., 1978-- . To be in 4 pts. In progress.

Bulletins and newsletters issued by businesses, associations, and government agencies are described in full detail. Each of the four parts contains approximately 750 items.

Also the sources in items 12.309 and 12.310 can be used to identify the publications, including newsletters, of relevant organizations.

The following sources are useful for identifying future meetings to be held on the various aspects of suicide.

12.312 WORLD MEETINGS: OUTSIDE U.S.A. AND CANADA. Prepared by the World Meeting Information Center, distributed by Macmillan Information, 1968-- . Completely updated quarterly issues.

> Meetings planned to take place within the next two years are registered by this service. Full information on plans for the meetings are given, which includes sponsors, source of general information, sections and short meetings scheduled, number of papers to be presented, projected attendance, availability of abstracts or papers, and data on exhibits. Five indexes are helpful: date of the meeting, keyword, location, abstract or paper, and sponsor.

> Consult: Suicide

12.313 WORLD MEETINGS: UNITED STATES AND CANADA. Prepared by the World Meeting Information Center, distributed by Macmillan Information, 1963-- . Completely updated quarterly issues.

> This work has the same arrangement as item 12.312 above.

> Consult: Suicide

Items 12.309 and 12.310 provide information on upcoming meetings of suicide organizations on national and international levels.

12.4 CONFERENCES AND CONFERENCE PROCEEDINGS ON SUICIDE: NATIONAL AND INTERNATIONAL

Most national and international professional and service organizations have conferences or congresses periodically, usually from one to three years apart. The proceedings and papers of the conferences are usually published within a year after each conference ends. However, in some cases, publication of the proceedings and papers may be delayed, for various reasons, until two to five years after the conference, even up to ten years in rare cases. This seriously affects dissemination of the information from the conference. This lag should be kept in mind when one is searching for the proceedings of conferences. In the meanwhile, the newsletters and journals of the organizations provide some information on the conferences.

One can expect that, for organizations such as those in items 12.301 and 12.302 whose main purposes are to further suicide research and prevention, the conferences and the published proceedings and paper will be on suicide research and prevention. Therefore, the researcher or investigator can keep up with developments in these areas by attending the conferences and securing the published proceedings, and other materials from the organization. Other national and international organizations, such as described in item 12.306, have suicide as only one out of many related areas of interest. Occasionally they may devote an entire conference to the study of suicide and suicidal behavior; or they may have several papers given per meeting on suicide out of perhaps sixty papers presented. These may be very significant, but they may be "lost" in the published proceedings and papers of the conference, unless certain indexing sources are used to locate them.

Principal sources for locating information on suicide from published conference proceedings and papers are described in this section.

12.401 CONFERENCE PAPERS INDEX. Louisville, Ky.: Data Courier, 1973-- .
Monthly, with cumulative quarterly and annual indexes.

This index provides the scientific, technical, and medical professions with the latest ongoing research and development information provided at meetings throughout the world. This source largely overcomes the time lag mentioned above, with information appearing within weeks after the worldwide conferences have ended. This is because the information included in the index is taken from the final programs or abstract publications of conferences, supplemented by responses to questionnaires sent by the CPI staff. Indexes provided are a subject index (each title is indexed under an average of five subject headings chosen by computer), an author index, date of meeting index, and an index by World Meetings Registry Number (from 12.312 and 12.313). This is a good source for conference papers on suicide, within its scope. This source can be computer searched; refer to items 5.301 and 5.302.

Consult: Suicide

12.402 DIRECTORY OF PUBLISHED PROCEEDINGS. Series SSH-SOCIAL SCIENCES/HUMANITIES. Harrison, N.Y.: InterDok Corp., 1968-- .
Quarterly, with annual cumulated index.

The published proceedings of congresses, conferences, symposia, meetings, seminars, and summer schools that have been held around the world are indexed in this directory. The contents are arranged in chronological order, giving the source, location, topic, and cost of the printed proceedings. There are indexes for the subject/sponsor, editor, and location of the published proceedings. The October issue contains the cumulated index.

Consult: Suicide

Special Resources

12.403 INDEX TO SCIENTIFIC AND TECHNICAL PROCEEDINGS. Philadelphia: Institute for Scientific Information, 1978-- . Monthly, with semiannual cumulations.

This work indexes approximately three thousand published proceedings a year, including over ninety thousand conference papers, from conferences throughout the world. It covers all forms of proceedings, including those in periodicals, multiauthored books, and report series. Proceedings appear in this index within one or two months of their receipt by ISI. Special issue indexes include category index of conference topics, subject index by title-words, author/editor index, sponsor index, meeting location index, and organizational affiliates of the author.

Consult: The list of words in item 5.133, remembering these may change over time, and new ones added.

12.404 INDEX TO SOCIAL SCIENCES AND HUMANITIES PROCEEDINGS. Philadelphia: Institute for Scientific Information, 1979-- . In progress.

This will be very similar to item 12.403 above in format and organization.

12.405 PROCEEDINGS IN PRINT. Arlington, Mass.: 1964-- . 6 issues per year, with an annual cumulated index.

An index to the proceedings of conferences, symposia, lecture series, congresses, hearings, seminars, courses, colloquia, and meetings in all languages on all subjects, this work is arranged by title of the conference, and indexed by editor, subject, and sponsor. It also gives the source, address, and cost when available. Prior to 1967, this directory indexed only proceedings on aerospace technology.

Consult: Suicide

The following ongoing works also index selected proceedings: BIORESEARCH INDEX (5.104), EDUCATION INDEX (5.111), RESOURCES IN EDUCATION (6.302), SCIENCE CITATION INDEX (5.133), SOCIAL SCIENCES CITATION INDEX (5.134), and SOCIOLOGICAL ABSTRACTS (5.225).

Part II

SELECTED REFERENCES ON THEORIES OF SUICIDE

Chapter 13
CLASSIFYING SUICIDAL BEHAVIORS

Theories of suicide vary according to the manner in which suicidologists classify and define suicide and suicidal behaviors. Although it may seem clear to the layman what is suicidal behavior and what is not, suicidologists have a great deal of difficulty in agreeing on this among themselves. There are four main issues involved in this disagreement.

13.1 COMPLETED SUICIDE VERSUS ATTEMPTED SUICIDE

Completed suicide refers to actions where the person actually dies. Attempted suicide refers to actions where the person survives the suicidal attempt. The following articles discuss relationships between the two behaviors.

13.101   Davis, Frederick B. "The Relationship between Suicide and Attempted Suicide." PSYCHIATRIC QUARTERLY 41 (October 1967): 752-65.

Refer to 13.105.

13.102   Kreitman, Norman; Philip, A.E.; Greer, Stephen; and Bagley, C.R. "Parasuicide." BRITISH JOURNAL OF PSYCHIATRY 115 (June 1969): 746-47.

Kreitman and his colleagues in the United Kingdom suggest renaming the behavior of attempted suicide as "parasuicide," to stress the fact that, although attempted suicide appears to be similar to completed suicide, it is not similar. It is merely mimicking completed suicide.

13.103   Lester, David. "Relation between Attempted Suicide and Completed Suicide." PSYCHOLOGICAL REPORTS 27 (December 1970): 719-22.

Lester argues that completed suicide and attempted suicide are similar behaviors, differing only in the lethality of the action. He argues that one can learn about completed suicides by studying attempted suicides, an important point since it is easier to study the latter as they remain alive.

Classifying Suicidal Behaviors

13.104   Lester, David; Beck, Aaron T.; and Trexler, Larry. "Extrapolation from Attempted Suicides to Completed Suicides." JOURNAL OF ABNORMAL PSYCHOLOGY 84 (October 1975): 563-66.

Lester and his colleagues illustrate his argument in an empirical manner, trying to show that it is possible to make generalizations about completed suicides from a study of attempted suicides.

13.105   Wilkins, James. "Suicidal Behavior." AMERICAN SOCIOLOGICAL REVIEW 32 (April 1967): 286-98.

Wilkins and Davis (13.101) review available evidence and conclude that, although there is some overlap, the two behaviors of completed and attempted suicide are best viewed as different behaviors.

13.2 GENERAL SELF-DESTRUCTIVE BEHAVIOR AS SUICIDE

There is a good deal of disagreement as to which self-destructive behaviors should be classified as suicidal. If the broad view is taken, then research can be conducted on a wide variety of behaviors in order to learn about suicide.

13.201   Farberow, Norman L.; Stein, Kenneth; Darbonne, Allen; and Hirsch, Sophie. "Indirect Self-Destructive Behavior in Diabetic Patients." HOSPITAL MEDICINE 6 (May 1970): 123-33.

These investigators studied diabetic patients who were remiss in taking their medication.

13.202   Goldstein, Kurt. HUMAN NATURE IN THE LIGHT OF PSYCHOPATHOLOGY. Cambridge, Mass.: Harvard University Press, 1940. 258 p.

Goldstein takes a very narrow view as to what constitutes suicide. He believes that a person must know the effects of his self-destructive actions and intend to die before his death can be called suicide.

13.203   Lester, David. "Self-Mutilating Behavior." PSYCHOLOGICAL BULLETIN 78 (August 1972): 119-28.

In this article, Lester reviews research on the various kinds of self-mutilating behavior and looks for parallels with true suicidal behavior.

13.204   Menninger, Karl. MAN AGAINST HIMSELF. New York: Harcourt, Brace & World, 1938. 429 p.

Menninger takes a very broad view of suicide and classi-
fies self-mutilating behavior as suicidal (focal suicide) as
well as long-term self-destructive behaviors such as alcoholism (chronic suicide).

13.205 Roberts, Albert R. SELF-DESTRUCTIVE BEHAVIOR. Springfield, Ill.:
Charles Thomas, 1975. 215 p.

Chapters in this book examine the suicidal motivations involved in auto accidents, drug abuse, alcoholism, and obesity.

13.206 Tabachnick, Norman, ed. ACCIDENT OR SUICIDE? DESTRUCTION
BY AUTOMOBILE. Springfield, Ill.: Charles Thomas, 1973. 262 p.

13.207 Tabachnick, Norman; Litman, Robert E.; Osman, Marvin; Jones, War-
ren L.; Cohn, Jay; Kasper, August; and Moffat, John. "Comparative
Psychiatric Study of Accidental and Suicidal Deaths." ARCHIVES OF
GENERAL PSYCHIATRY 14 (January 1966): 60-68.

Many car crashes of people alone in their cars are thought
to be suicide attempts. In this study, Tabachnick and his
colleagues compare the psychological characteristics of true
suicides and single car crash fatalities.

13.3 TAXONOMIES OF SUICIDE AND DEATH

A number of investigators have expressed dissatisfaction with the way in which
we classify death in general, and suicide in particular. Several alternative
classifications have been proposed.

13.301 Beck, Aaron T.; Davis, Joseph H.; Frederick, Calvin J.; Perlin,
Seymour; Pokorny, Alex; Schulman, Robert E.; Seiden, Richard H.;
and Wittlin, Byron J. "Classification and Nomenclature." In SUI-
CIDE PREVENTION IN THE SEVENTIES, edited by H.L.P. Resnick
and Berkley Hathorne, pp. 7-12. Washington, D.C.: Government
Printing Office, 1972. HE20.2402:Su 3.

This publication reports the results of a conference on the
classification of suicidal behavior. The report represents
the conclusion of the committee.

13.302 Kalish, Richard A. "A Continuum of Subjectively Perceived Death."
GERONTOLOGIST 6 (June 1966): 73-76.

Here Kalish proposes a distinction between different kinds
of death, defining the states of biological, psychological,
social, and anthropological death.

13.303   Pokorny, Alex D. "A Scheme for Classifying Suicidal Behaviors."
         In THE PREDICTION OF SUICIDE, edited by Aaron T. Beck, H.L.P.
         Resnick, and D.J. Lettieri, pp. 29-44. Bowie, Md.:   Charles Press,
         1974.

         Pokorny, who was also a member of the committee which
         authored item 13.301, here described his view as to what
         the standardized nomenclature should be for suicidal be-
         haviors.

13.304   Shneidman, Edwin S. "Classifications of Suicidal Phenomena." BUL-
         LETIN OF SUICIDOLOGY (July 1968): 1-9.

13.305   _____. "Orientation toward Cessation." JOURNAL OF FORENSIC
         SCIENCES 13 (January 1968): 33-45.

         In these articles (13.304 and 13.305), Shneidman proposes
         a new classification for all death and an alternative clas-
         sification for suicidal behavior that is based upon the per-
         son's motivations.

13.4 CERTIFICATION AND CLASSIFICATION OF DEATH

Social scientists studying suicide commonly make use of decisions made by coroners and medical examiners as to which deaths were suicide and which were
not. A good deal of research has been done on this decision process.

13.401   Barraclough, Brian M. "The Effect that Coroners Have on the Suicide
         Rate and the Open Verdict Rate." In PSYCHIATRIC EPIDEMIOLOGY,
         edited by E.H. Hare and J.K. Wing, pp. 361-65. London: Oxford
         University Press, 1970.

         Refer to 13.407.

13.402   Barraclough, Brian M.; Holding, Trevor; and Fayers, Peter. "Influence
         of Coroners' Officers and Pathologists on Suicide Verdicts." BRITISH
         JOURNAL OF PSYCHIATRY 128 (May 1976): 471-74.

         This study showed that certification of a death as suicide
         or not as suicide in England did not depend upon the par-
         ticular investigating officer, nor on the pathologist who
         conducted the autopsy.

13.403   Brooke, Eileen M. SUICIDE AND ATTEMPTED SUICIDE. Geneva:
         World Health Organization, 1974. 127 p.

         In this book, medical examiners from several European na-
         tions are given the same cases of death to certify and dif-
         ferences in their decisions are examined. English and

Danish methods are compared in detail using selected cases, and it is found that English coroners prefer open verdicts more than Danish coroners.

13.404   Curphey, Theodore J.   "The Psychological Autopsy."   BULLETIN OF SUICIDOLOGY (July 1968): 39-45.

A medical examiner discusses the process of the psychological autopsy which is an aid in certifying the mode of death.   In a psychological autopsy, a team of social scientists tries to reconstruct the behaviors and psychological state of the deceased in order to ascertain whether the behavior and state of the deceased prior to death resembled that of the suicidal person. In this way, for example, a drug death can be more accurately classified as accidental, murder, or suicide.

13.405   Douglas, Jack D. THE SOCIAL MEANINGS OF SUICIDE. Princeton, N.J.: Princeton University Press, 1967. 398 p.

Douglas reviews the differences from region to region, both within and between countries, on certifying death. As a result he argues that official statistics on suicide from different regions are simply not comparable. Medical examiners do not follow standardized procedures. If deaths cannot be certified accurately, and if psychological autopsies are rarely carried out, then official statistics may be quite inaccurate.

13.406   Litman, R.E.; Curphey, Theodore; Shneidman, Edwin; Farberow, Norman; and Tabachnick, Norman.   "Investigations of Equivocal Suicides." JOURNAL OF THE AMERICAN MEDICAL ASSOCIATION 184 (22 June 1963): 924-29.

Here the staff of the Los Angeles Suicide Prevention Center and the Medical Examiner discuss the contributions that a suicide prevention center can make to the accurate certification of death.

13.407   Sainsbury, Peter, and Barraclough, Brian M.   "Differences between Suicide Rates." NATURE (London) 220 (21 December 1968): 1252.

In this article and in item 13.401, Barraclough and his colleague produce evidence to indicate that differences in the certification of death from one locale to another do not appear to have much of an effect on the suicide rate reported.

13.408   Stengel, E., and Farberow, Norman L.   "Certification of Suicide around the World."   In International Conference for Suicide Prevention,

4th, 1967, PROCEEDINGS, edited by Norman L. Farberow, pp. 8-15. Los Angeles: Suicide Prevention Center, 1968.

In this article, the authors compare how deaths are certified and the criteria used in different countries.

13.409 Weisman, Avery, and Kastenbaum, Robert. THE PSYCHOLOGICAL AUTOPSY. Community Mental Health Monograph, no. 4. New York: Behavioral Publications, 1968. 59 p.

In order to carry out a psychological autopsy, a number of standardized procedures have been described. Weisman is one of the leaders in this field, and this monograph describes his techniques, in which a team of mental health professionals can conduct an analysis of the last few weeks of a deceased person's life in order to come to some conclusions about the circumstances leading to his death.

Chapter 14
SOCIOLOGICAL THEORIES OF SUICIDE

Sociologists have proposed a number of theories of suicide. These theories tend to be more formal than the psychological theories. Typically, the sociologist makes more clear his assumptions, postulates, and formal deductions. There have been three major theories (Durkheim, Gibbs and Martin, and Henry and Short) with a large number of critical contributions to these theories, and two minor theories (Douglas and Palmer).

14.1 THE MAJOR AND MINOR SOCIOLOGICAL THEORIES OF SUICIDE

14.101   Douglas, Jack D.   THE SOCIAL MEANINGS OF SUICIDE.   Princeton, N.J.:   Princeton University Press, 1967.   398 p.

> Douglas advances a theory that focuses upon the meaning of the word "suicide" in a society, rather than upon its rate of occurrence.

14.102   Durkheim, Emile.   SUICIDE.   Edited by G. Simpson.   Translated by J.A. Spaulding and G. Simpson.   Glencoe, Ill.:   Free Press, 1951.   405 p.

> This is the earliest theory of suicide proposed by a sociologist which still has contemporary relevance.   This relevance is ensured by the importance of Durkheim's thought for modern sociology.

14.103   Gibbs, Jack P., and Martin, Walter T.   STATUS INTEGRATION AND SUICIDE.   Eugene: University of Oregon Press, 1964.   225 p.

> This work is a simplified and more quantitative version of Durkheim's theory, and it is now recognized as a theory in its own right.

14.104   Henry, Andrew F., and Short, James F.   SUICIDE AND HOMICIDE. New York: Free Press, 1954.   214 p.

This theory is quite different from that of Durkheim, and and is noteworthy for its attempt to include and reconcile both sociological and psychological theories and for its attempts to test the theory with empirical evidence.

14.105 Palmer, Stuart. THE VIOLENT SOCIETY. New Haven, Conn.: College and University Press, 1972. 223 p.

A sociological theory of suicide is presented that tries to incorporate previous theories under two main concepts: the degree to which a person is integrated into a society and the degree to which his interactions with others are reciprocal. Palmer applied this theory to suicide and homicide, tries to show that it encompasses previous theories, and explains the variation of suicide rates with sociological variables.

14.2 CRITIQUES OF SOCIOLOGICAL THEORIES OF SUICIDE

Several writers have reviewed sociological theories of suicide in general and have made comments and evaluations of them.

14.201 Douglas, Jack D. THE SOCIAL MEANINGS OF SUICIDE. Princeton, N.J.: Princeton University Press, 1967. 398 p.

14.202 Lester, David. WHY PEOPLE KILL THEMSELVES. Springfield, Ill.: Charles Thomas, 1972. 353 p.

14.203 Wilkins, James. "Suicidal Behavior." AMERICAN SOCIOLOGICAL REVIEW 32 (April 1967): 286-98.

There have been several major critical articles on Durkheim's theory (14.102):

14.204 Dohrenwend, Bruce P. "Egoism, Altruism, Anomie, and Fatalism." AMERICAN SOCIOLOGICAL REVIEW 24 (August 1959): 466-73.

14.205 Ginsberg, Ralph B. "Anomie and Aspirations: A Reinterpretation of Durkheim's Theory." Unpublished Ph.D. dissertation, Columbia University, 1966. (DAI 27/11A, p. 3945). 67-05820.

14.206 Johnson, Barclay D. "Durkheim's One Cause of Suicide." AMERICAN SOCIOLOGICAL REVIEW 30 (December 1965): 875-86.

14.207 Powell, Elwin H. "Occupation Status and Suicide." AMERICAN SOCIOLOGICAL REVIEW 23 (April 1958): 131-39.

There have also been two systematic attempts to test the validity of Durkheim's theory (14.102) empirically:

14.208   Miley, James D., and Micklin, Michael. "Structural Change and the Durkheimian Legacy." AMERICAN JOURNAL OF SOCIOLOGY 78 (November 1972): 657-73.

This reports an attempt to test Durkheim's theory of suicide with data from a sample of modern nations.

14.209   Rootman, Irving. "A Cross-Cultural Note on Durkheim's Theory of Suicide." LIFE THREATENING BEHAVIOR 3 (Summer 1973): 83-94.

A test of whether social regulation and social integration do affect the suicide rate of primitive cultures in the way that Durkheim proposed that they would.

There have been several articles critical of the theory proposed by Gibbs and Martin (14.103):

14.210   Chambliss, William J., and Steele, Marion F. "Status Integration and Suicide." AMERICAN SOCIOLOGICAL REVIEW 31 (August 1966): 524-32.

14.211   Hagedorn, Robert, and Labovitz, Sanford. "A Note on Status Integration and Suicide." SOCIAL PROBLEMS 14 (Summer 1966): 79-84.

Replies by Gibbs and Martin include:

14.212   Gibbs, Jack P., and Martin, Walter T. "On Assessing the Theory of Status Integration and Suicide." AMERICAN SOCIOLOGICAL REVIEW 31 (August 1966): 533-41.

Several critiques of the theory proposed by Henry and Short (14.104) include:

14.213   Lester, David. "Henry and Short on Suicide." JOURNAL OF PSYCHOLOGY 70 (November 1968): 179-86.

14.214   Maris, Ronald W. SOCIAL FORCES IN URBAN SUICIDE. Homewood, Ill.: Dorsey, 1969. 214 p.

In addition, book reviews of these major theories have appeared in AMERICAN SOCIOLOGICAL REVIEW and in THE AMERICAN JOURNAL OF SOCIOLOGY, as well as other sociological journals. These reviews will incorporate critiques of the theories. Refer to section 3.5 for sources of book reviews.

Chapter 15
PSYCHOLOGICAL THEORIES OF SUICIDE

The major psychological theory of suicide is proposed by Freud, and it is by far the dominant psychological viewpoint about suicide. Although Freud himself did not formally address himself to suicide in detail, other psychoanalysts have formulated a theory of suicide based upon his general theory of human behavior.

15.1 SIGMUND FREUD AND PSYCHOANALYSIS

15.101   Friedman, Paul, ed. ON SUICIDE. New York: International Universities Press, 1967. 141 p.

   This includes the discussions of the Vienna Psychoanalytic Society in a symposium in 1910, with contributions from Sigmund Freud and other psychoanalysts.

15.102   Litman, Robert E. "Sigmund Freud on Suicide." BULLETIN OF SUICIDOLOGY (July 1968): 11–23.

15.103   _____. "Sigmund Freud on Suicide." PSYCHOANALYTIC FORUM I (1966): 206–21.

   Litman conducted a search through Freud's writings and extracted Freud's statements about suicide. Litman then organized these into a coherent theory.

15.104   Meerloo, Joost A.M. SUICIDE AND MASS SUICIDE. New York: Grune & Stratton, 1962. 153 p.

   Some thoughts on aspects of suicidal behavior are presented by a psychoanalyst.

15.105   Menninger, Karl. MAN AGAINST HIMSELF. New York: Harcourt, Brace & World, 1938. 429 p.

   This is an excellent account of suicidal behavior by a leading psychoanalyst.

15.2 OTHER VIEWPOINTS

15.201 Farber, Maurice L. THEORY OF SUICIDE. New York: Funk &
Wagnalls, 1968. 115 p.

A modern theory of suicide based primarily upon the psychological concept of hope and the social variable of
available resources for the distressed person.

15.202 Farberow, Norman L. "Crisis, Disaster, and Suicide." In ESSAYS
IN SELF-DESTRUCTION, edited by Edwin S. Shneidman, pp. 373-98.
New York: Science House, 1967.

Refer to item 15.206.

15.203 Henry, Andrew F., and Short, James F. SUICIDE AND HOMICIDE.
New York: Free Press, 1954. 214 p.

Henry and Short proposed what is primarily a sociological
theory of suicide. But included in their book is an excellent account of the psychological factors that might lead
people to internalize their aggression (as in suicidal behavior) rather than externalize their aggression (as in homicidal behavior). See also item 14.104.

15.204 Hillman, James. SUICIDE AND THE SOUL. London: Hodder and
Stoughton, 1964. 191 p.

This is an analysis of suicidal behavior written from the
framework of Carl Jung's theory of human behavior.

15.205 Leonard, Calista V. UNDERSTANDING AND PREVENTING SUICIDE.
Springfield, Ill.: Charles Thomas, 1967. 351 p.

A theory of suicide is proposed here that is based on the
description of three different kinds of suicidal individuals,
with a clinical description of the developmental factors
that lead to these styles of behavior.

15.206 Tabachnick, Norman. "The Crisis Treatment of Suicide." CALIFOR-
NIA MEDICINE 112 (June 1970): 1-8.

The staff of the Los Angeles Suicide Prevention Center
were the first group to view suicidal behavior from the
standpoint of crisis theory. In this article and in item
15.202, two different members of the staff present their
viewpoint.

See also item 22.201.

Part III

SELECTED REFERENCES ON SOCIAL AND
ENVIRONMENTAL CORRELATES OF SUICIDE

Chapter 16
SOCIOLOGICAL AND ENVIRONMENTAL VARIABLES

This chapter focuses on the study of variables that are of most interest to sociologists, although research into suicidal behavior usually transcends the artificial barriers set up by social scientists between their different disciplines. The studies listed typically examine the suicide rates in different social categories (e.g., males and females, single and married people), and the differences in the suicidal behaviors of these various social categories.

16.1 GENERAL EPIDEMIOLOGICAL SURVEYS

16.101   Kramer, Morton; Pollak, Earl S.; Redick, Richard W.; and Locke, Ben Z. MENTAL DISORDERS/SUICIDE. Cambridge: Harvard University Press, 1972. 301 p.

> An excellent epidemiological study of suicide that examines recent trends in the United States and the relationship of suicide rates and methods for committing suicide with such variables as sex, age, geographic region, marital status, social class, religion, mental illness and migration.

16.102   Schwab, John J.; Warheit, George J.; and Holzer, Charles E. "Suicidal Ideation and Behavior in a General Population." DISEASES OF THE NERVOUS SYSTEM 33 (November 1972): 745-48.

> The only survey to ascertain the frequency of suicidal ideation and suicide attempts in a population, a county in Florida. They also explore the demographic variables that are associated with these frequencies.

16.2 SPECIFIC VARIABLES

Age—General

16.201   Massey, James T. SUICIDE IN THE UNITED STATES, 1950-1964.

th Publication no. 100, series 20, no. 5. Washington,
. Public Health Series, 1967. FS 2.85/2:20/5. 34 p.

provides accurate data, for the United States and
rate states, that permit conclusions about how the
rate varies with age in whites and nonwhites and
in males and females.

Age—The Young

16.202 Finch, Stuart M., and Poznanski, Elva O. ADOLESCENT SUICIDE.
Springfield, Ill.: Charles Thomas, 1971. 66 p.

>A brief review for professionals of some factors and issues
associated with suicide in adolescents.

16.203 Glaser, Kurt. "Suicidal Children." AMERICAN JOURNAL OF PSY-
CHOTHERAPY 25 (January 1971): 27-36.

>A discussion of suicide in children with particular attention
paid to causes and treatment.

16.204 Haim, Andre. ADOLESCENT SUICIDE. New York: International
Universities Press, 1974. 310 p.

>A thorough and competent review of knowledge about sui-
cidal behavior in adolescents.

16.205 Jacobs, Jerry. ADOLESCENT SUICIDE. New York: Wiley, 1971.
147 p.

>This book reviews the literature on suicidal behavior in
adolescents and presents the results of an analysis of those
factors that lead to suicide in adolescents. The study reported in the book is one of the best conducted on suicidal
behavior in youth.

16.206 Klagsbrun, Francine. TOO YOUNG TO DIE. Boston: Houghton-
Mifflin, 1976. 201 p.

>A discussion of suicidal behavior in children, written for
the educated layman.

16.207 McAnarney, Elizabeth R. "Suicidal Behavior in Children and Youth."
PEDIATRIC CLINICS OF NORTH AMERICA 22 (August 1975): 595-604.

>A discussion of the incidence, prevention, and management
of suicide in children. Cases are included.

16.208   Seiden, Richard H. SUICIDE AMONG YOUTH: A REVIEW OF THE
LITERATURE, 1900-1967. A supplement to the BULLETIN OF SUI-
CIDOLOGY. Chevy Chase, Md.: National Institute of Mental
Health, 1969. Public Health Service Publication, no. 1971. 62 p.
HE 20.2413/2:Y8.

This book contains an excellent review of information about
suicidal behavior in youth.

16.209   Toolan, James M. "Suicide in Children and Adolescents." AMERICAN
JOURNAL OF PSYCHOTHERAPY 29 (July 1975): 339-44.

A discussion of the symptoms of suicidal preoccupation in
children and possibilities for treatment.

See also section 6.219

Age—The Old

16.210   Bock, E. Wilbur, and Webber, Irving L. "Social Status and Rela-
tional System of Elderly Suicides." LIFE THREATENING BEHAVIOR
2 (Fall 1972): 145-59.

16.211   _____. "Suicide among the Elderly." JOURNAL OF MARRIAGE
AND THE FAMILY 34 (February 1972): 24-31.

A study of suicide in the elderly and the variables that
affect the likelihood of suicidal behavior, such as widowhood, social class and the strength of social relationships.

16.212   Farberow, Norman L., and Moriwaki, Sharon Y. "Self-destructive
Crises in the Older Person." GERONTOLOGIST 15 (August 1975):
333-37.

A good discussion of suicidal behavior in the elderly, with
cases and suggestions for agency intervention.

16.213   Farberow, Norman L., and Shneidman, Edwin S. "Suicide and Age."
In CLUES TO SUICIDE, edited by Edwin S. Shneidman and Norman L.
Farberow, pp. 41-49. New York: McGraw-Hill, 1957.

Farberow and Shneidman explore the different motives for
suicide in people of different ages.

Race

16.214   Bagley, Christopher, and Greer, Steven S. "Black Suicide." JOUR-
NAL OF SOCIAL PSYCHOLOGY 86 (April 1972): 175-79.

A study of attempted suicide among blacks and whites in England that throws doubts on the conclusions drawn by Hendin (16.215).

16.215 Hendin, Herbert. BLACK SUICIDE. New York: Basic Books, 1969. 176 p.

Hendin makes some suggestions as to the motives and circumstances that characterize suicidal behavior in American blacks.

16.216 Massey, James T. SUICIDE IN THE UNITED STATES 1950-1964. Public Health Publication no. 100, series 20, no. 5. Washington, D.C.: U.S. Public Health Service, 1967. 34 p. FS 2.85/2:20/5.

Massey reports accurate suicide rates for whites and nonwhites in the United States during 1950-64.

See also sections 6.202 and 6.205.

Sex

16.217 Beck, Aaron T.; Lester, David; and Kovacs, Maria. "Attempted Suicide by Males and Females." PSYCHOLOGICAL REPORTS 33 (December 1973): 965-66.

Refer to item 16.218.

16.218 Davis, Frederick B. "Sex Differences in Suicide and Attempted Suicide." DISEASES OF THE NERVOUS SYSTEM 29 (March 1968): 193-94.

These two articles (16.217 and 16.218) examine differences in the characteristics of male and female suicidal people.

16.219 Gove, Walter. "Sex, Marital Status and Suicide." JOURNAL OF HEALTH AND SOCIAL BEHAVIOR 13 (June 1972): 204-13.

Gove examines the role of social stress on females and males and proposes that marriage insulates men more than women from suicidal inclinations.

16.220 Lester, David. "Suicidal Behavior in Men and Women." MENTAL HYGIENE 53 (July 1969): 340-45.

Refer to item 16.221.

16.221 _____. "Suicide." In GENDER AND DISORDERED BEHAVIOR, edited by Edith Gomberg, and V. Franks. New York: Brunner-Mazel, forthcoming.

In these two articles (16.220 and 16.221) Lester reviews research findings on the reasons for the difference in the suicide rates between males and females.

16.222   Linehan, Marsha M.   "Suicide and Attempted Suicide."   PERCEPTUAL AND MOTOR SKILLS 37 (August 1973):   31-34.

Linehan examines the attitudes of people toward suicidal behavior and concludes that completed suicide is seen as a masculine behavior whereas attempted suicide is seen as a feminine behavior.   These attitudes may shape behavior.

16.223   Wetzel, Richard D., and McClure, James N.   "Suicide and the Menstrual Cycle."   COMPREHENSIVE PSYCHIATRY 13 (July-August 1972): 369-74.

Some theories of the difference in suicidal behavior of men and women are based on biological differences.   This paper reviews work and presents data on the relationship between the menstrual cycle in women and fluctuations in their suicidal inclinations.

See also section 6.214

Religion

See section 6.218

Social Condemnation of Suicide

16.224   Douglas, Jack D.   THE SOCIAL MEANING OF SUICIDE. Princeton, N.J.:   Princeton University Press, 1967.   398 p.

Douglas argues that social views on suicide are likely to affect whether deaths are recorded accurately as suicide or not.

16.225   Farber, Maurice L.   THEORY OF SUICIDE. New York: Funk and Wagnalls, 1968.   115 p.

Farber explores the possibility that the negative views held by members of a society toward suicide may reduce the suicide rate.

Social Class

16.226   Maris, Ronald W.   SOCIAL FORCES IN URBAN SUICIDE. Homewood, Ill.:   Dorsey, 1969.   214 p.

The suicide rates of people from different social classes in Chicago are reported.

16.227 Porterfield, Austin L., and Gibbs, Jack P. "Occupational Prestige and Social Mobility of Suicides in New Zealand." AMERICAN JOURNAL OF SOCIOLOGY 66 (September 1960): 147-52.

The suicide rates of people from different social classes in New Zealand are reported.

16.228 Stengel, Erwin. SUICIDE AND ATTEMPTED SUICIDE. Baltimore: Penguin, 1964. 135 p.

Stengel provides data on the suicide rates on people from different social classes in England.

Social Mobility

16.229 Breed, Warren. "Occupational Mobility and Suicide among White Males." AMERICAN SOCIOLOGICAL REVIEW 28 (April 1963): 179-88.

Refer to item 16.230.

16.230 Porterfield, Austin L., and Gibbs, Jack P. "Occupational Prestige and Social Mobility of Suicides in New Zealand." AMERICAN JOURNAL OF SOCIOLOGY 66 (September 1960): 147-52.

These reports (16.229 and 16.230) examine whether suicidal persons are more likely to undergo a change in social class or social status during their lifetime than are nonsuidical persons, and whether they experience change in social class or social status from that of their fathers.

Rural-Urban Residence

16.231 Capstick, Alan. "Urban and Rural Suicide." JOURNAL OF MENTAL SCIENCE 106 (October 1960): 1327-36.

Capstick studied the differences in the urban and rural suicide rates in Wales, and reports that the urban rate is usually higher.

16.232 Schroeder, W. Widrick, and Beegle, J. Allen. "Suicide." RURAL SOCIOLOGY 18 (March 1953): 45-52.

A study conducted in Michigan indicates that the rural suicide rate is higher than the urban suicide rate.

Sociological and Environmental Variables

16.233 Shneidman, Edwin S., and Farberow, Norman L. "A Socio-Psychological Investigation of Suicide." In PERSPECTIVES ON PERSONALITY RESEARCH, edited by Henry P. David and J.C. Brengelmann, pp. 270-93. New York: Springer, 1960.

> Shneidman and Farberow classified the different parts of Los Angeles by type of community and social class and describe the kinds of suicidal behaviors that are found in each area.

Community Growth

16.234 Lynn, R. "National Rates of Economic Growth, Anxiety and Suicide." NATURE 222 (May 3, 1969): 494.

> Refer to item 16.235.

16.235 Quinney, Richard. "Suicide, Homicide, and Economic Development." SOCIAL FORCES (March 1965): 401-8.

> These two studies (16.234 and 16.235) compare nations with increasing and decreasing rates of industrialization and urbanization for their suicide rates.

16.236 Wechsler, Henry. "Community Growth, Depressive Disorders, and Suicide." AMERICAN JOURNAL OF SOCIOLOGY 67 (July 1961): 9-16.

> Wechsler compares communities near Boston which are rapidly growing in size with those which are not, and reports on the rates of various psychiatric disorders, including suicide, in the two groups of communities.

Occupation

16.237 Blachly, P.H.; Disher, William; and Roduner, Gregory. "Suicide by Physicians." BULLETIN OF SUICIDOLOGY (December 1968): 1-18.

> These authors report on the suicide rates of physicians with different specialities.

16.238 Labovitz, Sanford, and Hagedorn, Robert. "An Analysis of Suicide Rates among Occupational Categories." SOCIOLOGICAL INQUIRY 41 (Winter 1971): 67-72.

> These authors report the suicide rates of workers in various occupations.

Sociological and Environmental Variables

16.239 Tuckman, Jacob; Youngman, William F.; and Kriezman, Garry.
"Occupation and Suicide." INDUSTRIAL MEDICINE AND SURGERY
33 (November 1964): 818-20.

These authors report the suicide rates for workers in a
variety of occupations.

See also items 7.201-7.206 and 5.117.

Unemployment

16.240 Edwards, J.E., and Whitlock, F.A. "Suicide and Attempted Suicide
in Brisbane." MEDICAL JOURNAL OF AUSTRALIA 1 (1 June 1968):
932-38.

An investigation of the incidence of unemployment in suicidal people in a town in Australia.

16.241 Robin, A.A.; Brooke, Eileen M.; and Freeman-Browne, Dorothy, L.
"Some Aspects of Suicide in Psychiatric Patients in Southend." BRITISH
JOURNAL OF PSYCHIATRY 144 (June 1968): 739-47.

These authors investigate whether suicidal people in a
town in England are more likely to be unemployed than
nonsuicidal people.

16.242 Tuckman, Jacob, and Youngman, William F. "A Scale for Assessing
Suicidal Risk of Attempted Suicides." JOURNAL OF CLINICAL PSY-
CHOLOGY 24 (January 1968): 17-19.

Tuckman and Youngman investigate whether being unemployed makes it more likely that someone who has attempted
suicide in an American city will subsequently kill himself.

Economic Fluctuations

16.243 Henry, Andrew F., and Short, James F. SUICIDE AND HOMICIDE.
Glencoe, Ill.: Free Press, 1954. 214 p.

The variation of the suicide rates in America with the
economy over time is analyzed in detail in this book.

16.244 MacMahon, Brian; Johnson, Samuel; and Pugh, Thomas F. "Relations
of Suicide Rates to Social Conditions." PUBLIC HEALTH REPORTS 78
(April 1963): 285-93.

The variation of the suicide rate with the economy in
America is examined, with special attention given to the
Great Depression.

Sociological and Environmental Variables

16.245 Pierce, Albert. "The Economic Cycle and the Social Suicide Rate."
AMERICAN SOCIOLOGICAL REVIEW 32 (June 1967): 457-62.

Refer to 16.246.

16.246 Simon, Julian L. "The Effect of Income on the Suicide Rate."
AMERICAN JOURNAL OF SOCIOLOGY 74 (November 1968): 302-3.

These two papers (16.245 and 16.246) analyze the variation
of the suicide rate with economic fluctuations in America
in greater detail.

Social Disorganization

The studies cited below each explore the relationship of the suicide rate to
various indexes of social disorganization in the different areas of a city. The
indexes include such variables as overcrowded housing, delinquency rates, and
the divorce rate. Lester reported on Buffalo, Maris on Chicago, and McCulloch
and his colleagues on Edinburgh, Scotland.

16.247 Lester, David. "Social Disorganization and Completed Suicide." SO-
CIAL PSYCHIATRY 5 (July 1970): 175-76.

16.248 McCulloch, J.W., and Philip, A.E. "Social Variables in Attempted
Suicide." ACTA PSYCHIATRIC SCANDINAVIA 43 (1967): 341-46.

16.249 McCulloch, J.W.; Philip, A.E.; and Carstairs, G.M. "The Ecology
of Suicidal Behavior." BRITISH JOURNAL OF PSYCHIATRY 113
(March 1967): 313-19.

16.250 Maris, Ronald W. SOCIAL FORCES IN URBAN SUICIDE. Homewood,
Ill.: Dorsey, 1969. 214 p.

Migration—Emigration and Immigration

16.251 Breed, Warren. "Suicide, Migration, and Race." JOURNAL OF SO-
CIAL ISSUES 22 (January 1966): 30-43.

Breed compares the circumstances of the suicidal deaths of
those who migrated to an American city with the circumstances of those who were native born.

16.252 Sainsbury, Peter, and Barraclough, Brian. "Differences between Suicide Rates." NATURE 220 (21 December 1968): 1252.

This article reports on a cross-national study of suicide
rates. The suicide rates of immigrants to America are compared to the suicide rates of the native countries.

16.253 Schmid, Calvin F. "Suicide in Minneapolis." AMERICAN JOURNAL OF SOCIOLOGY 39 (July 1933): 30-48.

Refer to item 16.255.

16.254 Whitlock, F.A. "Migration and Suicide." MEDICAL JOURNAL OF AUSTRALIA 2 (23 October 1971): 840-48.

This study of the suicide rate of immigrants to Australia includes a discussion of the possible causes for higher rates among immigrants.

16.255 Yap, P.M. "Suicide in Hong Kong." JOURNAL OF MENTAL SCIENCE 104 (April 1958): 266-301.

These two reports (16.253 and 16.255) present data that immigrants have a higher suicide rate than native-born people.

War

16.256 Lunden, Walter A. "Suicide in France: 1910-1943." AMERICAN JOURNAL OF SOCIOLOGY 52 (January 1947): 321-34.

An examination of the change in the suicide rate in France during the First and Second World Wars.

16.257 MacMahon, Brian; Johnson, Samuel; and Pugh, Thomas F. "Relation of Suicide Rates to Social Conditions." PUBLIC HEALTH REPORTS 78 (April 1963): 285-93.

Refer to item 16.259.

16.258 Rojcewicz, Stephen J. "War and Suicide." LIFE THREATENING BEHAVIOR 1 (Spring 1971): 46-54.

Rojcewicz tests three hypotheses as to why suicide rates drop during wartime. He presents evidence that indicates that the hypothesis which proposes an increase in social integration during wartime is valid.

16.259 Yessler, P.G. "Suicide in the Military." In SUICIDAL BEHAVIORS: DIAGNOSIS AND MANAGEMENT, edited by H.L.P. Resnik, pp. 241-54. Boston: Little, Brown, 1968.

These two articles (16.257 and 16.259) examine the suicide rate of Americans during World War II, by sex, for civilians and those in the military service.

Weather

Common sense tells us that the weather affects our mood greatly. Whether the sun is shining when we wake up or whether it is raining can have an impact on our mood for the day. The notion that the weather may affect suicidal behavior has intrigued scholars for a long time, and in recent years some sound research has been conducted to explore this idea. In items 16.261-16.264, Pokorny analyzes data from Texas to rule out the influence of almost all meteorological variables on suicidal behavior. Pokorny concludes that there is no evidence that such variables are related to suicidal behavior. The findings in item 16.260, however, differ from those of Pokorny.

16.260   Digon, Edward, and Block, H. Barrett. "Suicide and Climatology."
ARCHIVES OF ENVIRONMENTAL HEALTH 12 (March 1966): 278-86.

Digon and Block report on data from Philadelphia and find
a couple of significant findings among their various analyses.
The variables that they report to be related to suicidal behavior were not found to be associated by Pokorny in his
studies.

16.261   Pokorny, Alex D. "Suicide and Weather." ARCHIVES OF ENVIRON-
MENTAL HEALTH 13 (August 1966): 255-56.

16.262   Pokorny, Alex D. "Sunspots, Suicide and Homicide." DISEASES OF
THE NERVOUS SYSTEM 27 (May 1966): 347-48.

16.263   Pokorny, Alex D.; Davis, Fred; and Harberson, Wayne. "Suicide,
Suicide Attempts, and Weather." AMERICAN JOURNAL OF PSY-
CHIATRY 120 (October 1963): 377-81.

16.264   Pokorny, Alex D., and Mefford, Roy B. "Geomagnetic Fluctuations
and Disturbed Behavior." JOURNAL OF NERVOUS AND MENTAL
DISEASE 143 (August 1966): 140-51.

Chapter 17
SOCIAL RELATIONSHIPS

People are social organisms and their behavior often is greatly affected by the behavior of others. Suicidal behavior typically is influenced by the social relationships that the individual has or has had in the past. This chapter is concerned with research on these variables.

Research on these variables in regard to suicide is not very common. Few studies have appeared that analyze these variables in detail and, unfortunately, many of those on the social relationships of suicidal people are to be found only in unpublished doctoral dissertations (see also item 6.207).

17.1 EFFECTS OF A SPOUSE AND CHILDREN

17.101   Bhagat, M. "The Spouses of Attempted Suicides." BRITISH JOURNAL OF PSYCHIATRY 128 (January 1976): 44-46.

This study of the spouses of attempted suicides indicates that the husbands of female attempted suicides seem normal; while the wives of male attempted suicides seem more independent than the average wife, suggesting that role reversal may characterize such marriages.

17.102   Dublin, Louis I. SUICIDE. New York: Ronald, 1963. 240 p.

Dublin presents data on the suicide rate of people who are single, married, divorced, and widowed, indicating that married people have the lowest suicide rate.

17.103   Dublin, Louis I., and Bunzel, Bessie. TO BE OR NOT TO BE. New York: Harrison Smith and Robert Haas, 1933. 443 p.

They presented data that indicated that presence of children reduces the risk of suicide in adults.

17.104   Henry, Andrew F., and Short, James F.   SUICIDE AND HOMICIDE.
         Glencoe, Ill.:   Free Press, 1954.   214 p.

         Henry and Short present several hypotheses as to why the
         suicide rate is high in those who are divorced.

17.105   MacMahon, Brian, and Pugh, Thomas F.   "Suicide in the Widowed."
         AMERICAN JOURNAL OF EPIDEMIOLOGY 81 (January 1965): 23-31.

         MacMahon and Pugh tried to see whether the bereavement
         itself was responsible for the high suicide rate in widowed
         persons or whether the less suicidal widows and widowers
         were more likely to remarry.   Their data support the theory
         that bereavement itself is crucial.

17.106   Shneidman, Edwin S., and Farberow, Norman L.   "Statistical Com-
         parisons between Committed and Attempted Suicides."   In THE CRY
         FOR HELP, edited by Norman L. Farberow and Edwin S. Shneidman,
         pp. 19-47.   New York: McGraw-Hill, 1961.

         The rate of attempted suicide for different marital groups
         is presented for Los Angeles.

17.2 SUICIDE AND SUGGESTIBILITY

17.201   Blumenthal, Sol, and Bergner, Lawrence.   "Suicide and Newspapers."
         AMERICAN JOURNAL OF PSYCHIATRY 130 (April 1973):   468-71.

         This article represents a study of the effects of a long
         newspaper strike in New York City on the suicide rate
         there.

17.202   Hankoff, Leon D.   "An Epidemic of Attempted Suicide."   COMPRE-
         HENSIVE PSYCHIATRY 2 (October 1961):   294-98.

         Hankoff reports that epidemics of attempted suicide do
         occur and describes one on a Marine base.   This suggests
         a contagion effect for suicide.

17.203   Kreitman, Norman; Smith, Peter; and Tan, Eng-Seong.   "Attempted
         Suicide in Social Networks."   BRITISH JOURNAL OF PREVENTATIVE
         AND SOCIAL MEDICINE 23 (May 1969):   116-23.

         Kreitman and his colleagues find that attempted suicides
         have more suicidal friends than nonsuicidal people have,
         and suggest that this could indicate a contagion effect for
         suicide.

17.204   Motto, Jerome A. "Newspaper Influence on Suicide." ARCHIVES OF GENERAL PSYCHIATRY 23 (August 1970): 143-48.

Refer to item 17.205.

17.205   _____. "Suicide and Suggestibility." AMERICAN JOURNAL OF PSYCHIATRY 124 (August 1967): 252-56.

Motto (17.204 and 17.205) examines the suicide rates in cities where newspaper strikes prevented the reporting of suicidal deaths. He found some tentative support for a reduction in the suicide rate for some groups during such strikes.

17.206   Phillips, David P. "The Influence of Suggestion on Suicide." AMERICAN SOCIOLOGICAL REVIEW 39 (June 1974): 340-54.

This analysis provides data that reports of suicidal deaths on the front page of newspapers lead to an increase in the suicide rate in the next two months. The analyses cover 1946-68 in the United States, and show that the same phenomenon occurs in England.

17.3 RECENT STRESS AND THE PRECIPITATION OF SUICIDE

It is clear that certain events often appear to be precipitants of suicide action. Such events can include loss of a loved one, failure at a job, a threat of arrest, or onset of a terminal illness. However, very little research has ever been conducted into these precipitating events, and only one study has appeared that bears upon this topic.

17.301   Paykel, Eugene S.; Prusoff, Brigitte A.; and Myers, Jerome K. "Suicide Attempts and Recent Life Events." ARCHIVES OF GENERAL PSYCHIATRY 32 (March 1975): 327-33.

An analysis of precipitating events in suicidal behavior, which indicates that stresses increase in frequency for the suicidal person prior to the attempt. Such a build-up is not found for nonsuicidal depressed patients.

17.4 INTERPERSONAL BEHAVIOR AND SUICIDE

17.401   Ganzler, Sidney. "Some Interpersonal and Social Dimensions of Suicidal Behavior." Ph.D. dissertation, University of California, Los Angeles, 1967.

Ganzler investigates the social isolation and powerlessness of suicidal people and finds such feelings to be very high in these people.

17.402   Hattem, Jack V. "Precipitating Role of Discordant Interpersonal Re-
         lationships in Suicidal Behavior." Ph.D. dissertation, University of
         Houston, 1964.

         Hattem explores the relationship between the suicidal adult
         and the spouse. The suicidal partner is more sensitive to
         criticism, more dependent, and more unstable.

17.403   Jacobs, Jerry. ADOLESCENT SUICIDE. New York: Wiley, 1971.
         147 p.

         Refer to item 17.404.

17.404   Jacobs, Jerry, and Teicher, Joseph D. "Broken Homes and Social
         Isolation in Attempted Suicide of Adolescents." INTERNATIONAL
         JOURNAL OF SOCIAL PSYCHIATRY 13 (Spring 1967): 139-49.

         Jacobs (17.403 and 17.404) explores the relationships be-
         tween suicidal adolescents and their parents, and how these
         relationships change prior to the suicidal crisis.

17.405   Lester, David. "Resentment and Dependency in the Suicidal Individual."
         JOURNAL OF GENERAL PSYCHOLOGY 81 (July 1969): 137-45.

         Lester explores the dependencies of suicidal people and
         finds them to resent those upon whom they depended more
         than nonsuicidal people did.

17.406   _____. WHY PEOPLE KILL THEMSELVES. Springfield, Ill.: Charles
         Thomas, 1972. 353 p.

         Chapter 15 of this book contains a review of the more minor
         studies conducted into the social relationships of suicidal
         people.

17.407   Peck, Michael L. "The Relation of Suicidal Behavior to Character-
         istics of the Significant Other." Ph.D. dissertation, University of
         Portland, 1965.

         Peck studies the spouses of suicidal people and finds them
         more likely to use double-bind communications than their
         spouses.

17.5 EFFECTS OF SUICIDE ON THE BEREAVED

After a person kills himself or herself, his or her problem cease. However,
the suicidal death creates problems for others. First, the death must be classified accurately (see section 13.4). More important, those who are bereaved
by the suicide must be taken care of. In recent years, both of these issues
have been the focus of some attention.

17.501   Cain, Albert C., ed. SURVIVORS OF SUICIDE. Springfield, Ill.:
         Charles Thomas, 1972.   305 p.

> A series of articles on the effects of a suicide on the
> family members. One section deals with the effects on
> the surviving children. There is a section on how to help
> the survivors of a suicide and one that presents detailed
> case studies.

17.502   Shepherd, D.M., and Barraclough, Brian M. "The Aftermath of
         Parental Suicide for Children." BRITISH JOURNAL OF PSYCHIATRY
         129 (September 1976): 267-76.

> Shepherd and Barraclough look at the effects on children
> that result from the suicidal death of a parent.

17.503   _____. "The Aftermath of Suicide." BRITISH MEDICAL JOURNAL
         2 (15 June 1974): 600-603.

> A study of spouses of people who had killed themselves,
> which explores their reactions to the inquest, the stigma
> that they felt, and their adjustment. Surviving spouses
> were equally likely to be better off and worse off after
> the death.

17.504   Wallace, Samuel E. AFTER SUICIDE. New York: Wiley, 1973. 269 p.

> Wallace interviewed twelve women whose husbands com-
> mitted suicide. He describes and analyzes the problems
> facing the survivors of a suicide and reports a fair amount
> of his interviews with the bereaved wives.

Chapter 18
SUICIDE IN OTHER CULTURES

It is far from easy to obtain regular information about suicidal behaviors in other nations and cultures. For detailed information about suicide in a particular culture, a search of INDEX MEDICUS (5.115) will frequently locate one or more articles written by suicidologists in the country of interest, usually in that language. Also the Human Relations Area Files (2.207) are an outstanding source for information on suicide in other cultures, nations, and areas. Hastings's ENCYCLOPEDIA OF RELIGION AND ETHICS (4.108) is an excellent early source for scholarly information on suicide in primitive societies and ancient cultures. Farberow (18.204) is a good recent source for suicide information in different cultures. In this chapter, major sources of information on suicide in other cultures that are available in the English language are reviewed.

18.1 SUICIDE RATES IN OTHER COUNTRIES

The United Nations has been coordinating the collection of demographic data throughout the world since World War II. One aspect of this project is the summarization of current census data and vital statistics from nearly every country in the world in its annual publications. Suicide is reported as one of the causes of death, that is, as part of the death statistics. Hence the two United Nations volumes described below (18.102 and 18.103) are excellent sources of worldwide suicide statistics. Other sources of brief data are described in various of the almanacs and yearbooks cited in chapter 4, section 2.

18.101   Brooke, Eileen M.   SUICIDE AND ATTEMPTED SUICIDE.   Geneva: World Health Organization, 1974.   127 p.

This book provides suicide rates for some nations before its date of publication.

18.102   DEMOGRAPHIC YEARBOOK.   New York: United Nations, 1948-- . Annual.

This annual is a basic source of suicide statistics from nearly eighty countries and territories. The 1974 volume contains special tabulations on suicide. See also item 7.303.

18.103　WORLD HEALTH STATISTICS ANNUAL.　Geneva:　World Health Organization, 1962-- .　Annual.

>This work gives the suicide rates by nation annually from 1965 to date.　Separate rates are normally given for males and females and for different age groups.　See also item 7.308.

Three investigators have tried to estimate suicide rates for primitive or non-literate cultures whose members do not keep statistical records.　Each investigator used a different technique and each technique is probably unreliable. However, their data have been utilized for cross-cultural research in primitive societies.　The three sources are:

18.104　Krauss, Herbert H., and Krauss, Beatrice J.　"Cross-Cultural Study of the Thwarting Disorientation Theory of Suicide."　JOURNAL OF ABNORMAL PSYCHOLOGY　73 (August 1968):　353-57.

>The raw data upon which the Krausses' paper is based is included in the original copy of his doctoral dissertation (section 6.205).

18.105　Naroll, Raoul.　DATA QUALITY CONTROL.　Glencoe, Ill.:　Free Press, 1962.　198 p.

18.106　Palmer, Stuart.　"Murder and Suicide in 40 Nonliterate Societies." JOURNAL OF CRIMINAL LAW, CRIMINOLOGY AND POLICE SCIENCE　56 (September 1965):　320-24.

The original sources from which the above three investigators drew their data are to be found in the Human Relations Area Files (2.207).

18.107　Ruzicka, L.T.　"Suicide, 1950 to 1971."　WORLD HEALTH STATISTICS REPORT　29 (1976):　396-413.

>This article contains comparative data on suicide for about thirty countries in the past two decades.

18.108　"Suicides by Means Used, 1950-1969."　WORLD HEALTH STATISTICS REPORT　26 (1973):　164-280.

>The means used for committing suicide in various countries are analyzed in this extensive report.

18.2 STUDIES OF SUICIDE IN PARTICULAR CULTURES

18.201　Bohannon, Paul, ed.　AFRICAN HOMICIDE AND SUICIDE.　Princeton, N.J.:　Princeton University Press, 1960.　292 p.

Suicide in Other Cultures

This book explores behavior in a number of African tribes. There is an appendix in which individual cases of suicide in these tribes are listed, with relevant details such as method and motive.

18.202 Dizmang, Larry H., and Swenson, David D., eds. SUICIDE AMONG THE AMERICAN INDIANS. Public Health Service Publication, no. 1903. Washington, D.C.: National Institute of Mental Health, Indian Health Service, 1969. 37 p. FS2.22:Su3/2.

This publication reports the papers given at two workshops convened to discuss suicidal behavior in American Indians. Suicidal behavior is examined among the Oglala Sioux and in the Cheyenne River Reservation. Suggestions are made for providing mental health facilities to deal with the problem.

18.203 Farber, Maurice L. THEORY OF SUICIDE. New York: Funk and Wagnalls, 1968. 115 p.

In this book, Farber proposes a psychological theory of suicide and illustrates it with examples from Scandinavia.

18.204 Farberow, Norman L., ed. SUICIDE IN DIFFERENT CULTURES. Baltimore: University Park Press, 1975. 304 p.

This is a collection of articles by experts on suicidal behavior among Anglo-Americans, Black-Americans, Japanese-Americans, and Mexican-Americans, and in addition the British, Dutch, Italians, Austrians, Bulgarians, Israelis, Indians, Taiwanese, Japanese, Scandinavians, and South Americans. The chapters present facts about the suicidal behavior of the different cultures and explores reasons for the differences between the different cultures.

18.205 Farberow, Norman L., and Simon, M.D. "Suicides in Los Angeles and Vienna." PUBLIC HEALTH REPORTS 84 (May 1969): 389-402.

A comparison of the suicides in the two cities using psychological autopsies, a standardized way for investigating the circumstances and motives behind suicidal behavior.

18.206 Firth, Raymond. "Suicide and Risk-Taking in Tikopia Society." PSYCHIATRY 24 (February 1961): 1-17.

An analysis of suicidal behavior in a culture in the South Pacific.

18.207 Hendin, Herbert. BLACK SUICIDE. New York: Basic Books, 1969. 176 p.

A study of attempted suicide by twenty-five blacks in New York City, with psychoanalytic speculation about the motives involved in suicide among blacks in America.

18.208 _____. SUICIDE AND SCANDINAVIA. New York: Grune and Stratton, 1964. 176 p.

This book was the first comparative study of suicide. Suicidal behavior in Sweden, Denmark, and Norway was examined by means of clinical interviews with patients in each of the countries and Hendin's reading of the literature in the three countries. Hendin proposed that very different motives underlie suicidal behavior in the three countries. See item 9.203

18.209 Iga, Mamoru. "Cultural Factors in Suicide of Japanese Youth with Focus on Personality." SOCIOLOGY AND SOCIAL RESEARCH 46 (October 1961): 75-90.

Iga has written extensively in English on the problem of suicide in Japan. This is one of his typical articles.

18.210 Leighton, Alexander H., and Hughes, Charles C. "Notes on Eskimo Patterns of Suicide." SOUTHWESTERN JOURNAL OF ANTHROPOLOGY 11 (Winter 1955): 327-38.

An examination of patterns of suicide among the Eskimos living on St. Lawrence Island, Alaska.

18.211 Meer, Fatima. RACE AND SUICIDE IN SOUTH AFRICA. London: Routledge & Kegan Paul, 1976. 319 p.

A study of suicidal behavior among the various racial groups in South Africa.

18.212 Ogden, Michael; Spector, Mozart I.; and Hill, Charles A., Jr. "Suicides and Homicides among Indians." PUBLIC HEALTH REPORTS 85 (January 1970): 75-80.

An examination of whether American Indians do have a high suicide rate or not.

18.213 Rudestam, Kjell E. "Stockholm and Los Angeles: A Cross-Cultural Study of the Communication of Suicidal Intent." JOURNAL OF CONSULTING AND CLINICAL PSYCHOLOGY 36 (February 1971): 82-90.

A comparison of the people who kill themselves in the cities of Los Angeles and Stockholm, and the ways in which they kill themselves.

18.214 Seward, Jack. HARAKIRI. Rutland, Vt.: Charles Tuttle, 1968.
        116 p.

>   An examination of ritual suicide (hara kiri) among the
>   Japanese.

18.215 Shore, James H. "American Indian Suicide." PSYCHIATRY 38
        (February 1975): 87-91.

>   An epidemiological study of American Indians in the North-
>   west United States, which permits estimations of the rates
>   of completed and attempted suicide.

See also sections 6.205 and 6.215.

Part IV

SELECTED REFERENCES TO PSYCHOLOGICAL

CORRELATES AND ANALYSES OF SUICIDE

Chapter 19

MENTAL ILLNESS

The most important psychological variable that is relevant to the study of suicide is mental illness, or psychiatric disorder. Many psychologists and psychiatrists believe that suicidal behavior in people is a clue to their psychiatric
state, and indeed may be a symptom of psychiatric disorder.

Many people ask whether suicidal people can be sane. Such a question cannot
be answered. Even if the person were judged to be sane a short time prior to
his suicidal action, his psychiatric condition may have changed by the time he
committed suicide.

We do not know therefore the psychiatric status of those about to kill themselves in the next few moments. We cannot answer questions about people at
that time in their lives. However, we can answer the following questions:
What is the suicide rate of those with specific psychiatric disorders? and How
does suicidal behavior differ in those with different psychiatric disorders?

19.1 SUICIDE RATES IN DIFFERENT PSYCHIATRIC DISORDERS

19.101   Beall, Lynette. "The Dynamics of Suicide." BULLETIN OF SUI-
CIDOLOGY (March 1969): 2-16.

> Beall describes several distinct types of suicidal motivation
> and relates these types to the psychiatric illnesses of the
> people.

19.102   Greer, Steven. "The Relationship between Parental Loss and Attempted
Suicide." BRITISH JOURNAL OF PSYCHIATRY 110 (September 1964):
698-705.

> Greer computes rates of attempted suicide in neurotics and
> psychopaths.

19.103   Johnson, Eva. "A Study of Schizophrenia in the Male." ACTA PSY-
CHIATRICA NEUROLOGICA SCANDINAVIA 33 (1958): supplement
no. 125.

Johnson computes rates of completed and attempted suicides in schizophrenics.

19.104 Ljunberg, Lennart. "Hysteria." ACTA PSYCHIATRICA NEUROLOGICA SCANDINAVIA 32 (1957): supplement no. 112.

Ljunberg computes rates of completed and attempted suicide for patients with hysterical neuroses.

19.105 Murphy, George E., and Robins, Eli. "Social Factors in Suicide." JOURNAL OF THE AMERICAN MEDICAL ASSOCIATION 199 (30 January 1967): 303-8.

Refer to item 19.106.

19.106 Robins, Eli, and O'Neal, Patricia. "Culture and Mental Disorder." HUMAN ORGANIZATION 16 (Winter 1958): 7-11.

Robins and his colleagues (19.105 and 19.106) compare the different stresses and precipitating events for suicidal behavior in alcoholics (and related disorders) and in manic-depressive psychotics (and related disorders).

19.107 Pokorny, Alex D. "Follow-up Study of 618 Suicidal Patients." AMERICAN JOURNAL OF PSYCHIATRY 122 (April 1966): 1109-1116.

Refer to item 19.108.

19.108 _____. "Suicide Rates in Various Psychiatric Disorders." JOURNAL OF NERVOUS AND MENTAL DISEASE 139 (December 1964): 499-506.

Pokorny in these two studies (19.107 and 19.108) computes the suicide rate of patients given various psychiatric disorders.

19.109 Temoche, Abelardo; Pugh, Thomas F.; and MacMahon, Brian. "Suicide Rates among Current and Former Mental Institution Patients." JOURNAL OF NERVOUS AND MENTAL DISEASE 138 (February 1964): 124-30.

Temoche and his colleagues reviewed research on studies of suicides to see how many were psychiatrically disturbed. Estimates ranged from 5 to 94 percent, suggesting bias in the opinions of the investigators. Temoche then followed up patients with differing psychiatric diagnoses and computed their actual suicide rates. He found that those with diagnoses of depressive psychoses had the highest suicide rate.

19.2 SUICIDES IN NEUROTICS AND PSYCHOTICS

19.201 Dorpat, Theodore L., and Boswell, John W. "An Evaluation of Suicidal Intent in Suicide Attempts." COMPREHENSIVE PSYCHIATRY 4
(April 1963): 117-25.

Dorpat and Boswell presented data indicating that neurotics
make less serious attempts than do psychotics.

19.202 Lester, David. "Suicidal Behavior, Sex, and Mental Disorder." PSY-
CHOLOGICAL REPORTS 27 (August 1970): 61-62.

Lester reviewed the available data on the association between a diagnosis of neurosis and psychosis and the type
of suicidal behavior. In addition, he suggested that sex
was related to this association. Females are more prone
to neurosis and attempted suicide, whereas males are more
prone to psychosis and completed suicide.

19.203 Menninger, Karl. MAN AGAINST HIMSELF. New York: Harcourt,
Brace, and World, 1938. 429 p.

Menninger suggested that neurotics were more likely to
attempt suicide, whereas psychotics were more likely to
complete suicide.

19.3 DISTURBED THOUGHT PROCESSES IN THE SUICIDAL PERSON

19.301 Neuringer, Charles. "The Cognitive Organization of Meaning in Suicidal Individuals." JOURNAL OF GENERAL PSYCHOLOGY 76
(January 1967): 91-100.

Refer to item 19.303.

19.302 _____. "Dichotomous Evaluations in Suicidal Individuals." JOURNAL
OF CONSULTING PSYCHOLOGY 25 (October 1961): 445-49.

19.303 _____. "Rigid Thinking in Suicidal Individuals." JOURNAL OF
CONSULTING PSYCHOLOGY 28 (February 1964): 54-58.

In these articles (19.301, 19.302, and 19.303), Neuringer
explored the thinking of attempted suicides by giving them
psychological tests. He found that they were rigid and
tended to think in absolute dichotomies.

19.304 Shneidman, Edwin S., and Farberow, Norman L. "The Logic of Suicide." In CLUES TO SUICIDE, edited by Edwin S. Shneidman and
Norman L. Farberow, pp. 31-40. New York: McGraw-Hill, 1957.

Mental Illness

Shneidman and Farberow describe a type of illogical thinking that suicides show, which they call catalogic, in which
the suicide confuses himself, as experienced by himself,
with himself as experienced by others. They document this
with excerpts from suicide notes.

19.4 SUICIDE IN ALCOHOLICS

19.401 Koller, K.M., and Castanos, J.N. "Attempted Suicide and Alcoholism." MEDICAL JOURNAL OF AUSTRALIA 2 (9 November 1968):
835-37.

Refer to item 19.403.

19.402 Murphy, George E., and Robins, Eli. "Social Factors in Suicide."
JOURNAL OF THE AMERICAN MEDICAL ASSOCIATION 199 (30
January 1967): 303-8.

In this report, alcoholics who kill themselves are compared
with other suicides.

19.403 Ritson, E.B. "Suicide among Alcoholics." BRITISH JOURNAL OF
MEDICAL PSYCHOLOGY 41, pt. 3 (1968): 235-42.

These two articles (19.401 and 19.403) compare alcoholics
who complete suicide or attempted suicide with alcoholics
who are not suicidal.

19.404 Rushing, W.A. "Alcoholism and Suicide Rates by Status Set and Occupation." QUARTERLY JOURNAL OF STUDIES IN ALCOHOL 19
(June 1968): 399-412.

Refer to item 19.405.

19.405 _____. "Suicide and the Interaction of Alcoholism (Liver Cirrhosis)
with the Social Situation." QUARTERLY JOURNAL OF STUDIES IN
ALCOHOL 30 (March 1969): 93-103.

Rushing (19.404 and 19.405) reviews much of the evidence
indicating that suicidal behavior is more common in alcoholics than in other groups. He also tries to test whether
in fact alcoholism leads to suicide or whether both suicide
and alcoholism are expressions of some other variable (such
as social stress).

19.5 SUICIDE IN CRIMINALS

These publications discuss the suicidal behavior of offenders who are incarcerated
in prisons:

19.501 Beigel, Allan, and Russell, Harold E. "Suicide Attempts in Jails." HOSPITAL AND COMMUNITY PSYCHIATRY 23 (December 1972): 361-63.

19.502 Danto, Bruce L. JAILHOUSE BLUES. Orchard Lake, Mich.: Epic Publications, 1973. 325 p.

19.503 _____. "The Suicidal Inmate." POLICE CHIEF 38 (August 1971): 56-59.

19.504 James, I. Pierce. "Suicide and Mortality amongst Heroin Addicts in Britain." BRITISH JOURNAL OF ADDICTION 62 (December 1967): 391-98.

        James discusses suicidal behavior among heroin addicts.

19.505 Reiger, Wolfram. "Suicide Attempts in a Federal Prison." ARCHIVES OF GENERAL PSYCHIATRY 24 (June 1971): 532-35.

19.506 Tuckman, Jacob, and Youngman, William F. "Suicide and Criminality." JOURNAL OF FORENSIC SCIENCE 10 (January 1965): 104-7.

        Tuckman and Youngman found no difference in the criminal history of those who completed suicide and those who died from other causes.

Chapter 20
AGGRESSION IN SUICIDAL PERSONS

The most common psychological conception of suicide is that it is an act of aggression. The suicidal person is aggressing against himself or herself, an idea that stems from Sigmund Freud's views on depression and aggression (see section 15.1). This conception leads to the implication that people are likely to be either depressive and suicidal (turning aggression inwards) or assaultive and homicidal (turning aggression outwards), an idea that is developed in the sociological theory of suicide proposed by Henry and Short (see item 15.203). In this chapter, research is listed that is designed to test these ideas.

20.1 SUICIDE AS AN AGGRESSIVE ACT

20.101   Farberow, Norman L.; Shneidman, Edwin S.; and Neuringer, Charles. "Case History and Hospitalization Factors in Suicides of Neuropsychiatric Hospital Patients." JOURNAL OF NERVOUS AND MENTAL DISEASE 142 (January 1966): 32-44.

A study of psychiatric patients who killed themselves reveals that they are above average in violence while in the psychiatric hospital.

20.102   Henry, Andrew F., and Short, James F. SUICIDE AND HOMICIDE. Glencoe, Ill.: Free Press, 1954. 214 p.

Henry and Short take Freud's ideas on suicide and explore what societal constraints and which childhood experiences might lead some people to externalize anger while others internalize anger.

20.103   Lester, David. "Attempted Suicide as a Hostile Act." JOURNAL OF PSYCHOLOGY 68 (March 1968): 243-48.

Refer to item 20.106.

20.104   _____. "Henry and Short on Suicide." JOURNAL OF PSYCHOLOGY 70 (November 1968): 179-86.

Lester analyzes and comments upon the accuracy of the ideas proposed by Henry and Short.

20.105 _____. "Suicide: Aggression or Hostility?" CRISIS INTERVENTION 3, no. 1 (1971): 10-14.

Refer to item 20.106.

20.106 _____. WHY PEOPLE KILL THEMSELVES. Springfield, Ill.: Charles Thomas, 1972. 353 p.

In items 20.103, 20.105, and 20.106, Lester reviews the scattered research studies that contain information as to whether suicidal people are aggressive or not. He concludes that suicidal persons do not appear abnormal in this respect.

20.107 Litman, Robert E. "Sigmund Freud on Suicide." BULLETIN OF SUICIDOLOGY (July 1968): 11-23.

Refer to item 20.109.

20.108 _____. "Sigmund Freud on Suicide." In ESSAYS IN SELF-DESTRUCTION, edited by Edwin S. Shneidman, pp. 324-44. New York: Science House, 1967.

Refer to item 20.109.

20.109 _____. "Sigmund Freud on Suicide." PSYCHOANALYTIC FORUM 1, no. 2 (1966): 206-21.

Litman (20.107-20.109) organizes Freud's writings on suicide, and notes the importance of Freud's concept that suicide (and depression) results from aggression felt toward an external object that is now turned inward upon the self.

20.2 SUICIDE AND MURDER

20.201 Dorpat, Theodore L. "Suicide in Murders." PSYCHIATRIC DIGEST 27 (June 1966): 51-55.

Refer to item 20.206.

20.202 Lester, David. "The Relationship between Suicide and Homicide." CORRECTIVE AND SOCIAL PSYCHIATRY 23 (July 1977): 83-84.

This article reviews psychological and sociological research that attempts to see whether and in what way suicide and homicide are related behaviors.

20.203   Meerloo, Joost A.M. SUICIDE AND MASS SUICIDE. New York: Grune & Stratton, 1962. 153 p.

> Meerlo describes cases where people kill themselves partly in response to murderous wishes of others. Meerloo calls this phenomenon "psychic homicide."

20.204   Rosenbaum, Milton, and Richman, Joseph. "Suicide." AMERICAN JOURNAL OF PSYCHIATRY 126 (May 1970): 1652-55.

> A study of the role of aggressive death wishes on the part of relatives in precipitating suicidal behavior in people. Relatives and significant others often have death wishes for someone, who responds to these wishes by attempting suicide.

20.205   West, Donald J. MURDER FOLLOWED BY SUICIDE. Cambridge: Harvard University Press, 1966. 181 p.

> Refer to item 20.206.

20.206   Wolfgang, Marvin E. "An Analysis of Homicide-Suicide." JOURNAL OF CLINICAL AND EXPERIMENTAL PSYCHOPATHOLOGY 19 (September 1958): 208-17.

> In items 20.201, 20.205, and 20.206, the authors examine people who first kill someone else and then kill themselves. Dorpat and Wolfgang study American murderers, while West studies British murderers.

20.207   _____. "Suicide by Means of Victim-Precipitated Homicide." JOURNAL OF CLINICAL AND EXPERIMENTAL PSYCHOPATHOLOGY 20 (December 1959): 335-49.

> Wolfgang studies people who provoke and play a part in precipitating someone else to kill them. Wolfgang characterizes this behavior as committing suicide by getting someone else to murder you.

Chapter 21
SUICIDE NOTES AND OTHER COMMUNICATION

People who kill themselves leave few data for us to study, and therefore suicidologists usually turn to the study of those who attempt suicide but survive.
However, completed suicides often leave suicide notes, and these notes have
been the focus of much research. Can the study of these notes give us clues
as to the psychological state of the person about to kill himself or herself?

Suicide notes are a communication with the survivors. Suicidal people, however, often communicate their intent in other ways. These communications
have been the subject of much research, for if we understood the nature of
these communications better, we might be better able to identify potential suicides.

21.1 THE CONTENT OF SUICIDE NOTES

21.101   Shneidman, Edwin S., and Farberow, Norman L., eds. CLUES TO
         SUICIDE. New York: McGraw-Hill, 1957. 227 p.

>   In an appendix to this book, Shneidman and Farberow pub-
>   lish thirty-three genuine suicide notes. Each is paired with
>   a simulated suicide note written by someone of the same
>   age and sex as the suicide.

Six studies have appeared comparing the suicide notes published by Shneidman
and Farberow (item 21.101) for a variety of grammatical and content categories.
These studies are cited below.

21.102   Gottschalk, Louis A., and Gleser, Goldine C. "An Analysis of the
         Verbal Content of Suicide Notes." BRITISH JOURNAL OF MEDICAL
         PSYCHOLOGY 33, pt. 3 (1960): 195-204.

21.103   Ogilvie, Daniel M.; Stone, Philip J.; and Shneidman, Edwin S.
         "Some Characteristics of Genuine versus Simulated Suicide Notes."
         BULLETIN OF SUICIDOLOGY (March 1969): 27-32.

21.104 Osgood, Charles E., and Walker, Evelyn G. "Motivation and Language Behavior." JOURNAL OF ABNORMAL AND SOCIAL PSYCHOLOGY 59 (July 1959): 58-67.

21.105 Shneidman, Edwin A., and Farberow, Norman L. "Some Comparisons between Genuine and Simulated Suicide Notes in Terms of Mower's Concepts of Discomfort and Relief." JOURNAL OF GENERAL PSYCHOLOGY 56 (April 1957): 251-56.

21.106 Spiegel, Donald E., and Neuringer, Charles. "Role of Dread in Suicidal Behavior." JOURNAL OF ABNORMAL AND SOCIAL PSYCHOLOGY 66 (May 1963): 507-11.

21.107 Tuckman, Jacob, and Ziegler, Ralph. "Language Usage and Social Maturity as Related to Suicide Notes." JOURNAL OF SOCIAL PSYCHOLOGY 68 (February 1966): 139-42.

Other studies have taken samples of suicide notes and looked for differences in the motives for suicide of men and women, the young and the old, and those living in different kinds of communities.

21.108 Darbonne, Allen R. "Suicide and Age." JOURNAL OF CONSULTING AND CLINICAL PSYCHOLOGY 33 (February 1969): 46-50.

21.109 Farberow, Norman L., and Shneidman, Edwin S. "Suicide and Age." In CLUES TO SUICIDE, edited by Edwin S. Shneidman and Norman L. Farberow, pp. 41-49. New York: McGraw-Hill, 1957.

21.110 Lester, David. "Suicidal Behavior in Men and Women." MENTAL HYGIENE 53 (July 1969): 340-45.

21.111 Shneidman, Edwin S., and Farberow, Norman L. "A Socio-Psychological Investigation of Suicide." In PERSPECTIVES ON PERSONALITY RESEARCH, edited by Henry P. David and J.C. Brengelmann, pp. 270-93. New York: Springer, 1960.

Further studies on suicide notes include those below.

21.112 Frederick, Calvin J. "An Investigation of Handwriting of Suicidal People through Suicide Notes." JOURNAL OF ABNORMAL PSYCHOLOGY 73 (June 1968): 263-67.

Frederick found that handwriting experts could tell genuine suicide notes from copies made of them by nonsuicidal people.

21.113   Jacobs, Jerry. "A Phenomenological Study of Suicide Notes." SO-
CIAL PROBLEMS 15 (Summer 1967): 60-72.

Jacobs examines a sample of suicide notes to see whether
he can detect the various psychological states through which
a person has to pass in order to justify an act of suicide.

21.114   Lester, David. WHY PEOPLE KILL THEMSELVES. Springfield, Ill.:
Charles Thomas, 1972. 353 p.

This book contains the only review to date on all research
conducted into suicide notes.

21.2   SUICIDES AND THEIR PRIOR COMMUNICATIONS

21.201   Delong, W. Bradford, and Robins, Eli. "The Communication of Suicidal Intent prior to Psychiatric Hospitalization." AMERICAN JOUR-
NAL OF PSYCHIATRY 117 (February 1961): 695-705.

Refer to item 21.203.

21.202   Dorpat, Theodore L., and Boswell, John W. "An Evaluation of Suicidal Intent in Suicide Attempts." COMPREHENSIVE PSYCHIATRY 4
(April 1963): 117-25.

These investigators found that the more serious an attempt
at suicide, the more likely there was some prior attempt
at communication.

21.203   Robins, Eli; Gassner, Seymour; Kayes, Jack; Wilkinson, Robert H.;
and Murphy, George E. "The Communication of Suicidal Intent."
AMERICAN JOURNAL OF PSYCHIATRY 115 (February 1959): 724-33.

Robins and his associates (see also item 21.201) describe
over twenty-six ways in which suicidal people communicate
their suicidal intent prior to killing themselves. Typically,
such communication takes place, but typically those receiving these direct and indirect communications ignore the
message.

21.204   Yessler, Paul G.; Gibbs, James J.; and Becker, Herman A. "On the
Communication of Suicidal Ideas." ARCHIVES OF GENERAL PSY-
CHIATRY 3 (December 1960): 612-31.

Refer to item 21.205.

21.205   _____. "On the Communication of Suicidal Ideas." ARCHIVES OF
GENERAL PSYCHIATRY 5 (July 1961): 12-29.

Yessler and his colleagues (see also item 21.204) compared the
characteristics of suicides who do communicate prior to their
act and those who do not.

Chapter 22

CHILDHOOD EXPERIENCES

The most likely source of determinants of why some people become suicidal is their childhood. It is in these formative years that the path toward suicide is most likely to be taken, albeit unwittingly. However, suicides are not identi-fied until they are adult, and then their childhoods are obscured by the dis-tortions of memory. Thus, the study of childhoods of suicides is not easy. Too often, the suicidologist has to rely on data that are not reliable or valid, and the research that would be ideal, that is, direct observation of child-parent interactions, cannot be conducted.

22.1 PUNISHMENT EXPERIENCES

22.101   Gold, Martin.   "Suicide, Homicide, and the Socialization of Ag-
         gression."   AMERICAN JOURNAL OF SOCIOLOGY   63 (May 1958):
         651-61.

> Gold compared the suicide and homicide rates of various
> groups of the population (such as males and females, blacks
> and whites) to see whether the rates were consistent with
> Henry and Short's theory (22.102) and sociological expecta-
> tions about the incidence of physical punishment in these
> groups.

22.102   Henry, Andrew F., and Short, James F.   SUICIDE AND HOMICIDE.
         Glencoe, Ill.:   Free Press, 1954.   214 p.

> As part of their theory of suicide and homicide, Henry and
> Short propose that experience of love-oriented punishment
> leads to suicidal tendencies whereas experience of physical
> punishment leads to homicidal tendencies.

22.103   Lester, David.   "Punishment Experiences and Suicidal Preoccupation."
         JOURNAL OF GENETIC PSYCHOLOGY   113 (September 1968): 89-94.

> A study of the memories of suicidal and nonsuicidal college
> students pertaining to their punishment experiences.

22.104 _____. "Suicide, Homicide, and the Effects of Socialization."
JOURNAL OF PERSONALITY AND SOCIAL PSYCHOLOGY 5 (April 1967): 466-68.

> Lester looked at the use of love-oriented and physical techniques of punishment in primitive nonliterate societies and compared this with the reported suicide and homicide rates.

22.2 PARENTAL LOSS

22.201 Draper, Edgar. "A Developmental Theory of Suicide." COMPREHEN-SIVE PSYCHIATRY 17 (January-February 1976): 63-80.

> An alternative psychoanalytic theory which traces the genesis of suicidal behavior to loss of the mother's love during the age of four to twelve months. This loss may be through death or depression in the mother, or simply inattention. When the infant is later subject to loss in life, this loss rearouses the earlier traumatic loss and the person kills himself to escape the unbearable pain.

22.202 Greer, Steven, and Gunn, J.C. "Attempted Suicides from Intact and Broken Parental Homes." BRITISH MEDICAL JOURNAL 2 (3 December 1966): 1355-57.

> Greer and Gunn compared suicidal people who had experienced parental loss with those who had not and reported some differences.

22.203 Lester, David. WHY PEOPLE KILL THEMSELVES. Springfield, Ill.: Charles Thomas, 1972. 353 p.

> There have been a good many studies of attempted and completed suicides that look at the incidence of separation from parents. The only review to date of this scattered literature is in this book by Lester.

22.204 Lester, David, and Beck, Aaron T. "Early Loss as a Possible 'Sensitizer' to Later Loss in Attempted Suicides." PSYCHOLOGICAL RE-PORTS 39 (August 1976): 121-22.

> Lester and Beck explored whether experience of parental loss in childhood made it more likely that a person would become suicidal after interpersonal loss in adulthood.

22.3 BIRTH ORDER

22.301 Lester, David. "Suicide and Sibling Position." JOURNAL OF IN-
DIVIDUAL PSYCHOLOGY 26 (November 1970): 203-4.

This is the most recent review of data scattered in other
sources on the birth order of those who are suicidal.

22.4 FAMILY DYNAMICS

22.401 Hendin, Herbert. "Growing up Dead." AMERICAN JOURNAL OF
PSYCHOTHERAPY 29 (July 1975): 327-38.

Refer to item 22.402.

22.402 _____. "Student Suicide." JOURNAL OF NERVOUS AND MENTAL
DISEASE 160 (March 1975): 204-19.

A discussion of suicide in college students, focusing primarily upon the influence of the parents in setting up a
suicidal lifestyle for their children.

22.403 Jacobs, Jerry. ADOLESCENT SUICIDE. New York: Wiley, 1971.
147 p.

Refer to item 22.405.

22.404 Jacobs, Jerry, and Teicher, Joseph D. "Broken Homes and Social
Isolation in Attempted Suicide of Adolescents." INTERNATIONAL
JOURNAL OF SOCIAL PSYCHIATRY 13 (Spring 1967): 139-49.

Refer to item 22.405.

22.405 Margolin, N. Lionel, and Teicher, Joseph D. "Thirteen Adolescent
Male Suicide Attemptors." JOURNAL OF THE AMERICAN ACADEMY
OF CHILD PSYCHIATRY 7 (April 1968): 296-315.

Jacobs, Teicher, and Margolin (22.403-22.405) try to explore in more detail what goes on in the homes of adolescents who are suicidal. In particular, they try to fit
the suicidal behavior into a temporal progression of dis-
ruptive events in the family.

22.5 MENTAL ILLNESS IN THE FAMILIES OF SUICIDES

22.501 Lester, David. WHY PEOPLE KILL THEMSELVES. Springfield, Ill.:
Charles Thomas, 1972. 353 p.

This book contains the only review to date of the scattered data pertinent to the question of whether the families of suicidal people have an increased incidence of mental illness and of suicidal behavior.

Chapter 23
CASE STUDIES OF SUICIDAL PERSONS

Case studies of suicidal people provide a rich and less formal source of information about suicidal people. In chapter 9, the names of famous authors who had killed themselves were listed. Much has been written about these cases. There are also a number of case studies of suicidal people written by psychologists and psychiatrists. The more well known of these are described here. See also section 25.2.

23.101 Alvarez, Alfred. THE SAVAGE GOD: A STUDY OF SUICIDE. New York: Random House, 1971. 299 p.

> This book is written by a poet and a writer. It contains his review of what is known about suicide. However, it is prefaced by a good account of the last few years of the life of Sylvia Plath, an American poet and writer who committed suicide. Alvarez described his own attempt at suicide in an epilogue to the book.

23.102 Asinof, Eliot. CRAIG AND JOAN: TWO LIVES FOR PEACE. New York: Viking, 1971. 245 p.

> This book is written by a journalist and not a psychologist. However, it contains a detailed account of the events leading up to and following the deaths by suicide of two high school adolescents who killed themselves on Vietnam Moratorium Day in 1969.

23.103 Binswanger, Ludwig. "The Case of Ellen West." In EXISTENCE, edited by Rollo May, Ernest Angel, and Henri F. Ellenberger, pp. 237-364. New York: Basic Books, 1958.

> An existentialist psychologist describes the events leading up to the suicidal death of a patient, analyzing her death from an existential viewpoint.

23.104   Bosselman, Beulah C. SELF-DESTRUCTION: A STUDY OF THE SUI-
          CIDAL IMPULSE. Springfield, Ill.: Charles Thomas, 1958. 94 p.

          This book contains some psychiatric information about sui-
          cidal behavior and includes illustrative case studies.

23.105   Farberow, Norman L., and Shneidman, Edwin S., eds. THE CRY FOR
          HELP. New York: McGraw-Hill, 1961. 398 p.

          In this book, the case of a young man who attempted sui-
          cide is described in detail by a psychiatrist, and then six
          psychologists who have proposed theories of personality and
          psychotherapy each describe the case from the point of view
          of his or her theory.

23.106   Lester, Gene, and Lester, David. SUICIDE: THE GAMBLE WITH
          DEATH. Englewood Cliffs, N.J.: Prentice-Hall, 1971. 176 p.

          This book includes a chapter that describes the information
          collected in the course of a psychological autopsy on the
          suicidal death of a young man.

23.107   Niswander, G. Donald; Casey, Thomas M.; and Humphrey, John A.
          A PANORAMA OF SUICIDE. Springfield, Ill.: Charles Thomas,
          1973. 149 p.

          Nine cases of suicide are presented in detail, written from
          the point of view of a psychiatrist. Each one was investi-
          gated by means of a psychological autopsy and is presented
          in detail.

23.108   Reynolds, David K., and Farberow, Norman L. SUICIDE INSIDE AND
          OUT. Berkeley and Los Angeles: University of California Press, 1976.
          226 p.

          David Reynolds pretended to be a suicidal patient and was
          admitted to a psychiatric hospital. He describes what hap-
          pened to him in that setting. The book also contains a
          review of other participant-observer studies of psychiatric
          hospitals.

23.109   Russier, Gabrielle. THE AFFAIR OF GABRIELLE RUSSIER. New York:
          Knopf, 1971. 176 p.

          A discussion of a case of a French school teacher who com-
          mitted suicide in prison after being arrested for seducing one
          of her students. There is an account of the case and some
          letters that she wrote while in prison.

23.110   Shneidman, Edwin S., ed. DEATH AND THE COLLEGE STUDENT.
         New York: Behavioral Publications, 1972. 207 p.

         A series of essays written by Harvard University students,
         including essays on personal suicide attempts and the re-
         actions of the authors to the suicides of others.

Part V

SELECTED REFERENCES ON SUICIDE PREVENTION

Chapter 24
SUICIDE PREVENTION CENTERS

In recent years, many individuals in the United States have thought it important to prevent suicide, that is to prevent people taking their own lives. Part of their effort has been focused on educating the public about suicidal behavior, and the other part of the effort has been focused on setting up mental health agencies whose aim is to help prevent suicide. These agencies are primarily counseling services, with staff specifically trained to work with suicidal individuals, and which are run in a great variety of styles and under varied auspices.

24.1 SETTING UP A SUICIDE PREVENTION CENTER

24.101 Delworth, Ursula; Rudow, Edward H.; and Taub, Janet. CRISIS CEN-
TER HOTLINE. Springfield, Ill.: Charles Thomas, 1972. 144 p.

> A collection of papers that explains how to set up and ad-
> minister a crisis intervention center. Financing, day-to-day
> operations, legal issues, and evaluation are all discussed.
> This book contains the TRAINING MANUAL prepared by
> the staff of the Los Angeles Suicide Prevention Center in
> 1968, which has been the basic training manual for most
> suicide prevention centers.

24.102 Fisher, Sheila A. SUICIDE AND CRISIS INTERVENTION. New York:
Springer, 1973. 279 p.

> Most of this book is concerned with a survey of suicide
> prevention centers in the United States. The book describes
> their goals, funding, location, publicity, training, record
> keeping, and organization. An appendix contains examples
> of referral forms, brochures, counselor application forms,
> training manuals, log sheets, call report forms, and other
> suicide prevention center materials.

24.103 Lester, David, and Brockopp, Gene. CRISIS INTERVENTION AND
COUNSELING BY TELEPHONE. Springfield, Ill.: Charles Thomas,
1973. 322 p.

This book contains chapters that describe goals for suicide
prevention centers, the role that they should play in the
community, and the varieties of models that exist. There
are chapters on legal issues, selecting and training the
suicide prevention worker, specific problems that arise in
such services, such as callers who pose special problems,
and techniques to evaluate how effective the services are.

24.104 McGee, Richard K. CRISIS INTERVENTION IN THE COMMUNITY.
Baltimore: University Park Press, 1974. 307 p.

This book examines the founding and operation of ten crisis
intervention centers and suicide prevention centers. Ten
case histories are presented and their experiences analyzed.
McGee provides a set of guidelines for new centers based
upon the experiences of these centers.

24.105 Varah, Edward C. THE SAMARITANS. London: Constable, 1965.
246 p.

This book describes the suicide prevention movement in
England, where all suicide prevention centers are run by
the Samaritan organization. The book gives a history of
the organization, describes the centers, and illustrates their
counseling techniques.

24.106 World Health Organization. PREVENTION OF SUICIDE. Geneva:
1968. 84 p.

This work looks at the different kinds of suicide prevention
services, education programs, and training programs in
various countries.

See also sections 6.212 and 6.221

24.2 ARE SUICIDE PREVENTION CENTERS EFFECTIVE?

24.201 Bagley, Christopher. "The Evaluation of a Suicide Prevention Scheme
by an Ecological Method." SOCIAL SCIENCE AND MEDICINE 2
(March 1968): 1-4.

A comparison of towns in England with suicide prevention
centers and those without, which shows that the presence
of a suicide prevention center reduces the suicide rate.

24.202 Barraclough, Brian M. "A Medical Approach to Suicide Prevention."
SOCIAL SCIENCE AND MEDICINE 6 (December 1972): 661-71.

A discussion of why suicide prevention has proven effective
in England.

24.203 Barraclough, Brian M.; Jennings, C.; and Moss, J.R. "Suicide Prevention by the Samaritans." LANCET 2 (30 July 1977): 237-39.

Refer to item 24.205.

24.204 Bridge, T. Peter; Potkin, Steven G.; Zung, William W.K.; and Soldo, Beth J. "Suicide Prevention Centers." JOURNAL OF NERVOUS AND MENTAL DISEASE 164 (January 1977): 18-24.

This is a study in North Carolina counties that shows that the establishment of suicide prevention centers had no relationship to the suicide rate of the counties.

24.205 Jennings, C.; Barraclough, Brian M.; and Moss J. "Have the Samaritans Lowered the Suicide Rate?" PSYCHOLOGICAL MEDICINE 8 (August 1978): 413-22.

Items 24.203 and 24.205 report a study in England to check upon Bagley's findings that suicide prevention centers prevent suicide. These reports find that Bagley's conclusion was wrong.

24.206 Lester, David. "Effect of Suicide Prevention Centers on Suicide Rates in the United States." HEALTH SERVICE REPORTS 89 (January-February 1974): 37-39.

This comparison of cities in the United States with suicide prevention centers and those without, shows that the presence of a suicide prevention center does not affect the suicide rate of the city.

24.207 _____. "The Myth of Suicide Prevention." COMPREHENSIVE PSYCHIATRY 13 (November-December 1972): 555-60.

A discussion of the various reasons why suicide prevention centers have not reduced suicidal behavior in America.

Several of the books cited in section 24.1 have chapters on the evaluation of suicide prevention centers and crisis intervention centers. Cited below are two reviews of the work of those who have tried to evaluate the effectiveness of such centers.

24.208 Auerback, Stephen M., and Kilmann, Peter R. "Crisis Intervention: A Review of Outcome Research." PSYCHOLOGICAL BULLETIN 84 (November 1977): 1189-1217.

Refer to item 24.209.

24.209 Lester, David. "The Evaluation of Telephone Counseling Services." CRISIS INTERVENTION 4, no. 2 (1972): 53-60.

The article by Lester reviews research pertinent only to
telephone crisis intervention services, whereas the article
by Auerbach and Kilmann (24.208) reviews research pertinent to all kinds of crisis intervention services and is
more current.

24.3 STANDARDS FOR SUICIDE PREVENTION CENTERS

Suicide prevention centers are not presently licensed or inspected in any systematic way to see that they meet acceptable standards. However, some progress has been made toward setting up standards against which centers can be
judged. The following publications describe such standards.

24.301   Motto, Jerome A. "Development of Standards for Suicide Prevention
         Centers." BULLETIN OF SUICIDOLOGY (March 1969): 33-37.

24.302   Ross, Charlotte P., and Motto, Jerome A. "Implementation of Stan-
         dards for Suicide Prevention Centers." BULLETIN OF SUICIDOLOGY
         (Fall 1971): 18-21.

The work by Motto and his colleagues has more recently been written up more
extensively in book format:

24.303   Motto, Jerome A.; Brooks, Richard M.; Ross, Charlotte P.; and Allen,
         Nancy J. STANDARDS FOR SUICIDE PREVENTION AND CRISIS
         CENTERS. New York: Behavioral Publications, 1974. 114 p.

24.4 WHY PREVENT SUICIDE?

Not all investigators believe that suicide should be prevented. Some argue that
people have a right to kill themselves if they choose.

24.401   Lester, David. "The Concept of an Appropriate Death." PSYCHOL-
         OGY 7 (November 1970): 61-66.

         Refer to item 24.402.

24.402   _____. "Suicide as a Positive Act." PSYCHOLOGY 6 (August
         1969): 43-48.

         Lester argues that suicide may, in some circumstances, be
         an appropriate choice and that the behavior should not
         always be prevented.

24.403   Novak, David. SUICIDE AND MORALITY. New York: Scholars
          Studies, 1975. 136 p.

          Novak explores three philosophical arguments that favor
          prohibiting suicide.

24.404   Noyes, Russell. "Shall We Prevent Suicide?" COMPREHENSIVE
          PSYCHIATRY 11 (July 1970): 361-70.

          A general discussion of whether suicide should be considered
          good or bad and whether it should be prevented.

24.405   Pretzel, Paul W. "Philosophical and Ethical Considerations of Suicide
          Prevention." BULLETIN OF SUICIDOLOGY (July 1968): 30-38.

          Pretzel takes the position that suicide should be prevented
          and that rational suicides do not exist.

See also section 6.209

24.5 THE TREATMENT OF SUICIDAL PERSONS

24.501   Barraclough, Brian M. "A Medical Approach to Suicide Prevention."
          SOCIAL SCIENCE AND MEDICINE 6 (December 1972): 661-67.

          A good discussion of the medical approach to treatment,
          focusing on the role of the general practitioner and psy-
          chiatrist.

24.502   Comstock, Betsy S., and McDermott, Margaret. "Group Therapy for
          Patients Who Attempt Suicide." INTERNATIONAL JOURNAL OF
          GROUP PSYCHOTHERAPY 25 (January 1975): 44-49.

          Refer to item 24.503.

24.503   Frederick, Calvin J., and Farberow, Norman L. "Group Therapy with
          Suicidal Persons." INTERNATIONAL JOURNAL OF SOCIAL PSY-
          CHIATRY 16 (Spring 1970): 103-11.

          These two articles (24.502 and 24.503) discuss the use of
          group therapy in treating suicidal people.

24.504   Kiev, Ari. "Psychotherapeutic Strategies in the Management of De-
          pressed and Suicidal Patients." AMERICAN JOURNAL OF PSYCHO-
          THERAPY 29 (July 1975): 345-54.

          A discussion of the use of crisis intervention, chemotherapy,
          and supportive psychotherapy with suicidal patients. Kiev
          discusses in detail his format for crisis intervention, which
          involves teaching strategies for daily living.

24.505 Lesse, Stanley. "The Range of Therapies in the Treatment of Severely Depressed Suicidal Patients." AMERICAN JOURNAL OF PSYCHO-THERAPY 29 (July 1975): 308-26.

> Lesse discusses the qualities that a successful therapist should have for treating suicidal people, the aims of therapy at each phase of treatment, and appropriate techniques, including medication, electroconvulsive shock, and psychotherapy.

24.506 Maltsberger, John T., and Bule, Dan H. "Countertransference Hate in the Treatment of Suicidal Patients." ARCHIVES OF GENERAL PSYCHIATRY 30 (May 1974): 625-33.

> This article discusses the hostility that the therapist may feel toward suicidal patients, how it may be deleterious to the patient's health, and what steps the therapist may take to deal with it.

24.507 Mintz, Ronald S. "Basic Considerations in the Psychotherapy of the Depressed Suicidal Patient." AMERICAN JOURNAL OF PSYCHO-THERAPY 25 (January 1971): 56-73.

> A good discussion of the techniques of therapy useful for suicidal people and some of the problems encountered with them.

24.508 Schwartz, Donald A.; Flinn, Don E.; and Slawson, Paul F. "Treatment of the Suicidal Character." AMERICAN JOURNAL OF PSYCHO-THERAPY 28 (April 1974): 194-207.

> A discussion of the treatment of the person who is chronically suicidal, but who is otherwise not psychiatrically ill.

24.509 Tabachnick, Norman. "The Crisis Treatment of Suicide." WESTERN JOURNAL OF MEDICINE 69 (June 1970): 1-8, and CALIFORNIA MEDICINE 112 (June 1970): 1-8.

> A good discussion of suicide as a crisis and the crisis intervention approach to treatment.

See also items 1.107, 1.108, 1.111, 1.112, and 1.113.

Chapter 25
THE PREDICTION OF SUICIDE

In order to prevent suicide, it is useful to be able to predict which people are likely to kill themselves in the future. Much research has been directed toward developing this capability. In addition to analysis of the psychological and social correlates of suicide (parts III and IV of this book) as means of suicide prediction, special techniques and tests have been developed to identify potential suicides.

25.1 IDENTIFICATION OF SUICIDAL POTENTIAL

25.101 Brown, Timothy, and Sheran, Tamara J. "Suicide Prediction." LIFE THREATENING BEHAVIOR 2 (Summer 1972): 67-98.

Refer to item 25.104.

25.102 Conference on Identifying Suicide Potential. IDENTIFYING SUICIDE POTENTIAL: CONFERENCE PROCEEDINGS. Edited by Dorothy B. Anderson, and Lenora J. McClean. New York: Behavioral Publications, 1971. 112 p.

This series of papers given by experts at a conference cover the problem of suicidal behavior in various special groups such as college students, blacks, and alcoholics. There are two chapters on the prevention of suicide. Despite its title, the book does not systematically explore how to identify suicide potential in any quantitative way.

25.103 Lester, David. "Attempts to Predict Suicidal Risk Using Psychological Tests." PSYCHOLOGICAL BULLETIN 74 (July 1970): 1-17.

Refer to item 25.104.

25.104 Murphy, George E. "Clinical Identification of Suicidal Risk." ARCHIVES OF GENERAL PSYCHIATRY 27 (September 1972): 356-59.

These three articles (25.101, 25.103, and 25.104) provide independent reviews of recent research on the problem of prediction. They also survey a wide variety of psychological tests that have been used for this purpose.

25.105   Neuringer, Charles. PSYCHOLOGICAL ASSESSMENT OF SUICIDAL RISK. Springfield, Ill.: Charles Thomas, 1974. 240 p.

A review by various experts on the use of psychological tests and scales based on personal and social characteristics to predict suicide.

25.106   _____. "The Rorschach Test as a Research Device for the Identification, Prediction and Understanding of Suicidal Ideation and Behavior." JOURNAL OF PROJECTIVE TECHNIQUES AND PERSONALITY ASSESSMENT 29 (March 1965): 71-82.

In this article, Neuringer reviews research on the use of the Rorschach Ink Blot Test as a means of predicting suicidal behavior, and in doing so identifies most of the important issues that must be addressed by investigators.

25.107   THE PREDICTION OF SUICIDE. Edited by Aaron T. Beck; Harvey L.P. Resnik; and Dan J. Lettieri. Bowie, Md.: Charles Press, 1974. 249 p.

This book contains a collection of articles from leading authorities on suicide prediction. They present data on the very latest developments of special scales to predict suicidal behavior, and there are articles from leading critics and commentators on the topic of prediction.

Scales designed especially to predict suicidal behavior have recently been developed. Examples may be found in the book by Beck et al., above (25.107). The first scale of this type was developed by the Los Angeles Suicide Prevention Center and a revised version of this scale may be found in item 25.108.

25.108   Lester, David. "The Physician and Suicide." SANDORAMA, no. 2, 1972, pp. 19-21.

25.109   Whittemore, Kenneth R. TEN CENTERS. Atlanta: Lullwater Press, 1970. 82 p.

See also section 6.2111.

25.2 FOLLOW-UPS OF ATTEMPTED SUICIDES

Much of the work on suicide prediction involves identifying attempted suicides and exploring which variables predict which of these persons will subsequently kill themselves.

25.201 Alpert, George, and Leogrande, Ernest. SECOND CHANCE TO LIVE. New York: DeCapo Press, 1975. Unpaged.

A journalistic and photographic study of several people who tried to kill themselves but survived.

25.202 Retterstol, I. Nils. LONG-TERM PROGNOSIS AFTER ATTEMPTED SUICIDE. Springfield, Ill.: Charles Thomas, 1970. 112 p.

In this book, Retterstol conducted a more general study of what happens to a group of people who tried to kill themselves. He reports on their state several years after their initial suicide attempt.

INDEXES

NAME INDEX

This index lists all names associated with the items included in this information guide, with the exception of commercial publishers. It lists, therefore, personal authors, coauthors, editors, and compilers, as well as agencies, including government agencies, associations, libraries, organizations, and institutions. References are to entry numbers for the corresponding items in the guide. Alphabetization is letter by letter.

A

Abbiati, David L. 6.215
Abraham, Yair 6.203
Adam, Kenneth S. 2.301
Aeschylus 9.204
Aiken, Conrad 9.204
Ainsworth, William H. 9.204
Akey, Denise 12.104
Albee, Edward 9.204
Aldington, Richard 9.204
Aleman, Mateo 9.204
Allen, Nancy J. 24.303
Alpert, George 25.201
Alternative Press Center 10.201
Alvarez, Alfred 1.101, 23.101
Amberg, William F. 6.212
American Association of Law
   Libraries 8.503
American Association of Suicidology
   12.301
American Dental Association 5.117
American Film Institute, The 11.101
American Hospital Association 5.113
American Journal of Nursing 5.126
American Library Association 4.303,
   5.129, 9.601, 9.608, 9.701

American Psychological Association
   5.219
American Society of Hospital Pharma-
   cists 5.127
American Theological Library Asso-
   ciation 5.221
Amicis, Edmondo de 9.204
Amis, Kingsley 9.204
Anderson, Dorothy B. 25.102
Anderson, Maxwell 9.204
Anderson, Sherwood 9.204
Andress, LaVern R. 6.215
Andrews, Eva L. 9.608
Andric, Ivo 9.204
Annunzio, Gabriele d' 9.204
Ansel, Edward L. 6.212
Arieti, Silvano 4.101
Aristotle 9.902
Arnold, Matthew 9.204
Artsybashev, Mikhail 9.204
Ash, Lee 12.103
Asinof, Eliot 23.102
Aslib 6.101
Asturias, Miguel 9.204
Auden, W.H. 9.204
Auerback, Stephen M. 24.208
Augustine 9.902
Aurelius, Antonius Marcus 9.902

Name Index

Azuela, Mariano 9.204

B

Bagley, Christopher R. 13.102,
16.214, 24.201
Baldwin, James 9.204
Balzac, Honore de 9.204
Barbier, Auguste 9.204
Barclay, John 9.204
Barnes, Thomas J. 6.211
Barraclough, Brian M. 13.401,
13.402, 13.407, 16.252, 17.502,
17.503, 24,202, 24.203, 24.205,
24.501
Barrie, James M. 9.204
Barrios, Eduardo 9.204
Barth, John 9.204
Bartman, Erwin R. 6.221
Bates, Mary E. 9.502
Bax, Clifford 9.204
Beall, Lynnette 2.302, 19.101
Beaumont, Francis 9.204
Beck, Aaron T. 13.104, 13.301,
13.303, 16.217, 22.204, 25.107
Becker, Herman A. 21.204
Beckett, Samuel 9.204
Beddoes, Thomas Lovell 9.1, 9.204
Beegle, J. Allen 16.232
Beerbohm, Max 9.204
Behn, Aphra 9.204
Beigel, Allan 19.501
Belanger, Robert R. 6.212
Bell, Don E. 6.201
Bellow, Saul 9.204
Bennett, Arnold 9.204
Bergner, Lawrence 17.201
Berk, Norman 6.213
Bernanos, Georges 9.204
Bernard, William Bayle 9.204
Besterman, Theodore 2.101
Beyle, Marie Henri 9.204
Bhagat, M. 17.101
Bierce, Ambrose 9.1, 12.105
Bilboul, Roger R. 6.109
Billings, James H. 6.221
Binswanger, Ludwig 23.103
BioSciences Information Service
5.104, 5.205
Bjornson, Bjornstjerne 9.204

Blachly, P.H. 16.237
Black, Dorothy M. 6.102
Black, Kimball D. 6.215
Block, H. Barrett 16.260
Blok, Aleksandr 9.204
Blumenthal, Sol 17.201
Boccaccio, Giovanni 9.204
Bock, E. Wilbur 16.210, 16.211
Bohannon, Paul 18.201
Bosselman, Beulah C. 1.201,
23.104
Boswell, James 9.902
Boswell, John W. 19.201, 21.202
Bourget, Paul 9.204
Bouwman, Robert E. 6.206
Bowen, Elizabeth 9.204
Bowles, Stephen E. 11.301
Bradshaw, Alfred D. 6.215
Braine, John 9.204
Brecht, Bertolt 9.204
Breed, Warren 16.229, 16.251
Brengelmann, J.C. 16.233
Bridge, T. Peter 24.204
Brigham Young University Library
5.121
Bristol, Roger P. 3.303
British Museum. Department of
Printed Books 3.101
Brockopp, Gene 24.103
Broke, Arthur 9.204
Bronte, Anne 9.204
Bronte, Emily 9.204
Brooke, Eileen M. 1.102, 2.201,
13.403, 16.241
Brooks, Richard M. 24.303
Brown, Charles Brockden 9.204
Brown, George Douglas 9.204
Brown, Irving R. 6.213
Brown, Timothy R. 6.211, 25.101
Browning, Robert 9.204
Bruncken, Herbert 9.602
Bruntjen, Carol 3.304
Bruntjen, Scott 3.304
Buchanan, William W. 8.302
Buchner, Georg 9.204
Buckley, K.A.H. 7.108
Bule, Dan H. 24.506
Bunin, Ivan 9.204
Bunzel, Bessie 17.103
Bureau of the Census. See U.S.
Bureau of the Census

Name Index

Data Courier 12.401
Daudet, Alphonse 9.204
David, Henry P. 16.233
Davies, Mark I. 6.217
Daviot, Gordon. See MacKintosh, Elizabeth
Davis, Andre 9.204
Davis, Fred 16.263
Davis, Frederick B. 13.101, 16.218
Davis, Joseph H. 13.301
Davis, Robert 6.215
Dazai, Osamu 9.1
Defoe, Daniel 9.204
Dekker, Edward D. 9.204
Dekker, Thomas 9.204
de la Mare, Walter 9.204
Delong, W. Bradford 21.201
Delworth, Ursula 24.101
Demi, Alice M. 6.220
Demmer, Charles C. 6.215
Demopulos, Alexander 6.218
Dennis, Nigel 9.204
Devries, Alcon G. 6.211
Diamond, Harriet A. 6.214
Dickens, Charles 9.204
Digon, Edward 16.260
Disher, William 16.237
Dizmang, Larry H. 18.202
Documentation Associates 2.305
Dohrenwend, Bruce P. 14.204
Doroff, David R. 6.219
Dorpat, Theodore L. 19.201, 20.201, 21.202
Dos Passos, John 9.204
Dostoyevsky, Fyodor 9.204
Douglas, George. See Brown, George Douglas
Douglas, Jack D. 6.216, 13.405, 14.104, 14.201, 16.224
Draper, Edgar 22.201
Dreiser, Theodore 9.204
Dryden, John 9.204
Dublin, Louis I. 1.104, 17.102, 17.103
Dumas, Alexandre 9.204
Du Maurier, Daphne 9.204
Dunn, Olav 9.204
Duranty, Louis Edmond 9.204
Durham, Thomas W. 6.211
Durkheim, Emile 14.102, 14.103, 14.204 to 14.212

Durrell, Lawrence 9.204

E

Educational Film Library Association 11.302
Educational Resources Information Center. See U.S. Educational Resources Information Center
Edwards, J.E. 16.240
Edwards, Paul 4.107
Egger, Norman L. 6.212
Eliot, George 9.204
Elliott, Thomas B. 6.213
Epictetus 9.902
ERIC. See U.S. Educational Resources Information Center
Erickson, Gustave A. 6.221
Esenin, Sergei 9.204
Esler, Harold D. 6.213
Euyripides 9.202, 9.204, 9.902
Evans, Charles 3.306
Excerpta Criminologica Foundation 5.202

F

Faber, Melvin D. 6.217, 9.1, 9.201, 9.202, 9.204, 9.904
Farber, Maurice L. 15.201, 16.225, 18.203
Farberow, Norman L. 1.105, 1.117, 2.202, 6.213, 12.101, 13.201, 13.406, 13.408, 15.202, 16.212, 16.213, 16.233, 17.106, 18.204, 18.205, 19.304, 20.101, 21.101, 21.105, 21.109, 21.111, 23,105, 23.108, 24.503
Faulkner, William 9.204
Faux, Eugene J. 1.108
Faxon, Frederick W. 9.502
Fayers, Peter 13.402
Fedden, Henry R. 1.202
Ferguson, Charlotte G. 6.216
Fernandez, Ramon 9.1
Feuchtwanger, Lion 9.204
Fidell, Estelle A. 9.303
Fielding, Henry 9.204, 9.902
Finch, Stuart M. 16.202
Firkins, Ina Ten Eyck 9.503
Firth, Raymond 18.206

Name Index

Jarrell, Randall 9.1, 9.204, 12.103, 12.105
Jeffers, Robinson 9.204
Jellicoe, Ann 9.204
Jennings, C. 24.203, 24.205
Jensen, Johannes V. 9.204
Johnson, Barclay D. 14.206
Johnson, Eva 19.103
Johnson, Samuel 16.244, 16.257
Johnson, Uwe 9.204
Jokai, Maurus (Mor) 9.204
Jones, Henry Arthur 9.204
Jones, Leonard A. 8.502
Jones, Ronald B. 6.211
Jones, Warren L. 13.207
Jonson, Ben 9.204
Joyce, James 9.204
Juechter, Joanne K. 6.212
Jung, Carl 15.204

K

Kalish, Richard A. 13.302
Kanely, Edna M. 8.302
Kant, Immanuel 9.902
Kasper, August 13.207
Kastenbaum, Robert 13.409
Kayes, Jack 21.203
Kazantzakes, Nikos 9.204
Keckeissen, Rita G. 4.303
Kees, Weldon 9.1, 12.103, 12.105
Kelly, James 3.308
Kendra, John M. 6.211
Kennedy, Adrienne 9.204
Kent, Francis L. 6.109
Kesey, Ken 9.204
Kiev, Ari 24.504
Kilmann, Peter R. 24.208
Kilpatrick, Diane C. 6.213
Kinsinger, John R. 6.211
Kirk, Alton R. 6.202
Klagsbrun, Francine 16.206
Kleist, Heinrich von 9.1
Knickerbocker, David A. 6.212
Kochansky, Gerald E. 6.213
Koller, K.M. 19.401
Korella, Karl 6.219
Kovacs, Maria 16.217
Kramer, Morton 16.101
Krauss, Beatrice J. 18.104

Krauss, Herbert H. 6.205
Kreitman, Norman 13.102, 17.203
Kriezman, Garry 16.239
Krohn, Marvin D. 6.216
Kyd, Thomas 9.204

L

Labovitz, Sanford 14.211, 16.238
Land, Brian 12.307
Larsson, Tage 1.119
Lawrence, D.H. 9.204
Lee, Mercile J. 6.213
Le Fanu, Joseph S. 9.204
Leighton, Alexander H. 18.210
Lemerond, John N. 6.211
Leogrande, Ernest 25.201
Leonard, Calista V. 1.203, 15.205
Lermontov, Mikhail 9.204
Le Sage, Alain-Rene 9.204
Leshem, Ariel 6.201
Leshem, Yonina 6.201
Lesse, Stanley 24.505
Lester, David 1.109, 1.204, 2.303, 6.213, 9.203, 13.103, 13.104, 13.203, 14.202, 14.213, 16.217, 16.220, 16.221, 16.247, 17.405, 17.406, 19.202, 20.103 to 20.106, 20.202, 21.110, 21.114, 22.103, 22.104, 22.203, 22.204, 22.301, 22.501, 23.106, 24.103, 24.206, 24.207, 24.209, 24.401, 24.402, 25.103, 25.108
Lester, Gene 1.109, 23.106
Lettieri, Dan J. 6.213, 13.303, 25.107
Levenson, Marvin 6.213
Lewis, Marianno O. 12.204
Lewis, Sinclair 9.204
Lewis, Wyndham 9.204
Li, Hsing-Tao 9.204
Library Association (London) 4.304, 5.105
Library Association of the United Kingdom 5.129
Library of Congress. See U.S. Library of Congress
Lie, Jonas 9.204
Lindsay, Vachel 9.1, 12.103, 12.105

Name Index

Linehan, Marsha M. 6.214, 16.222
Litman, Robert E. 12.101, 13.207, 13.406, 15.102, 15.103, 20.107 to 20.109
Ljunberg, Lennart 19.104
Ljungstedt, Nils 1.119
Llewellyn, Richard 9.204
Lloyd, David 8.202
Locke, Ben Z. 16.101
Locke, John 9.902
Lockheed Information Systems 5.301
Lockridge, Ross F., Jr. 9.1, 9.204
Logasa, Hannah 9.505
London, Jack 9.1, 12.103, 12.105
Lowry, Malcom 9.204
Lucan 9.1
Lucretius Carus, Titus 9.902
Lum, Doman 6.221
Lunden, Walter A. 16.256
Lynn, R. 16.234

M

McAnarney, Elizabeth R. 16.207
McClean, Lenora J. 25.102
McClure, James N. 16.223
McCoy, Horace 9.204
McCullers, Carson 9.204
McCulloch, James W. 1.205, 16.248, 16.249
Macculloch, John Arnott 9.903
McDermott, Margaret 24.502
McEvoy, Theodore L. 6.213
McGee, Richard K. 24.104
McGrath, Marcia K.K. 6.213
Machen, Arthur 9.204
McIlvaine, Eileen 4.303
Mackenzie, Henry 9.204
MacKinnon, Douglas R. 6.215
MacKintosh, Elizabeth 9.204
MacMahon, Brian 16.244, 16.257, 17.105, 19.109
Madame de Staell. See Stael-Hostein, Anna Louise Germaine de
Maeterlinck, Maurice 9.204
Malraux, Andre 9.204
Maltsberger, John T. 24.506
Mann, Thomas 9.204
Mapes, Bruce E. 6.219
Margolin, N. Lionel 22.405

Marie de France 9.204
Maris, Ronald W. 6.216, 14.214, 16.226, 16.250
Marks, Alan H. 6.215
Markson, D.S. 8.101
Marshall, James R. 6.215
Martin, Harry A. 6.211
Martin, Walter T. 14.103, 14.212
Massey, James T. 16.201, 16.216
Massinger, Philip 9.204
Masters, Edgar L. 9.204
Matthieson, Francis O. 9.1, 12.105
Maturin, Charles 9.204
Maugham, W. Somerset 9.204
Maupassant, Guy de 9.204
Mayakovski, Vladimir 9.1, 9.204
Meer, Fatima 18.211
Meerloo, Joost A.M. 15.104, 20.203
Mefferd, Roy B. 16.264
Melville, Herman 9.204, 9.902
Menninger, Karl 13.204, 19.203
Mercer, David 9.204
Metalious, Grace 9.1
Micklin, Michael 14.208
Middleton, Thomas 9.204
Miley, James D. 6.216, 14.208
Miller, Arthur 9.204
Miller, Dorothy H. 6.216
Miller, Henry 9.204
Miller, Marv 6.214
Milner, John R. 6.204
Milton, John 9.204, 9.902
Mintz, Ronald S. 24.507
Mishima, Yukio 9.1, 12.105
Moffat, John 13.207
Molnar, Ferenc 9.204
Monck, Maurine F. 6.210
Monkhouse, Allan 9.204
Montaigne, Michel Eyguem de 9.902
Montesquieu, Charles Louis de Secondat 9.902
Moore, G.F. 9.903
Moravia, Alberto. See Pincherle, Alberto
Morgan, Marilyn W. 6.205
Moriwaki, Sharon Y. 16.212
Morris, Adah V. 5.128
Morrison, Donald 2.207
Moss, J.R. 24.203, 24.205

Name Index

Stein, Kenneth 13.201
Steinbeck, John 9.204
Steinkerchner, Raymond E. 6.211
Stendhal. See Beyle, Marie Henri
Stengel, Erwin 1.118, 13.408,
16.228
Stephens, James 9.204
Stevenson, Robert Louis 9.204
Stone, Howard W. 6.220
Stone, Philip J. 21.103
Strindberg, August 9.204
Styron, William 9.204
Sudermann, Hermann 9.204
Sue, Eugene 9.204
Suicide Prevention Center of Los
Angeles 12.101
Superintendent of Documents. See
U.S. Superintendent of Documents
Sutherland, Anne C. 9.502
Sutro, Alfred 9.204
Sutton, Wiley D. 6.207
Swenson, David D. 18.202
Swift, Jonathan 9.204, 9.902
Synge, J.M. 9.204
Systems Development Search Service
5.302

T

Tabachnick, Norman 13.206, 13.207,
13.406, 15.206, 24.509
Tacitus, Cornelius 9.902
Tan, Eng-Seong 17.203
Tapper, Bruce P. 6.213
Taub, Janet 24.101
Tauber, Ronald K. 6.213
Teasdale, Sara 9.1, 12.105
Teicher, Joseph D. 17.404, 22.404,
22.405
Telephonic Emergency Help Services
12.305
Temoche, Abelardo 6.213, 19.109
Tennant, Donald A. 6.216
Tennyson, Alfred 9.204
Thomas, Robert C. 12.311
Thompson, Lois E.L. 6.212
Thomson, Ruth G. 9.507
Tod, Dorothea 3.314
Toller, Ernst 9.1, 12.105
Tolstoy, Leo 9.204, 9.902

Toolan, James M. 16.209
Toomey, Alice F. 2.101
Trakl, George 9.1
Traven, B. 9.204
Tremaine, Marie 3.315
Trexler, Larry 13.104
Trollope, Anthony 9.204
Tsao, Chan 9.204
Tucholosky, Kurt 9.1
Tuckman, Jacob 16.239, 16.242,
19.506, 21.107
Turgenev, Ivan 9.204
Twain, Mark 9.204

U

Undset, Sigrid 9.204
UNESCO (United Nations Educational
Scientific and Cultural Organiza-
tion) 3.401, 3.402, 5.124,
5.125
Union of International Associations
12.310
United Nations 7.102, 7.303
U.S. Air University. Library
5.139
U.S. Bureau of the Census 7.106,
7.107, 7.208
U.S. Census Office 7.201 to 7.206
U.S. Educational Resources Informa-
tion Center (ERIC) 6.302
U.S. Library of Congress 3.104,
11.210
U.S. Library of Congress. Catalog
Publication Division 10.304,
10.305
U.S. Library of Congress. Division
of Documents 7.305
U.S. Library of Congress. National
Referral Center 12.107
U.S. National Center for Health
Statistics 7.209 to 7.212,
7.217, 7.306
U.S. National Clearinghouse for
Mental Health Information
5.220, 5.503, 12.102
U.S. Office of Education 12.209
U.S. Office of Management and
Budget 12.210
U.S. Superintendent of Documents
3.107, 7.307, 8.303

260

Name Index

Z

Zeromski, Stefan 9.204
Ziegler, Ralph 21.107

Zola, Emile 9.204
Zung, William W.K. 24.204
Zweig, Stephan 9.1, 12.103, 12.105

TITLE INDEX

This index lists titles of all books, reports, periodical articles, documents, dissertations, sets, and series included in this information guide. Some titles are listed in shortened form. References are to the entry numbers for the corresponding items in the guide. Items in section 9.204 are indicated by page number. Alphabetization is letter by letter.

Title Index

Title Index

Title Index

Title Index

Title Index

Joyeux Pendu, Le   p. 128
Jude the Obscure   p. 123
Judgment of Suicide Lethality, The
  6.211
Judith Paris   p. 131
Julius Caesar   p. 129
Junior High School Library Catalog
  9.802
Justice   p. 121

K

Karl Ludwig's Window   p. 126
Kenilworth   p. 128
King, the Greatest Alcalde, The
  p. 131
King Horn   p. 116
King Lear   p. 129
Kings in Exile   p. 119
Kreutzer Sonata, The   p. 130
Kristin Lavransdatter   p. 130

L

Lady from the Sea, The   p. 124
Lady of Shalott, The   p. 130
Lady's Not for Burning, The   p. 121
L'Aiglon   p. 128
Lais of Marie de France, The   p. 125
L'Amorosa Fiametta   p. 117
Language Usage and Social Maturity
  as Related to Suicide Notes
  21.107
Last Athenian, The   p. 128
Last Chronicle of Barset, The   p. 130
Last Puritan, The   p. 128
Last Tycoon, The   p. 121
Late Mattia Pascal, The   p. 127
Lathrop Report on Newspaper Indexes
  10.302
Lay Volunteer and Professional
  Trainee Therapeutic Functioning
  and Outcomes in a Suicide and
  Crisis Intervention Service   6.212
Leave Her to Heaven   p. 131
Legal Research in a Nutshell   8.201
Legal Responsibility for Suicide
  8.104
Legend of Good Women, The   p. 118
Lethal Aggression Rate and the
  Suicide-Murder Ratio, The   6.216

Liability of Hospital and Psychiatrist
  in Suicide   8.102
Library Literature   4.305
Library of Congress Catalog. Books:
  Subjects   3.104
Library of Congress Catalogs: Films
  and Other Materials for Projec-
  tion   11.210
Library of Congress Catalogs--
  Subject Catalog   3.104
Lie Down in Darkness   p. 130
Life Line International Newsletter
  12.304
Life's Trial, A   p. 116
Ligeia   p. 127
Liliom   p. 126
List of Doctoral Dissertations
  Printed   6.103
Little Minister, The   p. 116
'Loci Communes' on Death and
  Suicide in the Literature of the
  English Renaissance   6.217
Lockheed Information Systems   5.301
Logic of Suicide, The   19.304
Longest Journey, The   p. 121
Long Journey, The   p. 124
Long Lent Loathes Light: A Study of
  Suicide in Three English Non-
  dramatic Writers of the Sixteenth
  Century   6.217
Long-Term Prognosis after Attempted
  Suicide   25.202
Lord Jim   p. 118
Lost Illusions   p. 116
Lost Weekend, The   p. 124
Lotos-eaters, The   p. 130
Lower Depths, The   p. 122
Loyalties, The   p. 121

M

Macbeth   p. 129
Madame Bovary   p. 121
Mad Hercules   p. 128
Madwoman of Chaillot, The   p. 121
Magazine Index   5.127
Maggie   p. 129
Maggie: A Girl of the Streets
  p. 118
Magic Mountain, The   p. 125

Title Index

Title Index

Title Index

Q

Quo Vadis p. 129

R

Race and Suicide in South Africa
18.211
Race Suicide 6.206
Rainbow, The p. 124
Raintree County p. 125
Range of Therapies in the Treatment of
Severely Depressed Suicidal
Patients, The 24.505
Rape of Lucrece, The p. 129
Reader's Digest Almanac and Yearbook
4.202
Readers' Guide to Periodical Litera-
ture 5.132
Rebecca p. 120
Reckoning p. 125
Red and the Black, The p. 117
Redburn p. 126
Red Room, The p. 130
Reference Catalogue of Current
Literature 3.202
Regional Comparison of Attitudes
toward Suicide and Methods of
Self-Destruction, A 6.215
Relation between Attempted Suicide
and Completed Suicide 13.103
Relation of Suicidal Behavior to
Characteristics of the Significant
Other, The 6.207, 17.407
Relationship between Bioelectric
Potential Differences and Suicidal
Behavior, The 6.210
Relationship between Certain Problem
Areas and Suicidal Thoughts of
Adolescents, The 6.213
Relationship between Lethality of
Suicidal Intentions, The 6.211
Relationship between Parental Loss
and Attempted Suicide, The
19.102
Relationship between Suicide and
Attempted Suicide, The 13.101
Relationship between Suicide and
Homicide, The 20.202
Relations of Suicide Rates to Social
Conditions 16.244

Religion Index/One: Periodicals
5.221
Religious and Theological Abstracts
5.222
Renee Mauperin p. 122
Research Centers Directory 12.106
Research in Education 6.302
Resentment and Dependency in the
Suicidal Individual 17.405
Resources in Education 6.302
Responding to Suicidal Communica-
tions 6.221
Retrospective Index to Theses of
Great Britain and Ireland 6.109
Return, The p. 119
Return of the Native, The p. 123
Revenge of Bussy D'Ambois p. 118
Revisions and Further Tests of the
Theory of Status Integration and
Suicide 6.216
Riders in the Chariot p. 132
Rigidity in a Risk-Taking Task among
Serious Suicide Attempters and
Nonsuicidal Psychiatric Patients
6.213
Rigid Thinking in Suicidal Individuals
19.303
Risk-taking and Hedonic Mood
Stimulation in Suicide Attempters
6.213
Role Failure and Suicide 6.216
Role of Acting-out and Identifica-
tion in Adolescent Suicidal
Behavior, The 6.219
Role of Dread in Suicidal Behavior
21.106
Role of the College Counselor and
Suicide among Students 6.212
Rolla p. 126
Romance of a Schoolmaster, The
p. 115
Romeo and Juliet p. 129
Romeus and Juliet p. 117
Room at the Top p. 117
Rorschach Study of a Suicide, A
6.211
Rorschach Test as a Research Device
for the Identification, Prediction
and Understanding of Suicidal
Ideation and Behavior, The
25.106

Title Index

Title Index

Title Index

SUBJECT INDEX

The subject headings and subheadings listed in this index are in relation to suicide, even though the word "suicide" may not appear in the heading. Following each heading and subheading are entry numbers referring to the corresponding items in this information guide. A few references are to specific chapters. Author names in parentheses have been inserted as an aid to the reader. Alphabetization is letter by letter.

A

Accidents. See Suicide by automobile; Suicide by aircraft
Addicts, heroin 19.504
Adolescent suicide. See Suicide, adolescent
Africa, suicide in 18.201
Age 6.215 (O'Connell), 16.101, 16.201 to 16.212, 21.108, 21.109. See also Numbers and rates of suicide--age
Aged, suicide among 4.111, 6.214 (Miller), 16.210 to 16.214
Aggression 6.211 (Kinsinger), 6.213 (Lester, Rutstein, Waugh), 6.216 (Whitt), 20.101 to 20.109, 22.101
Aircraft. See Suicide by aircraft
Alaska, suicide in 18.210
Alcoholics, suicide among 19.105, 19.106, 19.402, 19.403, 25.102
Alcoholism and suicide 4.108, 5.204, 13.204, 13.205, 19.401, 19.404, 19.405

American Indians, suicide among 6.205 (Morgan), 18.202, 18.212, 18.215
Anomie 6.213 (Greth), 14.204, 14.205
Anthropology. See Suicide-- anthropological aspects
Armed forces personnel, suicide among. See Military personnel, suicide among
Asphyxia, suicide by 6.215 (Hutcherson)
Assertive training 6.221 (Bartman)
Associations, national. See Organizations, national
Attempted suicide. See Suicide, attempted
Attitudes and opinions on suicide 6.201, 6.203 (Windsor), 6.207 (Shagoury), 6.213 (Lettieri), 6.215 (Marks), 10.401, 10.402
Audiovisuals 3.103, 5.103, 5.110, ch. 11, 12.102
Australia, suicide in 16.254
Authors, suicide among 9.1, 12.103, 12.105

Subject Index

Automobiles. See Suicide by automobiles
Autopsies. See Coroners and medical examiners
Autopsy, psychological 13.404, 13.409, 23.106, 23.107

B

Behavior modification 6.221 (Corte)
Bible and suicide 9.901. See also Religious aspects of suicide
Bibliographies ch. 2, 12.102
Bioelectric potential 6.210
Birth order 22.301
Blacks, suicide among 6.202, 6.215 (Davis), 16.201, 16.214 to 16.216, 18.204, 18.207, 22.101, 25.102. See also Numbers and rates of suicide-- race; Race
Boston, suicide in 16.236
Brisbane (Australia), suicide in 16.240
Broken homes 17.404
Buffalo (N.Y.), suicide in 16.247
Bulgaria, suicide in 18.204
Burial of suicides 4.102, 4.108, 4.112
Business aspects of suicide. See Economic aspects of suicide

C

Case studies. See Suicide--case studies
Catholics and suicide. See Roman Catholics and suicide
Chemotherapy 24.504
Chicago, suicide in 6.216 (Maris), 16.226
Childhood experiences 6.203, ch. 22
Children, suicide among 5.111, 5.208, 5.214, 6.219, 16.203, 16.206, 16.207, 16.209
Children as suicide deterrents 17.103
Children's literature, suicide in 9.601, 9.605 to 9.608, 9.801, 9.802
Church and suicide. See Religious aspects of suicide

Church of Jesus Christ of Latter-day Saints 5.121
Classification of death. See Death, classification of
Clearinghouses. See Research centers
Cleveland, suicide in 6.215 (Hutcherson)
Climate. See Weather
Cognition 1.116, 6.213 (Elliott, Geller, Lettieri, Levenson, Neuringer, and Wetzel), 19.301 to 19.304
Collections, research 6.302, 12.101 to 12.107
College students. See Students, college, suicide among
Communication of suicidal intent 6.205 (Rudestam), 6.221 (Cowgell), 21.201 to 21.205
Communication patterns 6.203 (Abraham), 6.207 (Shagoury), 6.213 (Darbonne), 17.407
Community growth 16.234 to 16.236
Computer. See Data banks, computer stored--Canada; Data banks, computer stored-- United States; Data bases, computer stored bibliographic
Conference proceedings. See Proceedings
Conferences, international 12.302, 12.305, 12.306, 12.309, 12.310, 12.312
Conferences, national 12.301, 12.309, 12.313
Consultants 12.101
Coroners and medical examiners 1.102, 6.215 (MacKinnon), 13.401 to 13.409
Correctional institutions. See Prisoners, suicide among
Counseling, suicide 1.111, 6.212 (Praul), 6.221 (Lum)
Countertransference 24.506
Crime and suicide 4.104, 4.108, 5.202, 5.203, 6.215 (Vincentnathan)
Criminals, suicide among. See Prisoners, suicide among

Subject Index

G

Geomagnetic fluctuations 16.264
Gerontology 5.213
Grants-in-aid. See Research, funding of
Grief 6.220 (Stone)
Group therapy 6.221 (Billings, Clanton, White), 24.502, 24.503. See also Treatment of suicidal persons

H

Handwriting analysis 21.112
Harakiri 18.214
Heroin addicts. See Addicts, heroin
Historical aspects of suicide--
bibliography 2.202, 2.203, 2.206
Canada 3.307, 3.314, 3.315
Great Britain 3.101, 3.309, 3.310
United States 3.301 to 3.306, 3.308, 3.311 to 3.313, 7.106, 7.201 to 7.206
History of suicide 1.110, 1.202, 4.108, 4.109, 5.102, 5.114, 5.115, 5.128, 5.401, 6.206
Hong Kong, suicide in 16.255
Hospital patients. See Mental hospital patients
Hospital responsibility 8.102, 8.104
Hostility 6.213 (Lester)
Humor 6.213 (Goldsmith)
Husbands 17.101. See also Married persons; Wives
Hysteria 19.104

I

Immigrants 7.203, 7.206, 16.251 to 16.255
Income 7.210, 16.246. See also Economic aspects of suicide
India, suicide in 18.204
Indian Americans. See American Indians
Information centers. See Collections, research; Research centers
Insurance, life 4.103, 4.104, 4.105, 5.106

Interpersonal relations 6.207, 14.105, 16.210, 17.203, 17.401 to 17.407
Israel, suicide in 18
Italy, suicide in 18.204

J

Jails. See Prisoners, suicide among
Japan, suicide in 18.204, 18.208, 18.214
Japanese-Americans, suicide among 18.204
Jews and suicide 4.106, 5.118. See also Religious aspects of suicide

L

Legal aspects of suicide
Canada 8.501, 8.503, 8.604
Great Britain 8.105, 8.502, 8.503, 8.603, 8.604
United States 1.116, 2.204, 4.103, 4.104, 5.103, 8.101 to 8.105, 8.301, 8.401 to 8.405, 8.502, 8.503, 8.601, 8.602
Legal research 8.201 to 8.203
Library collections and resources. See Collections, research
Life insurance. See Insurance, life
Literature, suicide in 1.101, 1.110, 1.114, 2.205, 5.102, 5.105, 5.107, 5.111, 5.114, 5.128, 5.129, 5.132, 5.401, 6.217, ch. 9
Los Angeles, suicide in 6.205 (Rudestam), 16.233, 18.205, 18.213

M

Madras (India), suicide in 6.215 (Vincentnathan)
Maine, suicide in 6.215 (Abbiati)
Males, suicide among 6.202 (Kirk), 6.213 (Cabiles), 6.214 (Miller), 6.221 (Erickson), 16.229, 19.103. See also Females, suicide among, Sex

Subject Index

Marital status 7.205, 7.206, 7.210, 7.211, 16.101, 16.219, 17.102, 17.106
Married persons, suicide among 17.101, 17.102
Mass suicide 20.203
Means of suicide 6.215 (Marks), 7.106, 7.107, 7.201 to 7.205, 7.207, 7.208, 7.212, 18.108, 18.202. See also Asphyxia; Drugs, suicide by means of; Poison, suicide by means of; Suicide by aircraft; Suicide by automobile
Media, nonprint. See Audiovisuals
Medical aspects of suicide 1.110, 2.204, 3.403, 4.105, 4.112, 5.103, 5.110, 5.113, 5.115, 5.117, 5.126, 5.209 to 5.216, 24.501, 25.108. See also Drugs, suicide by means of; Forensic aspects of suicide
Medical examiners. See Coroners and medical examiners
Medicine, forensic. See Forensic aspects of suicide; Coroners and medical examiners
Menstrual cycle 16.223
Mental hospital patients 6.211 (Durham), 6.213 (Farberow), 19.109, 20.101, 21.201
Mental illness 4.104, 4.111, 5.220, 6.213 (Temoche), 16.101, 19.101 to 19.203, 22.501. See also Mental hospital patients; Neurotics; Psychotics; Psychopaths; Schizophrenics
Methodists 5.138
Mexican-Americans, suicide among 18.204
Michigan, suicide in 16.232
Migration 16.101, 16.251 to 16.255
Military personnel, suicide among 5.139, 6.215 (Demmer), 16.259, 17.202
Miller, Arthur 6.217 (Slavensky)
Minneapolis, suicide in 16.253
Minnesota Multiphasic Personality Inventory (MMPI) 6.211 (Jones, Lemerond)

Missing persons 6.208
Missouri, suicide in 6.216 (Geisel)
Mobility, geographical. See Migration occupational or social. See Social mobility
Moral aspects of suicide. See Ethical aspects of suicide
Motion pictures 11.101 to 11.103. See also Films, educational
Motor vehicle accidents. See Suicide by automobile
Murder and suicide 20.102, 20.201 to 20.207
Myths, suicide 9.303, 9.304

N

National conferences. See Conferences, national
Native Americans. See American Indians
Navajos, suicide among 6.205 (Morgan)
Netherlands, suicide in the 18.204
Neurotics, suicide among 19.102, 19.201 to 19.203
New Hampshire, suicide in 6.216 (Humphrey)
Newsletters. See Organizations, national--newsletters; Organizations, international--newsletters
Newspapers ch. 10
Newspapers and suicide 17.201, 17.204 to 17.206
New York City, suicide in 17.201, 18.207
New Zealand, suicide in 16.227, 16.230
Nomenclature, suicide. See Taxonomy of suicide
Norway, suicide in 18.203, 18.204, 18.208
Notes. See Suicide notes
Novels. See Literature, suicide in
Numbers and rates of suicide
Canada 4.109, 7.101, 7.108, 7.207
Canada--Age 7.101, 7.207

289

Subject Index

Canada--Provinces 7.108, 7.207
Canada--Sex 7.101, 7.108,
 7.207
Great Britain 4.109, 7.103
Selected countries 4.201, 7.102,
 7.107, 7.303, 7.308, 18.107
Selected countries--Age 7.102,
 7.107, 7.303, 7.308
Selected countries--Sex 7.102,
 7.107, 7.303, 7.308
United States 4.109, 4.202,
 4.203, 7.106, 7.107, 7.201
 to 7.206, 7.208 to 7.212,
 7.301, 7.306
United States--Age 4.203, 7.201
 to 7.206, 7.208 to 7.210,
 7.212
United States--Cities 7.208
United States--Counties 7.212
United States--Race 4.203,
 7.106, 7.201 to 7.206, 7.208
 to 7.210, 7.212
United States--Sex 4.203, 7.106,
 7.107, 7.201 to 7.206, 7.208
 to 7.210, 7.212
United States--Standard Metropolitan Statistical Areas 7.212
United States--States 7.208,
 7.212. See also Statistics,
 suicide

O

Obese persons, suicide among 13.205
Occupation and suicide 6.214
 (Diamond), 6.216 (Miller),
 7.201, 7.205, 7.206, 7.208,
 14.207, 16.230, 16.237 to
 16.239, 19.404
Older persons. See Aged
Opinion polls. See Attitudes and
 opinions
Organizations
 international 12.302, 12.305,
 12.306, 12.309, 12.310
 international--newsletters 12.302,
 12.306, 12.309
 national 12.101, 12.301, 12.303,
 12.304, 12.307, 12.308,
 12.309

national--newsletters 12.301,
 12.304, 12.309, 12.311

P

Parental loss 19.102, 22.201 to
 22.204
Parental suicide, effects on children
 17.502
Pathology 5.212
Personality
 and suicide 6.202 (Salter),
 6.213 (Berk, Geller, Haws),
 6.219 (Cantor), 18.209
 tests 6.211 (Crasilneck, Devries),
 6.213 (Vogel), 25.103 to
 25.105. See also Minnesota
 Multiphasic Personality Inventory (MPPI), Rorschach,
 Thematic Apperception Test
 (TAT), Suicide prediction
 scales
 theory 1.105
Philadelphia, suicide in 6.215
 (Campion), 16.260
Philosophical aspects of suicide
 1.110, 1.114, 1.116, 1.202,
 1.207, 4.107, 5.102, 5.218,
 5.401, 6.209, 9.902, 23.103,
 24.403. See also Ethical
 aspects of suicide
Physician responsibility 8.102,
 8.104
Physicians, suicide among 16.237
Pittsburgh, suicide in 6.215 (Schmid)
Poems. See Literature, suicide in
Poison, suicide by means of 4.103
Powerlessness 17.401
Prediction, suicide. See Suicide
 prediction; Suicide prediction
 scales
Prevention, suicide. See Suicide
 prevention; Suicide prevention
 centers and programs
Prisoners, suicide among 19.501 to
 19.503, 19.505, 19.506,
 23.109
Proceedings 12.401 to 12.405
Psychiatry. See Suicide--psychologi-
 cal and psychiatric aspects

290

Subject Index

Slaves, suicide among 7.201
Social
  change 6.216 (Krohn, Miley),
    14.208
  class 4.111, 16.101, 16.210,
    16.226 to 16.228
  disorganization 6.216 (Krohn),
    16.247 to 16.250
  integration 6.216 (Peck)
  isolation 6.203 (Jacobs), 6.221
    (White), 17.401, 17.404
  mobility 6.202 (Holmes), 16.229,
    16.230
  services 5.216, 5.224
  status 16.210, 19.404
  structure 6.216 (Futrell, Miley,
    Reinhart), 14.208
  surveys. See Surveys, epidemi-
    logical
Sociology. See Suicide--sociological
  aspects; Surveys, epidemiological;
  Theories of suicide, sociological
Sound recordings. See Audiovisuals
South Africa, suicide in 18.211
South America, suicide in 18.204
Southend (England), suicide in 16.241
Southern Baptists 5.136
Statistics, suicide 1.104, 1.116,
    5.123, 5.131, 6.215 (Bradshaw,
    Marshall), ch. 7. See also
    Data banks, computer stored;
    Numbers and rates of suicide--
    Canada; Numbers and rates of
    suicide--Great Britain; Numbers
    and rates of suicide--selected
    countries; Numbers and rates of
    suicide--United States
Status integration 6.216 (Geisel,
    Tennant), 14.103, 14.105,
    14.210 to 14.212
Stigma 17.503. See also Suicide,
    social condemnation of
Stockholm, suicide in 6.205
    (Rudestam), 18.213
Stress 16.219, 17.301
Students, college--suicide among
    5.206, 5.207, 6.201 (Bell,
    Leshem), 6.212 (Praul), 6.213
    (Callender, Gerth, Haws, Kil-
    patrick, Lee), 6.215 (Black),

22.103, 22.401, 22.402,
    23.110, 25.102
Suggestibility and suicide 17.201 to
    17.206
Suicide
  adolescent 1.102, 1.108, 2.304,
    4.112, 5.111, 5.140, 5.207,
    6.203, 6.213 (Hynes), 6.219,
    9.201, 16.202, 16.204,
    16.205, 16.209, 18.209,
    23.102
  anthropological aspects 1.114,
    3.401, 4.108, 5.225
  attempted 1.102, 1.105, 1.118,
    1.119, 2.204, 4.101, 5.115,
    6.213 (Brown, Cohorn, Hynes,
    Jacobson, Kochansky, Lee,
    Pearson, Ruby, Scholz, Sharon,
    Vogel, Walker, Waugh, Welu),
    6.214 (Linehan), 6.216 (Wenz),
    6.219 (Cantor, Doroff, Francis,
    Walch), 6.221 (Bartman),
    13.101 to 13.105, 16.217,
    16.218, 16.222, 16.242,
    17.101, 17.106, 17.202,
    17.203, 17.301, 18.215,
    19.103, 19.104, 19.201 to
    19.203, 19.301 to 19.303,
    19.401, 19.403, 19.501,
    20.103, 20.204, 22.202 to
    22.204, 23.110, 25.201,
    25.202
  by aircraft 5.139
  by automobile 13.205 to 13.207
  case studies 1.105, 1.201,
    16.207, 17.501, 20.101,
    23.101 to 23.110
  counseling. See Counseling,
    suicide
  epidemics. See Epidemics, suicide
  in literature. See Literature,
    suicide in
  murder-suicide ratio 6.216 (Whitt)
  myths. See Myths, suicide
  notes 6.213 (Tauber), 19.304
    21.101 to 21.114
  prediction 6.211, 6.216
    (Futrell), ch. 25
  prediction scales 6.211 (Saltz-
    berg), 16.242, 25.107 to
    25.109

prevention 1.107, 1.108, 1.113, 1.116, 2.204, 4.101, 4.111, 5.115, 5.131, 5.133, 5.219, 6.212, 6.221 (Billings), 8.103, 15.205, 16.212, 24.401 to 24.405. See also Counseling, suicide

prevention centers and programs 4.101, 5.219, 6.212, 12.101, 12.302, 12.303, ch. 24. See also Suicide prevention--telephone counseling; Samaritans

prevention centers and programs, evaluation of 6.212 (Welu), 24.201 to 24.209

prevention centers and programs, standards for 24.301 to 24.303

prevention personnel 6.212 (Ansel, Belanger, Knickerbocker, Thompson)

prevention--telephone counseling 6.212 (Thompson), 12.304, 12.305, 24.103, 24.209

prevention, training for 1.113, 1.206, 5.101, 6.212 (Thompson), 12.101, 12.302, 24.101 to 24.103, 24.106

psychological and psychiatric aspects 1.110, 1.114, 1.201, 4.101 to 4.103, 4.111, 5.104, 5.133 to 5.135, 5.205, 5.215, 5.219, 5.402, 5.403, 6.213, 15.203. See also Mental illness; Theories of suicide, psychological

research 1.113, 1.116, 1.205. See also Collection, research; Research centers; Research, funding of; Research-in-progress, announcing and reporting of

research, reviews of 2.301 to 2.304, 16.205

social condemnation of 16.224, 16.225. See also Stigma

sociological aspects 1.104, 1.110, 1.114, 3.402, 5.105, 5.107, 5.134, 5.135, 5.223, 5.225, 5.403, 6.215, 6.216, 19.105. See also Theories of suicide, sociological

Sunspots 16.262

Surveys, epidemiological 6.214

(Andress), 16.101, 16.102, 18.215

Survivors 6.220, 17.501 to 17.504. See also Widows, widowers

Sweden, suicide in 18.203, 18.204, 18.208

T

Taiwan, suicide in 18.204

Taxonomy, suicide 1.113, 1.114, 6.213 (Perlman), 13.301 to 13.305

Television 10.204, 11.207

Thematic Apperception Test (TAT) 6.213 (McEvoy)

Theories of suicide psychological ch. 15. See also Suicide--psychological and psychiatric aspects sociological 6.216, ch. 14. See also Suicide--sociological aspects

Theory, crisis 15.202, 15.206

Tikopia, suicide in 18.206

Time perspectives 6.211 (Barnes), 6.213 (Flynn)

Tokyo 6.215 (Vincentnathan)

Tragedy, English 6.217 (Cleary, Hicks)

Tragedy, Greek 9.202

Treatment, crisis 15.202, 15.206, 24.504, 24.509

Treatment of suicidal persons 1.107, 1.113, 4.110, 6.221, 16.209, 24.501 to 24.509. See also Chemotherapy; Electroshock therapy; Group therapy; Psychotherapy; Treatment, crisis

U

Unemployment 6.215 (Hartman), 16.240 to 16.242. See also Economic aspects of suicide

United Methodists 5.138

Urban residence 6.216 (Wenz), 7.206, 7.208, 16.226, 16.231 to 16.233

Subject Index

V

Vampires 4.102
Vienna, suicide in 18.205
Vital statistics. See Statistics

W

Wales, suicide in 16.231
War 16.256 to 16.259
Washington, suicide in 6.215
   (Schmid)
Weather 6.204, 16.260 to 16.264
Widows, widowers 6.220 (Demi),
   16.210, 17.102, 17.105
   17.504. See also Survivors

Wives 17.101, 17.504. See also
   Husbands
Work. See Occupation; Unemploy-
   ment
World War I, suicide during
   16.256
World War II, suicide during
   16.256, 16.257, 16.259
Wyoming, suicide in 6.216
   (Nelson)